D1267727

Akan Christology

African Christian Studies Series (AfriCS)

This series will make available significant works in the field of African Christian studies, taking into account the many forms of Christianity across the whole continent of Africa. African Christian studies is defined here as any scholarship that relates to themes and issues on the history, nature, identity, character, and place of African Christianity in world Christianity. It also refers to topics that address the continuing search for abundant life for Africans through multiple appeals to African religions and African Christianity in a challenging social context. The books in this series are expected to make significant contributions in historicizing trends in African Christian studies, while shifting the contemporary discourse in these areas from narrow theological concerns to a broader inter-disciplinary engagement with African religio-cultural traditions and Africa's challenging social context.

The series will cater to scholarly and educational texts in the areas of religious studies, theology, mission studies, biblical studies, philosophy, social justice, and other diverse issues current in African Christianity. We define these studies broadly and specifically as primarily focused on new voices, fresh perspectives, new approaches, and historical and cultural analyses that are emerging because of the significant place of African Christianity and African religio-cultural traditions in world Christianity. The series intends to continually fill a gap in African scholarship, especially in the areas of social analysis in African Christian studies, African philosophies, new biblical and narrative hermeneutical approaches to African theologies, and the challenges facing African women in today's Africa and within African Christianity. Other diverse themes in African Traditional Religions; African ecology; African ecclesiology; inter-cultural, inter-ethnic, and inter-religious dialogue; ecumenism; creative inculturation; African theologies of development, reconciliation, globalization, and poverty reduction will also be covered in this series.

Akan Christology

An Analysis of the Christologies of
John Samuel Pobee and Kwame Bediako
in Conversation with the Theology of Karl Barth

CHARLES SARPONG AYE-ADDO

Foreword by
S. WESLEY ARIARAJAH

PICKWICK *Publications* · Eugene, Oregon

AKAN CHRISTOLOGY
An Analysis of the Christologies of John Samuel Pobee and Kwame Bediako in Conversation with the Theology of Karl Barth

African Christian Studies Series 5

Pickwick Publications
An Imprint of Wipf and Stock Publishers
199 W. 8th Ave., Suite 3
Eugene, OR 97401

www.wipfandstock.com

ISBN 13: 978-1-62032-155-3

Cataloging-in-Publication data:

Aye-Addo, Charles Sarpong.

Akan christology : an analysis of the christologies of John Samuel Pobee and Kwame Bediako in conversation with the theology of Karl Barth / Charles Sarpong Aye-Addo ; foreword by S. Wesley Ariarajah.

xxx + 208 p.; 23 cm—Includes bibliographical references and index.

African Christian Studies Series 5

ISBN 13: 978-1-62032-155-3

1. Jesus Christ—Person and offices. 2. Christianity—Africa, Sub-Saharan. 3. Africa, Sub-Saharan—Religion. I. Ariaraja, S. Wesley. II. Title. III. Series.

BT205 .A95 2013

Manufactured in the USA.

This volume is dedicated to my father and mother

Mr. Martin Glover Aye-Addo
&
Mrs. Gloria Akusika Aye-Addo

Contents

Foreword

"WHO IS HE?" AND "What does his life, death, and resurrection mean to us?" These are the two fundamental questions about Jesus Christ with which the Christian church has struggled through the centuries. There were some tentative answers given by the first disciples and the early church in their immediate Jewish environment. Later, as the church moved into the Greco-Roman world, perceptions and interpretations of Christ changed radically; new understandings about him and his significance were spelt out on the basis of Greek philosophy, accompanied by deep and divisive controversies. The classical Christology that the church inherited emerged as the result of the agreements that were reached in the Middle-Ages and had become an essential part of European theological traditions.

When Christianity began to expend into Africa and Asia from the seventeenth century, the missionaries brought with them and instilled in these churches the classical Christology that had been refined and reformulated in Europe. It is this Christology that is still the basis of the faith, worship life and mission of the churches in Africa.

It is significant, however, that from time to time, and especially since the liberation of the African nations from colonial rule, African theologians have been pointing out that the "white, blond, blue-eyed Christ" presented by the Christians missions somehow did not speak meaningfully within the African culture, and that if the reality of Christ is universal it should be possible to make interpretations of him and his significance that would arise from the cultural symbols and thought pattern that are native to Africa. This conviction had led some pioneering African theologians to venture into fresh interpretations of Christ with symbols that are taken from African culture. This had not been an easy task since they had the burden of having to deal with the biblical witness to Christ, the traditions of the church and an African interpretation that would be meaningful to the Christian peoples of Africa.

Some of the pioneers of African Christology had come from the Akan culture predominant in West Africa, and especially Ghana. In this work Charles Aye-Addo discusses the Christological contributions of John Samuel Pobee and Kwame Bediako as two of the representative thinkers of African Christology to examine the impact of their work on African theology, spirituality and church life. The significance of Aye-Addo's work is that he seeks to present the work of these two theologians in the form of a dialogue with Karl Barth, one of the foremost European theologians that had influenced Protestant theological and missionary thinking. Barth's strength is that he insisted on being biblical in his interpretation of Christ which is also one of the primary interests of Aye-Addo.

As a result we have here a fascinating window into some of the key concepts that are essential to West African culture, two of the struggles to interpret Christ within that culture, and a critical study of the result that is both informative and challenging. This volume makes a valuable contribution to contemporary explorations on Christology.

S. Wesley Ariarajah
Prof. of Ecumenical Theology
Drew University, School of Theology

Preface

CHRISTOLOGY HAS GRADUALLY BECOME the dominant theological issue in the development of African theology. Many theologians, in their attempt to construct theology for the African churches, have used some of the African cultural categories. Of interest for this dissertation are the works of John Pobee and Kwame Bediako who used Biblical sources and African cultural categories with special reference to the ancestral paradigm.

This work critically engages these two attempts to construct an authentic African Christology that uses indigenous religio-cultural concepts to speak of the Jesus encountered in the Bible. This project affirms and shares the concerns of this theological movement. However, it questions some of the assumptions and constructive moves: it also seeks to examine the extent to which these attempts have delivered on the promise of honoring both the biblical witness and indigenous thought.

Predominantly, the project critiques the appropriation of the Akan ancestor traditions in Akan Christological projects. Intriguingly, such an appropriation to make Jesus Christ "at home" in the African spiritual universe mirrors the Anglo-European identification of Christ with their own culture, which is identified by the African theologians as the source of the problem in the first place. Therefore, this study seeks to facilitate a conversation between the selected theologians and Karl Barth who, in the European context, made some methodological decisions to counter the easy identification of Christ with culture, in an attempt to recover the independence of biblical testimony.

This move is an attempt to shed light on the complexities of the challenge facing the construction of African theology. It also hopes to better enable African theologians to avoid some of the pitfalls of Anglo-European theologies in their very effort to distinguish Akan Christianity from Anglo-European cultural categories. This book suggests that in doing Akan Christology perhaps we should turn to Paul's vision of Christ in his Second Letter to the Corinthians, where he develops Christological formulation in the phrase, "God was in Christ." This understanding of the fullness of

God being made available in concrete terms, it is argued, is the function of Christology within the Akan tradition.

Charles Sarpong Aye-Addo, PhD
Founder and Executive Chancellor
Yeshua Institute of Technology
Accra, Ghana

Acknowledgments

THE MATERIAL IN THIS volume was originally written as a doctoral dissertation at the Drew University School of Theology. I would like to express my deep gratitude to Professor Chris Boesel, my main advisor, and to Professors Wesley Ariarajah and Robert Corrington who had accompanied the process and helped me to complete my work. I am also grateful to my good friends John and Winnie Kwofie who read the chapters and provided meaningful suggestions and to Professor John Samuel Pobee and Archbishop Emeritus Peter Kwasi Sarpong for their suggestions as I progressed in my work. Professor Katherine Brown had spared no effort in helping me in the preparation and finalizing of the text for which I am very grateful. I realize that this undertaking would not have been possible without the support, encouragement and even prodding on the part of my beloved wife Gertrude and my children Akusika, Nyansafo, and Nhyira, my friend Shyamala, my sister Theresa and the Rev. and Mrs. Christopher Yaw Annor.

Introduction

African Christology has gradually become the central issue of theological endeavor on the continent. Since the last quarter of the twentieth century the challenge has been the method on which to construct African theological endeavor. Various attempts have been made to construct indigenous theology based on African categories as a point of departure. Some have also attempted to integrate both biblical and African categories in their respective theological endeavors. Still others have continued to depend on Euro-American Christian theology. John Vernon Taylor (11 September 1914—30 January 2001) an Oxford Scholar, English Bishop, theologian and missionary to Mukano, Uganda made a statement that reflected the nature and character of the evangelistic encounter between the missionaries and Africans. Here is how he analyzed the situation:

> Christ has been presented as the answer to the questions a white man would ask, the solution to the needs that Western man would feel, the Savior of the European world-view, the object of the adoration and prayer of historic Christendom. But if Christ were to appear as the answer to the questions that Africans are asking, what would he look like?[1]

This statement has generated series of questions regarding theology, teaching, and Christian practices of the missioners who brought Christianity to the African continent in the seventeenth century. It has also prompted African theologians to attempt to construct Christologies that make Christ quite different from those received from the missionaries.

Kwame Bediako, Professor of theology and Director of Akrofi-Christaller Graduate School of Applied Theology, described the above statement as pointing out "the general character of western missionary preaching and teaching in Africa since the arrival of missionaries on our

1. J. V. Taylor, *Primal Vision*, 16.

continent during the 19th century."[2] For him and many other African theologians, this is an important issue that must be addressed by contemporary theologians, church leaders and Christians, who are convinced that the teaching they have so far received is inadequate to establish Jesus Christ, the universal Savior, as also the Savior of the African world.[3]

It is this concern that has motivated the rise of African theologies. Even though the attempt was to do theology, in general, undoubtedly African Christology has gradually become the central issue of theological endeavor on the continent. Kofi Appiah-Kubi, a theologian and sociologist, posits that "we demand to serve the LORD in our own terms without being turned into Euro-Semitic bastards before we do so."[4] Such statements, among others, reiterate the fact that Christianity brought to Africa was loaded with Anglo-Euro cultural assumptions and has become a major problem for the articulation of "an authentic African Christology."[5]

John Pobee poses the following questions to reveal the problem as distinctively Christological: "Who is Jesus Christ? What manner of man is he? How does he affect my life? Why should an Akan relate to Jesus of Nazareth, who does not belong to his clan, family, tribe, and nation?"[6] Thus, the general feeling was that the thought of Jesus Christ could not ring home adequately in the ears of the African. To this end, Kwame Bediako concurs with the sentiment and so writes:

> Western missionary enterprise did not achieve a genuine encounter between the Christian faith and, for example, his own people, the *Akans*[7] because the reception and articulation of the Christian faith was often restricted to models of Christian traditions of Europe—thus, the presentation of the Gospel was done in such a way that Christ could not inhabit the spiritual universe of the African consciousness except, in essence as stranger.[8]

Thus, for Bediako, because the presentation of Christianity was shrouded in the models of European cultures and traditions, Christ became

2. Bediako, *Jesus in Africa*, 20.

3. Ibid.

4. Appiah-Kubi and Torres, *African Theology En Route*, viii.

5. Pobee, *Toward an African Theology*, 2.

6. Ibid., 81.

7. The Akan tribe is the largest ethnic or tribal group in Ghana forming about 49 percent of the population.

8. Bediako, "Biblical Christologies," 125.

a stranger to the Akan. How then should the gospel be presented in order to achieve a genuine encounter between the Christian faith and the Akans? Can African Christology stand alone or should it be biblical, or both? How can Jesus inhabit the spiritual universe of African consciousness? Is Jesus Christ expected to inhabit the Akan spiritual universe to transform it or to be adapted to it? It is in response to these challenges that this dissertation seeks to articulate a Christology that is in the thought and language forms of the Akan.

Since the turn of the second half of the twentieth century, which also marked the beginning of the end of colonialism, determination of who Jesus is by Africans for African Christians, using indigenous categories has become imperative for theological enterprise. Pobee asserts that "the concern of African theology is to attempt to use African concepts and African ethos as vehicles for the communication of the gospel in an African context . . . and that whatever we evolve should be tested against the plumb line of the biblical faith."[9] It can be noted that what these African theologians want is African Christianity with a Christology grounded in indigenous African religio-cultural categories. They also seek to distinguish it from Christianity and a Christology embedded in Anglo-European religious and cultural categories. Both Pobee and Kwame Bediako, in their attempt to construct an African Christology, present Jesus Christ as Ancestor. Pobee proposes that we think of Jesus Christ as the Great and the Greatest Ancestor—in *Akan* language, *Nana,*[10] as well as Chief Linguist,[11] while Bediako maintains Christ as "the only real and true Ancestor and source of life for all humankind."[12]

Donald Guthrie suggests an intriguing and valuable insight in his book, *New Testament Theology,* for the exploration of Christologies:

> Most modern approaches to Christology begin from the human on the grounds that we must begin with what we know. But too many inadequate Christologies have been built on this process, as if the belief in the divine side of the nature of Jesus was the result of a long process of development. Yet to begin with the divine pre-existent Son makes better sense of the New Testament approach, especially of Paul and John. If we begin from 'above' we shall take

9. Pobee, *Toward an African Theology*, 9, 82.

10. Ibid., 94.

11. Ibid., 95.

12. Bediako, *Jesus in African Culture*, 27.

> account of revelation, whereas if we begin from 'below' we shall be concerned with concepts within our own experiences and develop them in accordance with our existent knowledge of humanity, which leaves little room for revelation.[13]

What kinds of resources should be the guiding principles for doing theology in Africa? Should they be rooted in indigenous cultural ideas? Alternatively, is it feasible to distinguish a Christology that is irreducible to indigenous cultural assumptions of any kind, yet, can be appropriated and expressed using available and pertinent resources of contemporary, local, and cultural idioms as vehicles to transform them?

For theology, this is fundamentally the methodological question related to two concerns: To what extent can an authentic Christology be rooted in indigenous traditional assumptions of any culture? And, to what extent can Christology be distinguished from indigenous cultural assumptions of either those communicating the central message of Christianity or those receiving it? This leaves us with the basic question of the whence of a relevant and authentic Christology—what are its origins? How does an authentic Christology come to us at all? Is it from a source that is not our own indigenous possession, cultural presupposition and experiences? Is it "received" in any sense and to that extent is indeed "news?" Or, is this precisely what renders Christianity "inauthentic" on African soil for someone like Pobee, who seeks to "turn the Christian Faith into genuine African categories?"[14] In other words, are the criteria for authentic Christology the extent to which it is rooted in indigenous cultural traditions and their assumptions, and is it not received from the "outside" in ways that confronts, addresses, and transforms the said cultural traditions?

We share in the critique of Pobee and Bediako and also sympathize with their disagreement with "African" Christology that is rooted in Euro-Anglo cultural and philosophical thought forms. On the other hand, we feel that their constructive proposal is itself problematic in specific ways, especially as seen in their use of indigenous ancestral and other cultural categories to reconstruct African Christologies. Such a constructive remedy can easily become a replacement of Euro-American cultural assumptions with traditional African Cultural conceptions as the sources and criteria for Christology. This obscures the possibility of the emergence of a Christology that would be distinguishable from cultural assumptions and would give

13. D. Guthrie, *New Testament Theology*, 402.

14. Pobee, *Toward an African Theology*, 81.

little room for assessing them on the basis of 'biblical faith' that they claim should be the 'plumb-line.' It would appear that they are repeating the problem of Euro-American theology they are critiquing rather than offering a genuine rectification. It would therefore be important, when their theologies are taken up for discussion, to examine what Pobee means by biblical 'plumb-line' and the actual role of the Bible in their respective theologies.

We are not arguing that Christian theology cannot use cultural categories as a vehicle at all to articulate the distinctive identity of Jesus Christ in an African context, but rather, as a methodological concern this project seeks to find out how such categories are employed, especially in the Akan Christological constructions of Samuel Pobee and Kwame Bediako. We would then seek to argue for a more authentic Akan Christology that could be faithful to indigenous thought, without moving away from a biblical framework. This will be done in conversation with the theology of Karl Barth who had faced this dilemma in his own theological struggles in the European context.

Karl Barth was "educated in the standard liberalism descending from Albrecht Ritschl and Adolf von Harnack, and was particularly instructed by Wilhelm Herrmann."[15] In his close examination, Barth found that liberalism based its assertions, not on the Bible, but on its belief in natural revelation. That is, instead of focusing on the Bible and on God, liberal theology concentrated on how the human being approaches, conceives and constructs the knowledge of God through investigating human existence, culture and history, particularly in German thought and philosophy.

However, World War I, which was justified by a major section of the German church, a significant number of intellectuals and some professors, alienated Barth from liberal thinking. For him, this reality proved the shallowness and bankruptcy of liberalism, humanism, and the European culture. It caused Barth to dissociate himself from liberal theology and sent him in the route of re-examining every theological doctrine he had assimilated.

World War II provided for Barth yet another set of problems. Whereas with the First World War he was alienated from the undue optimism of liberal theology of what humans can achieve by their own efforts, the rise of Nazism, and the support given by large sections of the German "Christians" to Hitler's regime and its ideology shook Barth. He was deeply troubled by

15. Erickson, *Christian Theology*, 187.

the uncritical Christian identification of Christianity with German nationalism, culture, and ethnicity.

Thomas F. Torrance reveals Barth's intention in this way:

> Convinced that the subordination of evangelical Christianity to 'cultural Protestantism,' and the appalling loss of depth and meaning that even God had for the prevailing theology were due to the assimilation of God to nature and of revelation to history, and thus the reduction of theology to anthropology, that had been going on since the end of the eighteenth century, Barth determined to call a halt to it by tearing up the Protestant syntheses and creating such a diastasis between God and man, that God could really be recognized as God in the sheer majesty of his divine nature and in his absolutely unique existence and power, while man, disenchanted of his pretended divinity could be free at last to be truly and genuinely human.[16]

Barth's protest against Christian uncritical identification with German culture and ethnicity is a warning to theologies aimed at bringing the gospel and culture together in any situation, including Africa. While mindful of Barth's warning, it is still my intention in this dissertation to seek to work towards an African Christology that would be meaningful in the African context. Whereas my theological endeavor would question a Christology built on the category of the Ancestor, it would not be my intention to tear down what has been done by theologians like Pobee, Bediako and others. Rather, on the basis of what they have done, I would seek to articulate and present Jesus Christ in a manner which I believe would be more relevant and accessible to African Christians. My dependence on Barth here is mainly on methodological questions, especially as they relate to issues of revelation and scripture.

Barth's special concerns and the way he approached them may help us in our own attempts to develop tools that would enable us to use African cultural resources in the articulation of Christology. At the same time, we might also discern the potential and the limits of such usage, especially as they relate to the special divine activity in the world, which has been central to traditional European Christology. In view of Barth's own historical and cultural location, he could become a conversation partner of this exploration rather than the one who provides the criteria.

16. Torrance, "Problem of Natural Theology in the Thought of Karl Barth," 121.

It is possible to argue that in as much as some of the African theologians, like Pobee and Bediako, indeed substitute African cultural assumptions in the place of Euro-American cultural assumptions as the source and criterion for "authentic" African Christology—rather than attempting to explore the possibility of a "biblical" Christology—they are methodologically still dependent on Euro-American cultural and philosophical assumptions of the modern-liberal theological tradition. I would, therefore, attempt to do Christology, which, while moving away from Euro-American pre-modern cultural assumptions, would be attentive to the biblical witness and to the need for Christianity in Africa to be part of the church universal.

It is this constructive African Christology, rooted both in the biblical witness and in indigenous religio-cultural presuppositions that this project seeks to engage. While some of the African theologians immerse themselves in African cultural traditions to develop an African Christology, others, as for instance, John Mbiti, holds that African Christologies need to be within the overall traditions of the church and that "Christologies emerging from Africa need to be assembled and engaged with the Church universal."[17] Theology and the theological methodology of Karl Barth are of interest to this exploration also on the issue of the relationship between the church local and the church universal.

While recognizing the influence of culture on all theological enterprise, Barth was deeply concerned with the way cultural assumptions of European Christianity undermined what he considered the central message of the Gospel as revealed in scripture. In his Church Dogmatics, Volume I, Part I, Barth expounds the doctrines of Revelation and the Word of God using theological-biblical exegetical interpretation to point out that "since God himself has spoken, and continues to speak, in Jesus Christ and through the Holy Spirit, attested in Holy Scripture, it would be presumptuous on humankind's part to speak his own word as regards the things that pertain to God, that is, to speculate about them."[18] Thus, Barth takes revelation and faith as his epistemological foundations to counter the assumption that Christological convictions can be achieved solely through "culture, religion and piety."[19]

17. Mbiti, *Bible and Theology in African Christianity*, 15; see Pobee, *West Africa: Christ Would Be an African Too*.

18. Barth, *Church Dogmatics* I/1, 98.

19. Ibid., 103.

No doubt, Barth's theology was dictated by its own historical and cultural context. However, the concern that Barth addressed resonates with the concerns raised by some of the African theologians doing theology in Africa with African resources. What this dissertation attempts to do is to examine whether the concerns that Barth had raised in his context and the methodological tools that he had used to address them can serve as a bridge-builder between the two distinct interests (African traditional categories and Biblical faith) within African theology. In this sense, this discussion addresses a very important issue in relation to the future of African theology and subsequently African Christianity.

In response to Mbiti's challenge that "the African Church lacks theological concern"[20] a proliferation of indigenous African theologies begun flooding the theological playground of Africa. In this section, we will explore some of the diversity of opinions in the construction of African theology, illustrate some key themes and dimensions of the problems encountered in the formation of theology, and also offer both the main historical antecedents and works of the selected theologians—Samuel Pobee, Kwame Bediako, and Karl Barth.

Kofi Appiah-Kubi approaches Christology firstly through the African Independent Churches, which he feels are closer to African culture than those founded by the European missions, and secondly, through the personal experiences of African Christians. He makes a very intriguing but critical assertion on the question of sources: "Our question must not be what Karl Barth, Karl Rahner, or any other Karl has to say, but rather what God would have us do in our living concrete condition . . . pointing out that it is time to answer the critical question of Jesus Christ: "Who do you (African Christians) say that I am?"[21]

Secondly, Charles Nyamiti, a notable Tanzanian Roman Catholic priest and theologian, offers to do theology from "the multiple African religious heritages that calls for deeper analysis of the ancestral beliefs and practices for theological purposes."[22] Therefore, he expounds Christian thought using the African category of ancestor as a point of departure for dogmatic theology, Christian morality, and spirituality. Bénézet Bujo, a priest of the Diocese of Bunia in the Northeast of the Democratic Republic of Congo and later, Professor of Moral Theology and Social Ethics at the University of

20. Mbiti, *African Religions and Philosophy*, 14.

21. Appiah-Kubi and Torres, *African Theology En Route*, viii.

22. Nyamiti, *Christ as Our Ancestor*, 12ff.

Fribourg in Switzerland, reveals his theological agenda in this question: "In which way can Jesus Christ be an African among the Africans according to their own religious experience?[23] With this mindset, Bujo builds up his entire ancestor theology on the presupposition of "ancestor-preoccupation as a typical, anthropocentric, African 'mode of thought.'"[24] In a similar manner, Abraham Akrong, a Presbyterian Clergyman and Professor of theology, using the Akan socio-cultural and religious structure, designates Jesus Christ as ancestor.[25] Another Ghanaian Protestant theologian, Emmanuel Martey, speaks of the ancestral image as theologically appealing because for him, "it fits—if you read the scripture, and the African concept of ancestry."[26] Furthermore, Kairie claimed that the ancestral image of Christ "makes people feel very much at home."[27]

On the contrary, Yusufu Ameh Obaje, a Nigerian Baptist Minister and Professor of Theology at the Baptist Theological Seminary, at Ogbomoso, Nigeria, and scholar from University of Edinburgh, developed an African Theocentric Christology based on mythological concepts of God. Ameh Obaje posits: "There is no longer any need for them to return in search of God of the traditional African world view . . . because the same God found in African myths is the God of all creation who has finally come in Jesus Christ."[28]

Obaje makes this assertion based on the myths of human alienation in African traditional religions. In this particular myth, according to Obaje, God used to descend to earth on a long chain to distribute the bounties of heaven and remain on earth a little while to settle disputes between warring factions and yet, maintained his identity as the Supreme Being, then went back to heaven. Though some of the African myths portray *Onyankopong*, the Supreme Being, in ways that makes his experience with the African more concrete and meaningful, we have not really explored them in terms of theological or Christological thoughts. For instance, in the case of Obaje, he does not advance this theocentric Christology any further.

23. Bujo, *African Theology in its Social Context*, 9.

24. Ibid., 76–77.

25. Akrong, "Christology from an African Perspective," 122.

26. Emmanuel Martey, quoted in Stinton, *Jesus of Africa*, 138.

27. Karie, quoted in Stinton Diane, *Jesus of Africa: Voices of Contemporary African Christology*, 139.

28. Yusufu, "Theocentric Christology," 50.

On the contrary, some other theologians, clergymen and clergywomen, as well as laity refute most of the proposals for the use of especially cultural-ancestral categories in any Christological endeavor. The catalogue of some of the rejections can be obtained from Diane Stinton's book on *Jesus of Africa*. For instance, a Kenyan Catholic clergyman Elijah Chege cautions the use of the term, ancestor, for Christ because: "somehow he is slightly different because he is God."[29] A Ghanaian Protestant clergywoman, Margaret Asabea, explains: "an ancestor in the context of the African is your kith and kin, mother, father, grandfather, and great-grandfather."[30] She maintains that "any attempts to construe Jesus as kindred to Africans are simply academic gymnastics."[31] Similarly, a notable Ghanaian Catholic Archbishop Emeritus, Peter Sarpong, stressed that "ancestor is very restrictive" because it is an "ethnocentric concept."[32]

In the socio-cultural and religious world of the Akans (Africans) the cult of the ancestors promotes the idea of life after death. Kwesi Otabil states that "death only extends the family relationship into the spiritual world. The ancestors are therefore active members of their living families. They are leaders and elders and preside over family meetings. They can summon their living relatives to appear before them to explain any misconduct, especially misappropriation of family property."[33] Kofi Asare Opoku points out that "the ancestors are believed to be everywhere, at any time; they continue to live but in another kind of existence."[34] Quarcoopome posits that the ancestors are believed to have acquired extra-human powers in the after-life and with these powers they are able to intervene in the lives of the living members of the society."[35] Thus, ancestors are revered as heroes and heroines in some sectors of the various African tribes.

It must, however, be emphasized that the socio-cultural and religious terrain of the Africans have changed in lieu of the fact that Christianity has gained much ground on the continent. Today, most Africans do not succumb to rituals and sacrifices offered to the fetish and idols anymore. Syncretism is not commonly found among African Christians. In his recent

29. Stinton, *Jesus of Africa*, 138.
30. Ibid., 132.
31. Ibid.
32. Ibid.
33. Otabil, *West African Traditional Religion*, 77.
34. Opoku, *West African Traditional Religion*, 36.
35. Quarcoopome, *West African Traditional Religion*, 43.

book on *Ghana's New Christianity—Pentecostalism in a Globalizing African Economy,* Paul Gifford points out, among other things: "the Charismatic and Pentecostal strands of Ghanaian Christianity are meeting the socio-religious needs of the adherents in various ways while projecting the biblical image of Jesus Christ."[36]

Pobee has advocated for a "functional Christology;"[37] a Christology that focuses on the existential approach that relates to the deeds of Jesus Christ in relation to the individual believer. For Pobee, the New Testament itself, unlike the creeds, expresses its Christology in terms of Jesus' activity. Pobee believes that this approach agrees with the Akan perspective, which "prefers concreteness to abstraction."[38] Though Pobee agrees that no matter the diversities of theologies found in the New Testament, the "divinity and humanity of Jesus Christ cannot be negotiated,"[39] he discusses Jesus' divinity in functional terms and through his humanity.

The survey above on the many voices of African theologians struggling to expound African theology and Christology for Africa shows three distinctive features. To begin with, there is a general disquiet about uncritically adopting the Euro-American theological traditions as the theology of the churches in Africa. There is growing awareness that the received theology is as culture-bound as any theology that might be developed in Africa. There is an acute search for a theology that is authentically African.

Secondly, a number of theologians are attracted to the figure of the Ancestor as perhaps the most promising cultural entry point to explore an African Christology. It is believed that the Ancestor, as one that has lived on earth and continues to live beyond the grave, and as one that is already venerated, can provide the basis for an African Christology. However, it is also clear that there are equally strong voices that warn against an uncritical adoption of the image of the ancestor for Christology because of the limitations it places on the understanding of Christ.

Thirdly, the survey above shows nervousness on the part of a number of theologians of moving away from the biblical witness to Jesus. They are concerned that without the limits imposed by the biblical witness, African theology and Christology can get lost in the cultural wilderness.

36. Paul, *Ghana's New Christianity*, 199.

37. Ibid., 81.

38. Ibid.

39. Ibid.

It is within these concerns that Karl Barth becomes a significant theological conversation partner, especially in view of the methodological issues he raises regarding the nature of the theological task. This move is an attempt at shedding light on the complexities of the challenge facing the construction of African theology. Samuel Pobee and Kwame Bediako, for instance, call for "using the biblical faith as plumb-line" as an important criterion for doing theology in Africa. It is an attempt to always keep before the theologian, the distinction between the challenges of the Gospel as witnessed to in the scriptures and the human cultural resources that one cannot avoid employing, as they attempt to do theology in context. This dissertation is set within this struggle and seeks to explore ways in which an African Christology can be both African and biblical.

The phenomenal growth of Christianity in the land of Africa cannot be overemphasized. The fact, however, is that much of indigenous African theological literature produced by African theologians like Samuel Pobee and Kwame Bediako, strictly speaking, has little or no influence in this development. Rather, it is the same Judeo-Christian thought or more precisely the Euro-American Evangelical strand that is facilitating the prevailing spiritual current.

Some of the reasons are evident. First, it is obvious that much of the African theological literature that seeks to employ African symbols and cultural elements move away from the religious world that has become part of the Christian ethos that has been accepted and adopted since the arrival of the missionaries. Christians find it difficult to move back into the cultural world that the African theologians attempt to create. Secondly, the various proponents of African theology appear to dissociate Christianity from its roots in the Bible. This creates a distance between African Christians and theologians, because from the very beginnings of the missionary enterprise in Africa it is the Bible that has been at the center of African Christianity. For an African Christian, the belief in Christ is rooted in nothing more than the biblical witness he is. Thirdly, most of the literature ascribes to Jesus Christ the place of a Great Ancestor (Pobee) Brother Ancestor (Nyamiti) and Ancestor (Bediako) which does not reverberate with most of the African Christians. They do not see a correspondence between their concept of the ancestor and the Christ in whom they believe.

Because of the complexity produced by the above reality, there are many dimensions to the significance of this project. First, even though numerous works have appeared on the subject of African Christology, there has not been adequate rigorous constructive critical analysis of the positions that have been presented. This project seeks to analyze and offer constructive criticism with the aim of improving some of the proposals that have appeared.

It also seeks to provide a dialogue between some of the prominent African theologians and one of the streams of European theology on a subject-matter that is pertinent to the development of Christianity on the African continent. In this case, an attempt is made to put some aspects of the theology of Karl Barth in critical conversation with selected African theologians, thereby bringing out what it means to be a Christian outside of Euro-American theological shadows, and yet, to be within the overall traditions of the church drawn out from the biblical message.

Finally, the project seeks to make its own contribution to knowledge of the theological method through the articulation and analysis of the fundamental theological issues entailed in the challenge of appropriating both biblical and Akan resources to elucidate a Christology that can be recognized as distinctively Christian and authentically African.

To accomplish this task the work is divided into five chapters. The first chapter deals with the general introduction. In the second chapter, we will attempt to set out the overall religio-cultural world view of the Akan people within which the Christological reflections need to take place. In order to do this, the first part of the chapter will explore the Akan concept of *Onyankopong* or the Supreme Being. This will be done by examining some of the myths and stories related to the Supreme Being or God, the belief in God related to the creation of the cosmos, and the attributes given to God, such as, omnipotence, omniscience, and omnipresence.

This chapter will also study the understanding of the Akan God as one who has the powers of deliverance and healing, which is significant in the light of the general African belief in all manner of spiritual forces that plague the life of the people. Other aspects that are covered in this chapter are the moral and ethical dimensions of the Akan belief in God, the concepts of spiritual forces, and the concept of community within the Akan culture. The chapter concludes with the study of the concept of the family with special emphasis on Ancestors, a theme that has played a major role in many African Christologies.

In chapter three, our explorative work takes us to the two main Akan theologians selected for this study. Here we present a detailed account of the Akan Christological endeavors of Samuel Pobee and Kwame Bediako.

By doing so, we attempt to determine how these two theologians adopt and use both biblical and Akan religio-cultural categories to expound their view of Jesus Christ within the paradigm of the Ancestor. The study then assesses the way the concept of ancestor has been used to explicate their Christologies and examines the strengths and weaknesses of their proposals.

The fourth chapter will focus on the theology of Karl Barth. Here we will look closely at two aspects of his theology, namely, the Revelation of God in the Bible and the Incarnation of the Word as objective revelatory activities through which God relates to the world. After tracing the development of Barth's theological thought, special attention is paid to his understanding of God's self-revelation in Jesus Christ as attested to in the Word of God, the Bible. Here it is also important to study Barth's concern to emphasize both the humanity and divinity of Christ and his exploration of the concept of the Trinity. Exploring these dimensions of Barth's theology helps us in our examination of the place of the Bible in the development of Akan Christologies and the relationship between Jesus Christ and the Supreme Being of the Akan religion.

This chapter also examines some of the critical issues faced within Akan theology in conversation with some of the theological and methodological options Barth had made in a similar situation. Here, our interest is to investigate the appropriateness of the image of the Ancestor as a useful paradigm for an Akan Christology.

The concluding chapter further examines the strengths and weaknesses of the image of Ancestor, and proceeds to make some proposals for an African Christology on the basis of the discussions in the earlier chapters. Some of the important dimensions of this discussion are the role of the Bible in constructing theology in Africa and the issues of some of the legitimate ways in which Christian theology in Africa can be made truly African. The chapter then moves to the question of this dissertation. If the Ancestor paradigm is not an appropriate one, are there other ways in which to explore the Christological issue to make Christ "at home" in Africa? What we hope to do is to make some proposals showing some of the directions in which one could move.

Even though the research does not put forward a fully developed new Christological proposal, it is hoped that we would be able to point to some of the biblical themes that can help us build a Christology from both biblical and African resources that speak meaningfully to the Christian community in Africa.

In an appendix section, we attempt to present an interview conducted by Diane Stinton, a scholar and theologian from her book *Jesus of Africa: Voices of Contemporary African Christology* on the agreement and disagreement of the use of the ancestral categories for the development of Akan Christology.

With this purpose in mind, we will now turn in to the next chapter for a general survey of the Akan religio-cultural world view within which we must explore an African Christology.

1

Akan Cosmology

Cultural anthropologists classify the indigenous people of the West African nation of Ghana into five main groups on the basis of language, culture and geographical location. These groups are the Akan, the Ewe, the Ga-Adangbe, the Guan and the Mole-Dagbani. The Akan group, which this dissertation seeks to study, occupies most of the whole of the south and west of the Black Volta of Ghana. Historically, the Akan group migrated from the north to occupy the forest and coastal belt of the south in the thirteenth century. Some of the Akan ended up in the eastern section of Côte d'Ivoire, where they created the Baule community.

The history of the Akan-speaking people of southern Ghana dates back to the 1600s.[1] Much of what we know about ancient Akan customs comes to us in the form of oral histories that have survived for several hundred years. Many of the objects recovered in archaeological studies are still produced in modified form by the Akan peoples today. The rise of the early Akan centralized states can be traced to the thirteenth century and it is likely to be related to the opening of trade routes established to move gold throughout the region.

It was not until the end of the seventeenth century, however, that the grand Asante Kingdom[2] emerged in the central forest region of Ghana,

1. The history of the Akan can be traced from all Ghanaian history books especially from *West African History* by F. K. Buah and *The History of Ghana* by Adu-Boahen.

2. The Asante Kingdom was established and organized under one of their illustrious Kings—Osei Tutu I. King Osei Tutu had a friend who was a great and revered

when several small states united under the Chief of Kumasi, in a move to achieve political freedom from the Denkyira.[3] Apart from the Asante, other Akan groups are the Akwapim in the southeastern part of Ghana, the Akyem and the Kwahu in the eastern part, and the Fante in the central regions of Ghana. The Akan constitutes about half the population of Ghana and their dialects includes Fante (fanti, mfantse) Akuapem (akwapem twi, twi, akuapim, akwapi) Asante (ashante twi, twi, asanti, achanti) Agona, Dankyira, Asen, Akyem bosome, Kwawu, and Ahafo. Benjamin Ray, a scholar and writer on African Religions, in his book, *African Religions: Symbol, Ritual and Community,* chimes that there are many regional similarities in the cultural and religious lives of Africans. He maintains that:

> The Baganda, Banyoro, Banyankole, Bayamwezi, and Banyarwanda of Uganda, Tanzania and Rwanda who live around the Lake Region of East Africa speak closely related languages and share a great many cultural and religious institutions, spirit medium, and kingship among them. The same is true for the Akan peoples of Ghana, even though they are divided into subgroups, such as the Akim, Asante, Fante, Akuapem, Kwahu, Bono and others...they all see themselves as belonging to a broader cultural heritage.[4]

The Akan people share a common religious heritage generally made up of Christianity, Islam, and Traditional Religion. A minimal percent adhere to Hinduism, Buddhism, Eckankar, Baha'i Faith and others. In addition, to this day, they share the common experience of the consequences of European exploitation, expansionism, colonialism, and slavery. John Mbiti, a leading African theologian, points out that Akans, like all other indigenous Africans, are "notoriously religious."[5] Kofi Opoku Asare, a Senior Research Fellow in the Religion and Ethics Department of the Institute of African Studies at the University of Ghana, Accra, concurs with the statement, and holds that "religion is at the root of African culture and is the

---

priest,—Okomfo Anokye, through whose assistantship the Asantes development into a strong, fortified, formidable ethnic group that conquered almost all the other ethnic groups in the nation of the then Gold Coast, now Ghana.

3. Denkyira is another ethnic group in Ghana that stood fiercely against the conquering Asante Kingdom. They were also a power group of people who would not in any way bow to any King. It is said that "Denkyira had a King who bore a name but never could be mentioned."

4. Ray, *African Religions*, ix.

5. Mbiti, *African Religions and Philosophy,* 2nd ed., 1.

determining principle of African life."[6] Another Ghanaian theologian, currently the dean of the Regent Divinity of the Regent University College of Science and Technology, Accra, Ghana, shares analogous sentiments when he stresses the point that "at the heart of the African past is her religion and therefore any meaningful study of the African past must necessarily start with her Indigenous Religion."[7]

As we explore the works of these theologians and religionists, we may see some discrepancies in their thoughts. Such differences do not in any way devalue what they present as African thought and philosophy. Rather, it reveals the problem of not having a sacred text, like the Christian Bible or the Muslim Qur'an that set some authoritative boundaries for the explication of the faith. It also shows the inefficiencies related to the absolute dependence on Oral Tradition for the transmission of faith from one generation to another. However, it may be noted, and even be argued, that the overall thought patterns of these writers are, to a large extent, compatible. We would not, however, engage in a critical assessment of their thoughts, because the purpose of this chapter is not to critically analyze the thoughts of different theologians, but to give a synoptic description of some of the main concepts that are central to African religion.

Thus, our concern here is not to justify or glorify African thought, culture and religion. The purpose of this chapter is similar to what Bolaji Idowu, a Professor of Religious Studies in the University of Ibadan, Nigeria, pointed out in the preamble of his book, *African Traditional Religion—A Definition:* " . . . to discover what Africans actually know, actually believe, and actually think about Deity and the supersensible world."[8] African Religion has not received an objective assessment from most of the Western missionaries and Christian investigators. This is mainly because their approach to African Traditional Religion was influenced by their attempts to Christianize the indigenous people. The recurrent negative approach to African Religion by Western missionary scholars is pointed out by many African scholars today. For instance, in Quarcoopome's volume on *West African Traditional Religion,* he exposes the continuous use of derogatory terminologies such as "primitive, paganism, fetishism, animism, idolatry and polytheism" in designating the Traditional Religion.[9]

6. Opoku, *West African Traditional Religion*, 1.
7. Quarcoopome, *West African Traditional Religion*, 10.
8. Idowu, *African Traditional Religion*, 106–7.
9. Quarcoopome, *West African Traditional Religion*, 1.

In this section an attempt is made to give a description of Akan traditional concepts that constitutes the Akan Traditional Religion as understood by the Akan theologians we would engage in this dissertation and, indeed, by most African theologians. We shall examine the mythological concepts and explicate how they inform the Akan belief in the Supreme Being who is celebrated as the Creator with all the attributes that go with his supremacy. We shall also study the concepts related to the nature of the universe. Subsequent sections endeavor to elucidate how certain concepts such as spirits, divinities, the living-dead, the powers of evil related to witchcraft, sorcery and magic etc. operate in African Religion. Also of significance is the role of medicine-men who function in their various capacities within the spiritual universe of the Akan.

The Akan believes that the phenomenal world does not exist without the dictating forces of the unseen, intangible, and indestructible world of mystical forces and powers. This will give us the opportunity to understand who the ancestors are and what roles they play in their new unseen, spiritual world. The exploration will be done with religious writing authorities such as Geoffrey Parrinder, Benjamin C. Ray, Bolaji Idowu, T. N. O. Quarcoopome, John Mbiti, and Kofi Asare Opoku. These theologians and religionists have written extensive works on African Traditional Religion over a long period of time.

Under the general heading—the power of evil, we will discuss the effects of witchcraft, sorcery and magic as they relate to the progress of the victims and how traditional religion is able to combat such evil practices. This discussion, among others, will augur well to find a Christology that can deal with such people with evil powers who have such ability to manipulate mystical forces to maim and kill fellow human beings. On the discussions of medicine-men, an attempt will be made to portray their effects as the unorthodox medical personnel and more importantly the deliverers and exorcists of the communities in which they reside.

We hope that this discussion will help us gain a fair understanding of the "spiritual universe"[10] of the Akan, its sources, and assumptions, and provide some of the epistemological tools necessary for an Akan Christian theological endeavor. It will also provide us with a basis to critically analyze, assess, and understand the contributions of Pobee and Bediako to Akan Christological thinking. For example, the understanding of the ancestral categories is pertinent to the study of both Pobee and Bediako because they

10. Bediako, *Jesus and the Gospel in Africa*, 20.

have constructed their Akan Christologies using these categories. It will also help to orient us towards the fundamental questions as to how much Jesus Christ needs to be adapted to the Akan spiritual universe, and how much this spiritual universe needs to be engaged and challenged by Christ for its own transformation.

The Akan Concept of God: Divine Attributes

Before we attempt to give a description of the Akan concept of God and the divine attributes associated with God, we will endeavor to look at some of the myths that form the basis of the Akan belief system. Myths about God in Akan Religion are intended to teach about God, especially his attributes as creator and controller of the universe.

Akan Myths about *Onyankopong*

According to T. N. O. Quarcoopome currently the Dean of the Regent Divinity School at the Regent University College of Science and Technology, Accra, Ghana, and author of *West African Traditional Region,* the word, myth, can simply be defined as "a channel for conveying a certain fact or a certain basic truth about man's experiences in his encounter with the created order and with regard to man's relation to the supersensible world."[11]

African religion has no sacred texts. It is through the myths, as handed down by oral tradition from generation to generation, that transmission of beliefs and concepts occur. Thus, Quarcoopome recounts: "a myth is a sacred story told to explain how people think about themselves and about the universe. It attempts to explain the existing conditions of things."[12] Africans accept their mythical stories as authentic sources of their beliefs from their forefathers. No one disputes any known myth. Though they are stories, they cannot be fabricated. In order words, one cannot make up a story today and declare it as an African myth. It must however be noted that sometimes the stories are not exactly the same as the writers report. For instance, Bolaji Idowu points out that the Yoruba[13] have more than one myth that explains the

11. Quarcoopome, *West African Traditional Religion*, 25.

12. Ibid.

13. Yoruba people (*Yorùbá* in Yoruba orthography) are one of the largest ethnic groups in West Africa. The majority of the Yoruba speak the Yoruba language (Yoruba: *èdèe Yorùbá*; èdè). The Yoruba constitute between thirty and fifty million individuals]

separation of God and humankind, though the objective may be the same. We shall give an account of two myths about God authored by T. N. O. Quarcoopome and Kofi Asare Opoku but drawn from the oral traditional sources of the Yoruba of Nigeria and the Akan of Ghana:

> In the beginning the world was marshy and watery, a waste place. The sky was above where *Olorun,* the owner of the sky lived with the other divinities. There were some spiders' web which extended to the earth like fairy bridges. The gods sometimes came down to play in the marshy waste, coming down through the spiders' web. There were no men and there was no solid ground. One day *Olorun* called the chief of the divinities, great god or *Orisanla,* and gave him a snail shell in which there were some loose earth, a pigeon and a hen with five toes. He came down to the marsh and threw the earth from the snail shell into a small space. Then the hen and the pigeon were put on the earth and started to scratch the soil about. They were able to cover much of the marsh and solid ground was formed.[14]

So, for the Ethnic Yoruba of Nigeria, this is how the owner of the sky formed the earth and thus became the owner of the earth as well. Through this myth both the vast sky and huge earth are controlled by the owner of the sky—*Olorun.* This is, however, not the full text of this Yoruba myth. It continues to say that *Olorun* sent the animal chameleon to inspect the earth to see if the work of creating the earth had been completed to its satisfaction. The myth states that after the first thorough inspection, it was reported that the earth was wide but not dry enough. He was sent back again, but this time it was dry.[15]

The second mythical story is obtained from the works of Kofi Asare Opoku about the Akans. The myth is told thus:

> God and men once lived very close together, and men could reach, touch, and feel Him. Then an old woman began to pound her fufuu regularly, using a mortar and a long pestle. She hit God every time she pounded fufuu, so He moved further and further away from men and went into the skies. When the people realized what had happened they tried to find ways to bring God back . . . .The

throughout West Africa and are found predominantly in South Western Region of Nigeria that represents approximatelytwenty-one percent of its total population. Some are also located in the South Eastern Region of Benin.

14. Quarcoopome, *West African Traditional Religion*, 25.

15. Ibid., 26.

> old woman suggested that they should all bring their mortars together and pile them one on top of another to form a 'ladder' to reach Him. They discovered that they needed just about one more mortar to make a ladder long enough. The old woman then suggested that they pull out the bottom-most mortar and put it on top. When they attempted to do this the whole construction collapsed on them and killed many.[16]

These myths give us a picture of some of the ideas and beliefs of the Akan and how they sought to understand the relationship between God and human beings. They also seek to give an account of how the world was created. In the subsection below, we will delve more into some of the concepts of God that has become part of the Akan religio-cultural heritage.

The Akan Concepts of God—*Onyankopong*

From the myths quoted above one realizes that the Akan has had a long relationship and experience with *Onyankopong*, the Great God, who is affectionately called *Odomankoma*, which means, the infinite, inventor, or creator of the universe. But the Akan, like many African tribes and ethnic groups, did not write these down as sacred texts. It was the community that maintained and passed down the faith:

> African knowledge of God is expressed in proverbs, short statements, songs, prayers, names, myths, stories and religious ceremonies. All these are easy to remember and pass on to other people, since there are no sacred writings in traditional societies. One should not, therefore, expect long dissertations about God. But God is no stranger to African peoples, and in traditional life there are no atheists. This is summarized in an Ashanti (Akan) proverb that 'No one shows a child the Supreme Being'. That means that everybody knows of God's existence almost by instinct, and even children know Him.[17]

The Akan have had a long experience with the Creator God as their myths and philosophy, proverbs, songs, prayers, given names, stories, short statements and religious ceremonies point out. Most of the ideas, assumptions and thoughts have been handed down from generation to generation through oral history and traditions. Akan primal understanding of the

16. Opoku, *West African Traditional Religion*, 24.
17. Mbiti, *African Religions and Philosophy*, 29.

nature of the universe is basically "theistic and theocentric; and the Supreme Being—God is at the center of every cultural or traditional thought."[18] In this section, an attempt is made to elucidate the concept of God among the Akans, the misconceptions that arose with the missionary enterprise, and the appropriate corrections that were made by African theologians.

One thing that is clear beyond any ambiguity is that for the Akan, the belief that the "Supreme Being created the universe is noncontroversial and unquestionable."[19] He is perceived as the owner of the whole creation and therefore father of all. As the Father, the masculine pronoun, "He," is used in reference to Him. He wields all spiritual power and nothing can be compared to His supremacy and authority. He is not perceived as just a cosmic force unrelated to humankind; as the myths stated above affirms. He has a long standing relationship with the Akan. The Akan perceive the Supreme Being as the one who directs all human affairs and that is why they have such dependence on Him. This is one of the reasons why the Akan (African) is perceived to be "religiously notorious."[20]

However, there had been much confusion in the past (especially during the period of the European missionary enterprise) and thereafter, especially because of some of the Western writers, as to who the Akan refers to as *Onyame* or *Onyankopong*. This has also contributed to some of the misconceptions on what African Religious Traditions really entail. Long before the arrival of the European Missionaries the terms— *Onyankopong*, and *Nyame* or *Nana Nyankopon* or *Nana Nyame* in the Akan language were terms used in reference to the Supreme Being or the Supreme Deity as the one who controlled the vast sky or the universe without any uncertainty or confusion.

Given the deep and thoughtful meaning of the Akan terminologies used to designate the Supreme Being, one of the writers of West African Religions, Geoffrey Parrinder, specifically and categorically argued that the Supreme Being was simply the same as "God the Omnipotent, Omnipresent and Omniscient Creator of the universe" as perceived in the Western world. [21] Contending with the derogatory depictions and fallacies that had characterized the investigations of the earlier research perpetrated by Western missionaries and colonialists, Geoffrey Parrinder rightly detected the

18. Parrinder, *West African Religion*, 14.

19. Ibid., 14.

20. Mbiti, *African Religions and Philosophy*, 1.

21. Ibid., 13.

general misperceptions and misconceptions of the explorers, colonialists, and missionaries to the land of Africa. He later wrote the very significant fact that had led to all the misperceptions: "People took it for granted that there was no idea of God in Africa before the arrival of the Europeans."[22] In fact, William Bosman, one of the early European missionaries and explorers, observed two hundred and sixty years earlier that "West Africans believed in a high God, though they did not worship him."[23]

Though it can be argued that Bosman's statement is also a form of misconception, yet, at least from the first part of his statement, one can observe that there were some early affirmations that West Africans believed in a Supreme God. Unlike his contemporaries, who postulated that West Africans "had no idea of God," he chose to affirm that they did, but surprisingly, held that they did not worship their God.

What does Bossman really mean by this statement? According to Parrinder, Bosman makes a subtle argument on behalf of the Africans, pointing out that "They (West Africans) have a faint idea of the true God, and ascribe to him the attributes of Almighty and Omnipresence; they believe he created the Universe, and therefore vastly prefer him before their idol-gods; but they do not pray to him, or offer any sacrifices to Him."[24] Did Africans have a faint idea of the true God? Clearly Bossman was reluctant to equate the African belief in the Supreme God to that of the Western Christians. We need to understand the period within which all these observations were made and the intent of the observers. Parrinder asserts that "this was written long before any missionaries, except travelling padres, began settled work in West Africa."[25]

Further clarification about the Supreme Being and God has been articulated by Geoffrey Parrinder. According to Parrinder, it was Sir A. B. Ellis (a missionary and critical writer on African Religions in the eighteenth century) who first realized his own misleading thought and later corrected himself and for posterity:

22. Ibid., 14.

23. Ibid.

24. Ibid., 14. Quoted from Bossman, *A New and Accurate Description of the Coasts of Guinea, Divided into the Gold, the Slave, and the Ivory Coasts* (1705) 348; Ghana named the Gold Coast—a name given to the nation by the European explorers. In the same manner Nigeria was given the name Slave Coast and La Côte d' Ivoire formally Ivory Coast. The Gold Coast was changed to Ghana on the eve of the Independence Celebration in 1957.

25. Ibid., 14.

> Sir A. B. Ellis at first thought that the Supreme Being was a 'loan-god', introduced by missionaries. He said that the people of Ghana 'added to their system a new deity, whom they termed *'Nana Nyankopon'*. This he pointed out was the God of the Christians, borrowed from them, and adapted under a new designation, meaning 'Lord of the Sky.'[26]

Parrinder maintains that Ellis later modified this opinion; writing of *Mawu* of the *Ewe* tribe of Ghana, Togo, and Benin, he said:

> While upon the subject of this God, I may as well say that from additional evidence I have since collected, I now think that the view I expressed concerning the origin of *Nyankopon,* the parallel god of the Tshi (Twi or Akan)-speaking peoples, was incorrect; and that instead of his being the Christian God borrowed and thinly disguised, I now hold he is like *Mawu (the name given to the Creator God by the indigenous Ewe people of Ghana)* the sky-god, or indwelling spirit of the sky; and that also like *Mawu,* he has been to a certain extent confounded with Jehovah."[27]

Later still, Parrinder points out what Ellis wrote about Yoruba religion: "Just as the missionaries have caused *Nyankopon (Akan God of creation of the universe) Nyonmo (Ga-Adangbe's name for the God of the universe) and Mawu* to be confused with Jehovah of the Christians, by translating these names as "God", so have they done with *Olorun.*"[28] Thus, we see here vividly that some of the missionaries misconstrued one of the supreme beliefs of the Akans and many other ethnic groups in Ghana and even some West African Countries. The correction made by Ellis is very important as many people even today fail to understand some of the beliefs and practices of the Akan and of Africans as a whole. It also points to the disregard some of the missionaries had for what the Akans had lived for and worked with for centuries. For instance, Parrinder also reveals the derogatory terminologies such as primitive, paganism, fetishism, idolatry, polytheism, native, animism, etc. that were used to describe Akan religion.

The focus of this research, however, is neither to defend nor to criticize positions held in the past on the Akan conception of God. However, it is important to arrive at a good understanding of God in the Akan culture

26. Ibid,, 13.

27. Ibid.

28. Ibid., 13. *Olorun* is for the Yoruba of Nigeria as *Onyankopong* is for the Akan of Ghana.

in order to arrive at an appropriate Christology for the Akan people. In his own defense of the Akan religion after a thorough study as a missionary, Parrinder emphatically hypothesizes that "the religion of West Africans often used to be referred to as 'primitive,' but this is an inaccurate term."[29]

Similarly, Joseph Boakye Danquah, a Ghanaian Scholar, researcher and author of *"Akan Doctrine of God,"* maintains that "regardless of the plethora of gods or lesser deities, the Akan religion is simply monotheistic."[30] Kwame Bediako points out that the misconceptions seen above about Akan belief in God may explain why the missionaries failed to reach out to the "spiritual universe of the Akans."[31] As we shall see later, Bediako addresses these inadequacies and attempts to resolve the issue by making his own proposals on how to relate the Christian faith to the spiritual universe of the Akan. We will return to this in due course to examine and critically analyze his proposal and to offer an alternative.

Kofi Opoku Asare states succinctly in his book, *West African Traditional Religion,* that "In traditional Africa, religion is life and life, religion."[32] Akans are no exception. They are deeply religious and most of the times seek to assign religious reasons for whatever circumstances prevails, whether positive or negative, to determine the cause thereof. According to him as well the Akan believe that "the universe was created by a Supreme Being, whom they refer to variously as *Oboadee* (Creator) *Nyame* (God) *Odomankoma* (Infinite, Inventor) *Ananse Kokuroko* (The Great Spider; The Great Designer)."[33] The Akan believe that the Supreme Being is the architect of the universe. The Akan call God—*Onyame, Onyamkopong, and Onyamkopong Kwame.*[34] He also holds that these names referred to the Supreme Being long before the coming and establishment of Christianity in the land of the Akans.

T. N. O. Quarcoopome, a research fellow and author of *West African Traditional Religion* and currently dean of the Graduate School of Divinity of the Regent University College of Science and Technology, Accra, Ghana, points out that "the divine name, *Onyame,* has become a household

29. Ibid., 14.

30. Danquah, *Akan Doctrine of God*, 18.

31. Bediako, *Jesus and the Gospel in Africa,* 48.

32. Opoku, *West African Traditional Religion*, 1.

33. G. M. Arthur and Robert Rowe, *Akan Cosmology* (1998–2001)—A paper presentation retrieved from internet sources dated May 25, 2010.

34. Quarcoopome, *West African Traditional Religion,* 62.

name uttered in various conversations and most of the time, especially in Akan songs."[35] The real meaning of *Onyame* in the Akan traditional view is not certain. However, Quarcoopome's suggestion is that it is made up of "*Nya*"—"To get" and "*Me*"—"To be full," which gives a clear indication of the God they believed in. He explains that *Onyame* means "the God of fullness, the God of ultimate satisfaction."[36]

Onyamkopong is also the name for God among the Akans. According to Quarcoopome, the name derives from "*Nyame* and '*Koro*' meaning Great and '*Pon*' meaning One, Only."[37] Thus for him, *Onyamkopong* means "The Only Great Onyame", that is "The Only Great God of fullness and of satisfaction with perfect attributes."[38] Also, *Kwame* is a personal name among the Akan for males born on Saturdays just as Kofi is given to a male born on Friday and Kwabena for a male born on Tuesday. Quarcoopome points out a belief of the Akans that God completed his work of creation on Saturday—hence he is given the name Kwame. Thus, for the Akan, God is *Onyamkopong Kwame*—"the God who appears on a Saturday."[39]

Quarcoopome further states that such a name, associated with the Supreme Deity, "makes him a personal and intimate being with whom the Akans can enter into communion and communication."[40] The Akan brings every endeavor he or she makes to *Onyankopong* in the form of simple prayers. When the Akan wakes up he or she prays to thank God for giving strength for yet another day, just as he oversaw the sleeping process. Prayers are offered before the meal is cooked and before the food is eaten. While undertaking a journey, God the *Onyamkopong* will be called for traveling mercies and protection. The farms are given to him to pour his rain in good time and to give good yields. Thus, the Akan relate to *Onyamkopong* closely.

This notion is buttressed by John Mbiti when he asserts the widely held belief that "God shows His providence through fertility and health of humans, cattle and fields, as well as through the plentiful-ness of children, cattle, food and other goods."[41] He points out further that many African

35. Ibid., 63.
36. Ibid.
37. Ibid.
38. Ibid.
39. Ibid., 63.
40. Ibid., 64.
41. Mbiti, *African Religions and Philosophy*, 41 and 42.

societies therefore pray to him for these items. For instance, the Nuba[42] says in prayer: "God we are hungry; Give us cattle, give us sheep."[43] The belief of Akans that *Onyame* is the creator of the universe and the dependable one who satisfies all the needs of humankind both spiritual and physical is fundamental to their religious systems.

Kofi Opoku Asare maintains that the idea of God as the creator of the universe and humankind, and the final authority in all matters is native to Africa and is not, as some early writers on the subject asserted, of foreign origin. For him, this idea is, "firmly entrenched in the religious beliefs of West Africans."[44] Since the Akan thoughts on God are normally concrete, and not abstract, some of the abstract attributes such as 'eternal' etc. to *Onyankopong* needs to be looked at. John Mbiti gives some thoughtful explanations to clarify the matter:

> These attributes (the eternal and intrinsic) of God (*Onyankopong*) are difficult to grasp and express, since they pertain more to the realm of the abstract than concrete thought forms. Broadly speaking, African thought forms are more concrete than abstract. We find, however, considerable examples of how African peoples conceive of the eternal nature of God.[45]

Our concern here is not to address the issue of the move from concrete to abstract. But it is important because the presence of abstract attributes give credence to Bossman's point that the African idea of the Supreme God was borrowed from the European Christian missionary enterprise, to make the 'African god' look the same as God in the European sense. However, we are far from reaching such a conclusion because of Mbiti's thoughtful point that there are numerous examples within the African societies depicting their long practical experience with divinity. Let us examine closely some of the examples Mbiti points out.

42. *Nuba* is a collective term used here for the peoples who inhabit the*Nuba* Mountains in the states of Southern Sudan, Africa. Although the term is used to describe them as if they composed a single group, the *Nuba* are multiple distinct peoples who speak different languages. Estimates of the *Nuba* population vary widely; the Southern Sudanese government estimated that they numbered 1.07 million in 2003.

43. Ibid., 42.

44. Parrinder, *West African Religion*, 14.

45. Mbiti, *African Religions and Philosophy*, 30.

Mbiti maintains that most African societies, including the Akan, consider "God to be omniscient, that is, to know all things,"[46] expressed in the Akan-Twi language as *'Onim ade nyinaa.'* This expression according to Mbiti also "confers upon God the highest possible position of honor and respect since wisdom commands great respect in African societies."[47] Again, Mbiti points out that in presenting *Onyankopong* this way "humankind admit that humanity's wisdom, however, great, is limited, incomplete and acquired."[48] *Onyankopong's* ability to knowing everything does not only sets him apart from humankind's limited knowledge, but rather, and in addition, it sets him far apart in everything from the lesser deities as well. Parrinder has this to say in connection with the lesser deities: "They are incomparable to the Akan's *Onyamkopong.*"[49] The fact that *Onyankopong* does not compare with the lesser deities in any way concludes the fact that we cannot distinguish Akan Christology from the divinities or the lesser deities.

Mbiti observes God's omniscience as absolute, unlimited and intrinsically part of His eternal nature and being. Respectively, he outlines from Zulu[50] and Banyarwanda[51] sources where "God is known as 'the Wise One' and to the Akan as 'He Who knows or sees all.'"[52] With this knowledge, Mbiti says "God is regarded as the Omniscient from whom nothing is hidden, since nothing can escape His vision, hearing or knowledge. He knows everything, observes everything and hears everything, without limitation and without exception."[53] Danquah maintains that the Yoruba says: "only God is wise and that He is the discerner of hearts, who sees both the inside and outside of man."[54] Yet, Mbiti says the metaphor of seeing and hearing explains the concept of God as omniscient in a concrete way, which is easy to grasp.

46. Ibid.

47. Ibid.

48. Ibid.

49. Parrinder, *West African Religion,* 15.

50. Zulu: a member of a Bantu people of southeast Africa, primarily inhabiting the northeast Natal province in South Africa.

51. Banyarwanda is an ethnic group from Rwanda is the Southern African Region.

52. Mbiti, *African Religions and Philosophy,* 31.

53. Ibid.

54. Danquah, *Akan Doctrine of God,* 55.

Furthermore, Mbiti also points out that these people consider God "to be simultaneously everywhere (Omnipresent),"[55] expressed in Akan-Twi language as "*Owo mann nyinaa.*" This is intriguing and quite revealing. But, how do Akans account for the Omnipresence of *Onyankopong?* According to both Quarcoopome and Opoku Asare, the Akan believe that God is everywhere to the extent that in a typical village, one can accidently drop his money on the street and go only to come back to find it lying there untouched. It is assumed that *Onyankopong* is watching you and he will communicate it to the priest or priestesses who will later find the thief and deal with him. Thus, it is difficult for people to steal from one another. Mbiti maintains that "the Akamba, Igbo, Yoruba, and Akan believe that wrong-doers cannot escape the judgment of God."[56]

The last of the three eternal and intrinsic attributes of God in Akan religion point to the fact that he is to be *"almighty,* (Omnipotent)"[57] expressed in the Akan-Twi language as "*Tumi nyinaa Wura.*" Mbiti points out that God the almighty is a concept easier to grasp than the attributes discussed above with many concrete examples from all over Africa. People actually speak of *Onyankopong* or *Onyame* as 'the All-powerful' or 'the Almighty' that is *Onyame Kokoroko.*'[58] He is also described as 'He who bends down even majesties,' and 'He who roars so that all nations are struck with terror.' The Akan also sees his omnipotence in his exercise of power over nature, and the way he deals with and controls spirits. For instance, "he is known as the one who makes mountains quake and rivers overflow." He is the one who protects people from witchcraft power and the enemies of progress.

Finally, the attributes of transcendence are treated together with immanence. For the Akan, posited Mbiti, "He is so 'far' (transcendental) that man cannot reach Him; yet, He is so 'near' (immanent) that He comes close to men."[59] As a way of critique, Mbiti remarks that "many foreign writers have gone astray here, in emphasizing God's remoteness to the exclusion of His nearness."[60] Among the Akan, various names describe the ways He is perceived. Kofi Opoku Asare has outlined some of them as follows:

55. Mbiti, *African Religions and Philosophy*, 30.
56. Ibid., 31.
57. Ibid., 30.
58. Ibid., 31.
59. Ibid., 32.
60. Ibid.

> *Onyame*—The Supreme Being, God the Creator of all things, the Deity; *Nana Onyankopong*—Grandfather (the name Grandfather makes God masculine and hence the 'he' pronoun designates him) *Nyame* who alone is the Great One; *Twereduampon*—The dependable; *Amowia*—Giver of the Sun or Light; *Amosu*—Giver of Rain; *Totrobonsu*—The One who causes rain to fall abundantly; *Amoamee*—Giver of Sufficiency; *Brekyirihunuade*—He who sees all, even from behind; *Abommubuwafre*—Consoler, Comforter who gives salvation; *Nyaamanekose*—He in whom you confide troubles which come upon you; *Tetekwaframoa*—he who is there now as from ancient times; *Nana*—Grand Ancestor; *Borebore*—Excavator, Hewer, Creator, Originator, Carver, Architect; *Odomankoma*—Creator; *Oboadee*—Creator.[61]

Accordingly, Opoku Asare postulates that the names given to *Onyankopong* or *Onyame* "are unlike the names given to other spiritual beings they recognize . . . . He is thought of as "the Supreme Being, the One who is pre-eminent in all things."[62] Other recognized names includes God the King, *Onyame ne Hene;* God the judge, *Onyame ne Otemufuo;* the dependable God, *Otwereduampong Nyankopong*; the compassionate God, *Ahunu mmoboro Agya.* For both Kofi Opoku Asare and Quarcoopome, the idea that God is the creator of the universe and all it contains is at the core of the religious beliefs of West Africans.[63] John Mbiti extends this assertion to cover the entire region of Africa when he points out that "the way God is viewed in Christianity, Islam, and Judaism, the three main monotheistic religions, is very much similar to that of Africans."[64] As Creator of the universe, he is also the Sustainer of creation, provider and protector of creation, who rules over the universe and supports justice.

Among the Akan there is a myth about creation handed down by ancestors and told a million times. In this myth, as reported by Kofi Opoku Asare and Quarcoopome,

> Odomankoma, Creator, first made the sky, and then the earth, rivers and plants. Finally he created human and animals. The animals fed on the plants already created and, in turn, provided food for humankind. Humankind also needed protection in his environment and for this, God created the spirits of the waters, forests and

61. Opoku, *West African Traditional Religion*, 15

62. Ibid., 14.

63. Ibid., 19, and Quarcoopome, *West African Traditional Religion*, 62.

64. Mbiti, *African Religions and Philosophy*, 29.

> rocks. Thus, according to the Akan, everything was created in an ordered fashion and every creature has its place and its special or particular function in the universe.[65]

According to Kofi Asare, the idea of order of creation of the world is also expressed in the myth of the Fon, a popular ethnic group in Dahomey, now called the Republic of Benin. Benin is located midway between Ghana and Nigeria. Their philosophy and cultural ideologies are similar to that of the Yoruba of Nigeria. They all claim that the Creator completed creation in four literal days. These quotes are not from any sacred text. As already indicated, African Religions do not have sacred texts. Every fact or story documented today has been preserved through oral traditional sources handed down from generation to generation. Below is the belief of the order of creation from the Fon ethnic group of the Republic of Benin:

> The Fon believe that the Creator followed a particular course in His creation of the world which took four days—hence they observe a four-day week to conform to the order of creation. On the first day, Mawu-Lisa set the world in order and created man. On the second day, He sent a special agent into the world to make it habitable for man. Then, on the third day, God gave man the gift of sight and speech as well as the ability to know and learn about the world around him. Finally, on the fourth day He gave man the skills to master his environment and make it a better place to live in.[66]

This statement again, concretizes the fact that creation is the sole prerogative of the Creator who happened to be *Onyankopong* for the Akan, *Mawu* for the Fon of the Republic of Benin, and Ewe of Ghana, only to mention a few.

It is also believed among the Akans that *Onyame* brought into being life, itself, as well as everything found in this world. He has great care and concern for his creatures and he shows his care and compassion for them by providing for all they need. Kofi Asare indicates this idea of God's care and compassion in two of Akans proverbial expressions: "*Aboa onni dua, Onyame na opra ne ho,* meaning, it is God who drives away the flies for the tailless animal, and *Onyame na owo basini fufuo ma no,* meaning, it

65. Opoku, *West African Traditional Religion,* 21–22 and Quarcoopome, *West African Traditional Religion,* 63.

66. Opoku, *West African Traditional Religion,* 23.

is God who pounds fufu for the one armed-person."[67] Again, Kofi Asare Opoku points to another Akan belief of God from a proverb—*"Onyame ma wo yare a, oma wo ano aduru,"*[68] which literally means: if God gives you sickness, he provides the medicine for its cure. The whole expression, according to Kofi Asare is that even if God is the cause of misery, he provides the remedy for the victim.

Similarly, the idea that God is just and fair is predominant in Akan belief system. Kofi Asare uses another proverb to convey this thought—"Since God does not like wickedness, he gave everybody a name."[69] This is reinforced with a thought in another West African tribe, the Yoruba of Nigeria: "Those (thieves) we cannot catch, we leave in the hands of God."[70] Kofi Asare further points out that among Akans there is the belief of God's constant care and protection. This is the reason the *"Ijaw* name, *Egbesu,* means, the Supreme Protector."[71] Finally, Kofi Asare makes reference to a saying of the Ewes of Ghana—"He is good, for he has never withdrawn from us the good things he gave us."[72] Moreover, the Akan underscores the point that God's goodness is also reflected in the fact that every creature is endowed with a special gift—*"Onyame amma asomfena bribi a, omaa no ahodannan,*that is if God did not give the swallow any gift, he gave her the gift of swiftness of movement (agility)."[73]

It is also a belief among the Akan that God's providence never fails. The Akans thus state: "If God gives you a cup of wine and an evil-minded person kicks it over, he fills it up for you again."[74] To indicate absolute dependence on God's providence, the Akan attribute most of their successes to their belief in him. The absolute dependence on *Onyankopon*g is non-negotiable because of the belief in the incessant attacks from opposing cosmic forces. In this vein, some Akan names are derived from the circumstances that surround the birth of a child or even the establishment of a farm or a company. For instance, the Akan name, "*Nyamekye,*"[75] means God's gift or

67. Opoku, *West African Traditional Religion*, 28.
68. Ibid.
69. Ibid.
70. Ibid.
71. Ibid.
72. Ibid.
73. Ibid.
74. Ibid.
75. Ibid., 29.

a gift from God or Gifty as later realized in English names. Other names includes: *Nyameye*—God is good or God shows goodness; *Nyamedom* or *Nyame Adom*—God's grace or the Gracious hand of God. All these names point to the fact that without the influencing hand of *Onyankopong*, the couple would not be able to have children of their own. Thus, such names are given to children who are born after years of marriage without children or after many miscarriages.

Similar names found in other ethnic groups are ascribed to God or derived from the Supreme Being as pointed out by Quarcoopome and Kofi Asare. For instance, among the Ewes of Ghana are the following:

> *Mawunyo*—God is just, or God is kind; *Mawuenyega*, God is great; *Sedina*, God listens to humankind's supplications; *Selome*, The Creator loves mankind or God is kind to people; *Senyo*, God is good, *Senagbe*, God is the giver of life; *Selenu*, God never sleeps; *Sefako*, God is a comforter; and *Setutsi*, God blesses us. The Yoruba of Nigeria have the following among others; *Olutooke*, the Lord deserves to be glorified; *Oluwasanmi*, God is good to me; *Olufunmilayo*, God gave me joy; *Olufemi*, God loves me; *Olusanya*, God compensates for suffering; *Olukoya*, The lord champions the cause of the suffering; and *Oluremilojun*, God consoles me in my weeping.[76]

Kofi Asare lists the following attributes from the Igbo of Nigeria:

> *Chukwuneke* or *Chukwukolu*, God creates; *Chukwunyelu*, God gave; *Chukwuma*, God knows; *Chukwumaijem*, God knows my steps or my journey; *Chukwuka*, God is greater; *Chukwunweike* or *Ikechukwu*, power is with God; *Chukwuka-odinaka*, It is all in God's hands; *Ifenayichukwu*, Nothing is impossible with God; *Chukwuemeka* or *Olise meka*, God has done much; *Kenechukwu*, Thank God; *Arinze-chukwu*, Thanks to God, ie were it not for God . . . ; *Ngozichukwu* or *Gnosis*, Blessings of God; *Chukwumailo*, God knows my enemies; *Chukwuzoba*, God saves; and *Chukwuagbanarinam*, may God not be far from me.[77]

Kofi Asare intimates that all these attributes reflect the awe in which God, the Supreme Being or Onyankopong is held by West Africans and further emphasizes the presence of God in their lives—as Living Reality, who is active in the world and in the lives of humankind. Thus, he points out that

76. Ibid.

77. Ibid.

this kind of presence of God in the life of the people also comes as a result of the myths and experiences of the people.

Worship of the Creator—*Onyankopong*/God

The issue as to whether Akans worshipped God before the coming of Christianity has been raised since the arrival of Christianity in the land of Akan. According to John Mbiti, the absence of shrines, temples and feast days, specifically dedicated to God among West Africans, has led many casual observers to conclude that God is not worshipped by the Akan. He maintains that such a cursory observation never takes into consideration that fact that West Africans did not regard such practices as necessary to worship God.

Both the Yoruba of Nigeria and Akan of Ghana, according to Kofi Asare, have an explanation to justify their stand. The Yoruba states that "*Oluron* is everywhere hence it is unwise to try to confine him to a temple."[78] Likewise the Akan of Ghana says: "If you want to speak to God, speak to the wind."[79] God is compared to the wind, which is everywhere; as the wind is everywhere, so *Onyankopong* is. Kofi Asare therefore concludes that since God is everywhere, and can hear our supplications at any time, He is not to be identified with anything in particular or with any place. This also explains why priests and priestesses are not found in the worship of God among Akans.

Actually, according to Asare Opoku, it is rare among West African societies, in general, to have priests and priestesses especially appointed for the worship of God. Among the Akan of Ghana, there is the belief that through the *okra*,[80] that is the soul of humankind, one can have a more meaningful and direct access to *Onyame* than to go through a designated person for daily or weekly worship. According to Asare Opoku, "the Akan believe that there is no priest or priestess who alone has access to *Onyame* and can manipulate Him to comply with human wishes. Every person, it is believed, has direct access to *Onyame* through possession of the *okra* (the soul)"[81]

78. Ibid., 30.
79. Ibid.
80. Ibid.
81. Ibid.

This could, in fact, be a critique of Christianity which has designated priests and priestesses to facilitate the worship of the Supreme Being, even though both Christianity and Traditional Religion of the Akan accept the concept of the soul's direct connection and access to the Supreme Being with or without an agent. Again, Asare Opoku makes us aware that worship to the African stems from the awareness that humankind is a creature of God and consequently depends on a power superior to him. Worship for the Akan is specifically directed towards the Supreme Being and not any other spiritual entity.

Akan Cosmology and Religious Practices

We have already noted above that the universe and all that is contained in it, including humankind, is the creation of Supreme Being—*Onyame* or *Onyankopong*. Though each group of people has its own peculiar cultural heritage, all concepts, beliefs, and practices are related to and are about this Supreme Being. Robert Baum, Chair of the Department of Religious Studies at University of Missouri, whose research includes his Doctoral Studies in African History and African Religions including African Traditional Religion, Christianity and Islam, makes this significant point in his writing in *Africana: The Encyclopedia of African and African American Experience*:

> While it is true that Africans do not have a word equivalent to the term 'religion' there are a number of terms in African languages that describe activities, practices, and a system of thought that corresponds closely to what most Westerners mean by religion. African religions are often closely associated with African peoples' concepts of ethnic identity, language and culture. They are not limited to beliefs in supernatural beings *[God and spirits]* or to ritual acts of worship, but affect all aspects of life, from farming to hunting, from travel to courtship.[82]

This analysis is buttressed with the description given by John Mbiti that all African cultures and societies, traditional (pre-colonial) and contemporary (post-colonial) across the continent and regardless of differences in national origin, language, or ethnicity are deeply religious. He states:

> Each people [society in Africa] has its own religious system with a set of beliefs and practices. Religion permeates into all the departments of life so it is not easy or possible to isolate it [from other

82. Baum, *Africana*, 57.

> aspects of African society and culture.] A study of these religious systems is, therefore a study of the peoples themselves in all the complexities of traditional and modern life.[83]

Africans are particularly concerned with the here and hereafter. The beliefs and practices do not only center on the phenomenal world but also the noumenal. In this manner, Robert Baum, an American whose research focuses on African and African American history and religions, opines that "Like most religious systems African religions focus on the eternal questions of what it means to be human; what is the meaning of life, and what are the correct relations among humans, between humans and spiritual powers, and with the natural world?"[84] Through ritual activities, music, dance and even at some festive occasions Africans demonstrates and celebrate their world in awe of the Supreme Being. Their religious activities also seek to deal with the incessant work of evil and suffering. It is indeed a fact that every activity of the African is inextricably intertwined with religio-cultural thought.

John Mbiti makes mention of the fact that "the spiritual world of African peoples is very densely populated with spiritual beings, spirits and the living-dead."[85] The Akan spiritual universe is no exception. To more fully articulate their religious ethos and philosophical perception, Mbiti says that "It is essential to consider their concepts of the spiritual world in addition to the concepts of God."[86]

Therefore, in this section we will be engaged in the exploration of the concepts of the spiritual beings, spirits, and the living dead and how these entities merge with concepts such as witchcraft, magic, sorcery, and others to the extent that it is sometimes difficult to draw a distinction among them. This investigation will explicate the overall spiritual universe of the Akan and also will be especially helpful in the task of formulating an Akan Christology.

83. Mbiti, *African Religions and Philosophy,* 74.

84. Baum, *Africana,* 57.

85. Mbiti, *African Religions and Philosophy,* 74.

86. Ibid.

The Akan Concept of Spiritual Beings

Mbiti holds that "The spirits in general belong to the ontological mode of existence between God and man"[87] He recognizes two categories of spiritual beings: "Those which were created as such, and those which were once human beings."[88] He then sub-divides them into "divinities and associates of God, ordinary spirits, and the living-dead."[89] The divinities, according to Mbiti, covers personifications of God's activities and manifestations of natural phenomena and objects, the so-called 'nature spirits,' deified heroes, and mythological figures.[90] Other writers, he points out, refer to the divinities as 'gods,' 'demigods,' 'nature spirits,' and 'ancestral spirits.'[91]

According to Mbiti, "divinities have been created by God and are in the ontological category of spirits."[92] But this issue of the creation of the divinities appears to generate some measure of discrepancies in the thought of some leading African theologians and religionists. One of these theologians and religionists, Bolaji Idowu, Professor of Religious Studies at the University of Ibadan, writes in his book, "*African Traditional Religion—A Definition*" that "from the point of view of the theology of African traditional religion, it will not be correct to say that the divinities were created."[93] A thorough explanation to this problematic issue is beyond the scope of this research. However, an engagement of the thoughts of these two experts will facilitate a thorough investigation into the spiritual universe of the Akan from whose traditional thoughts we desire to develop a Christology for Akan Christianity.

How has the concept of divinities evolved in African Religion? What is the precise definition for the divinities? Idowu asserts that "it will be correct to say that they were brought into being, or that they came into being in the nature of things with regard to the divine ordering of the universe."[94] At this point, we acknowledge the fact that both definitions of 'divinities,' whether they were created or they came into being in the divine order of things, suggest that they do not bear any pre-existent or self-existent char-

87. Ibid.
88. Ibid.
89. Ibid.
90. Ibid.
91. Ibid.
92. Ibid.
93. Idowu, *African Traditional Religion*, 169.
94. Ibid.

acteristics and are unlike the pre-existent status that the Prologue of St. John's Gospel gives to the *Logos*. Nonetheless, Idowu asserts:

> Orisa-nlá (arch-divinity among the Yoruba of Nigeria) is definitely a derivation partaking of the very nature and metaphysical attributes of Olódùmarè. Hence he is often known as Deity's son or deputy, vested with the power and authority of royal sonship. And this is why it has been possible in Bahia to syncretize his cult with Christianity and identify him as Jesus Christ. Olokun (Benin) is known as the Son of Osanobwa—the Son vested with power and majesty by his Father. All Akan divinities are called sons of Onyame. It is in consequence of this derivative relationship that these divine 'beings' are entitled to be called divinities or deities.[95]

This thinking is an intriguing thought because Idowu seems to have landed on something that presumably eluded his colleagues. In his second point, Idowu re-emphasizes the fact that "the divinities are derivatives from the Deity."[96] He then points out that the divinities have no absolute existence and that they are viewed as beings only in consequence of the being of the Deity. Even their powers and authority are meaningless without the Deity.

Following slightly the thought of Mbiti, Kofi Asare Opoku maintains that "the general belief concerning the divinities is that they were created by God to fulfill specific functions and that they did not come into existence on their own volition."[97] Though Idowu does not agree with this assertion, he does not say that the divinities developed out of their own volition. In fact, he maintains that they were derivatives of God. Thus, Kofi Asare Opoku seems to have introduced the new motion that "the divinities did not come into existence on their own volition."[98]

Quarcoopome, whose assertion could be said to be in line with that of Idowu or is derived from his thought, points out that "the divinities stand next in relation to God in the hierarchy of powers. They are God's children. They were not created but were brought into being with regard to the divine ordering of the universe. They were ministers of God with derived powers."[99] For now, we can safely assume that whether the divinities were created or uncreated, one thing stands out clearly among these writers—

95. Idowu, *African Traditional Religion*, 169.

96. Ibid.

97. Opoku, *West African Traditional Religion*, 54.

98. Ibid., 54.

99. Quarcoopome, *West African Traditional Religion*, 41.

they did not come into existence on their own accord and that whatever power and authority they wield is a derivative from the Deity—Supreme Being—*Onyame*. The source of the power of the divinities is not quite certain for many Africans.

Idowu explicates further that each divinity has his own local name in the local language, which is descriptive either of his allotted function or the natural phenomenon which is believed to be a manifestation or emblem of his being. Moreover, he posits: "The divinities were brought into being as functionaries in the theocratic government of the universe."[100] For instance, in the same Yoruba, where he has already pointed out issues concerning *Orinsha-nla,* he also make reference to a divinity, *Jakuta,* which is called to be representative of 'Wrath', that is,"one who hurls or fights with stones."[101]

The Igbo of Nigeria, according to Idowu, has an arch-divinity by the name *Ala* or *Ana* or *Ani.* She is the Earth-goddess because the name also refers to the earth or ground. He points out that in the Republic of Benin, *Mawu-Lisa,* the arch-divinity, apportioned the kingdoms of the sky, the sea, and the earth among six of his offspring, and the seventh, *Legba,* made the divine messenger and inspector-general of the African pantheons.[102] One of the issues that come to mind as we explore these divinities is the fact that, in our understanding, these divinities with local names are the same as the lesser deities or the gods of the local areas. Thus, one may argue that these are attempts to link the gods of the land to the Supreme deity.

Mbiti points out that the divinities are associated with God and often stand for his activities or manifestations, either as personifications or as the spiritual beings in charge of the major objects or phenomena of nature. None of these scholars assign hierarchical powers to the divinities, except Quarcoopome, who asserts that "they stand next in relation to God in the hierarchy of powers."[103] Among the Akan, he opines that they function as ministers of God with derived powers and specific duties but normally act as intermediaries between God and humankind.

Quarcoopome reveals their nature as spirit beings with some manifestations of divine attributes. He further states their habitat as inanimate objects in nature such as rivers, lakes, lagoons, streams, ponds, trees, forests, groves, mountains, hills, and valleys. He strongly emphasizes that, to some extent, God is worshipped indirectly through the divinities. This gives

100. Idowu, *African Traditional Religion,* 170

101. Ibid., 169.

102. Idowu, *Olódùmaré,* 80ff.

103. Quarcoopome, *West African Traditional Religion,* 41.

reason why the divinities are given periodic worship and are served by traditional priests and priestesses. If they are given periodic worship during which the worshippers indirectly relate to God, then it can be argued that the spirit agency of God is somehow present in such worship. But it is also understood that the spirit agencies that inhabit the inanimate objects listed above may not necessarily be the spirit agency of God, but rather, of other spiritual forces that inhabit the universe.

As Mbiti stated earlier, the African believes that there are myriads of spirits in the universe. Though these innumerable spirits are all creation of *Onyankopong,* the Supreme Being, not all of them are given ministerial status. Such issues call for further study but they are beyond the scope of this project. Are the divinities real or not? By playing around with this question, Idowu offers an answer that has general appeal to both sides of the argument. He states that to those who believe in them, and believe that they derive succor from their ministration or afflictions from their machinations, they are real; and to those who have outgrown them or to whom they have never had significance, they have no real, objective existence.

For Idowu, "It is wrong to hold that certain experience is impossible simply on the ground that certain people have not had such or are incapable of it and that it will be sheer presumption to claim that we know already all that there is to know about the fact of spiritual powers of the supersensible world."[104] Though Idowu's point may be right, it is possible for someone to also suggest that it should be equally wrong to hold that because certain experiences have been possible for some it should be true for all people. Deducing from African belief with regard to the reality of the divinities, Idowu offers three salient points that are helpful, also for the thesis of this research:

First is to affirm that there are realities that may be described as the 'divinities of heaven.'[105] Idowu holds that it could be so because the traditions may know times when they used to be on earth in human form, and because it holds that their very origins belong to the divine secret which is beyond man's probing."[106] Idowu may be right, but such Kantian thoughts may not gain much ground in the context of some African ideas about the hereafter.

104. Idowu, *African Traditional Religion,* 172.

105. Ibid.

106. Ibid.

The second thought is that divinities in African belief are conceptualizations of certain prominent attributes of the Deity, especially as discerned through natural phenomena. Idowu maintains that this is the reason why in some cults like the 'Solar and Thunder,'[107] divinity is so universal that it is linguistically or notionally connected or confused with Deity or *Onyankopong*. Third, Idowu explains the divinities are no more than ancestors and heroes who have become deified. However, he points out, their deification occurred through their absorption of the attributes of certain earlier divinities.

Mbiti shares quite a different view about the Akan with regard to the use of *abosom* or divinities:

> The Ashanti have a pantheon of divinities through whom God manifest Himself. They are known as *abosom*; are said 'to come from Him' and to act as His servants and intermediaries between Him and other creatures . . . Minor divinities protect individual human beings; and it is believed that God purposely created the *abosom* to guard men.[108]

The Akan words, *abosom* (divinities or lesser gods or lesser deities) or *abosomfor* (priests, priestesses and worshippers) brings out the meaning clearly, because worshippers know when they deal with divinities that they do not in any way relate to the Supreme Being but rather to other spirit beings that are the creation of the Supreme Being. This distinction must be well articulated. The English word, 'divinities,' is somewhat confusing because it does not help in making the necessary distinction between the realities that are translated as 'divinities' and the Supreme Being that is above them.

It is important to note how Kofi Asare assigns in detail some of the functions of the divinities. For him, they have wide powers but not unlimited as that of God; yet, each has his or her own area of competence and jurisdiction. Thus, there are the gods of war, fertility, epidemics, nation building, agriculture and various other spheres of human endeavor.

Asare maintains that in each area of specialization, each god has full power and control to act. He however postulates that on some occasions they fail human beings. Hence sometimes the attitude towards them is ambivalent. As is common among humanity, these divinities or gods are treated with great respect when they meet expectations but with scorn and disrespect when their predictions and works fail. In Akan thought, a god

107. Ibid.

108. Mbiti, *African Religions and Philosophy*, 74ff.

who has failed may even be burned, but such action does not represent a rejection of belief in the gods. Asare further points out that a god who fails is simply replaced by a more powerful one or one who promises greater satisfaction.

It has already been stated that whatever power that is wielded by the gods is limited. It does not measure to the controlling power of the Supreme Being. Asare's use of the words, 'full power and control,' is just to show how it is understood by the people who have tasted of such experiences with significant impact. One other thing that must be clarified is that for the Akan, the Supreme Being—*Onyankopong* never fails anyone. He works in his own time. Just as he brings the rain in its season so he gives *Adom*, grace. The gods have no such power and can fail anytime.

The Akan Concept of Spirits

Having dealt with the issue of the divinities, which are considered those "spiritual beings of a relatively high status,"[109] we now move to take a look at the other spiritual beings. Mbiti asserts that to pursue a hierarchical consideration, the spirits are the 'common' spiritual beings beneath the status of divinities, and above the status of humankind. According to him, myriads of spirits are reported among all African People, but they defy description almost as much as they defy the scientists' test tubes in the laboratory.

Mbiti points out that there is no clear information from the African peoples on the origin of the spirits. According to him, "some spirits are considered to have been created as a 'race' by the spirit themselves . . . and such spirits reproduce to add to their numbers."[110] He also says, however, that "most people seem to believe that the spirits are what remain of human beings when they die physically."[111] It is the second understanding of the origin of spirits that is known and is most acceptable to the Akan. This is because it is believed that spirits are the destiny of humankind and beyond them is the realm of God. In this case, the classification has only two realities of humans and spirits. However, in the societies that recognize divinities, they are regarded as a further group in the ontological hierarchy between spirits and God. Here, a more complex hierarchy is posited. For instance, we could have the following chain of command: The Supreme

109. Mbiti, *African Religions and Philosophy*, 77.

110. Ibid.

111. Ibid.

Being or God, Divinities, Spirits, and Ancestors or the Living-dead, and humans.

According to Mbiti, "man does not, and need not, hope to become a spirit; he is inevitably to become one."[112] Spirits, he points out, are invisible, but may make themselves visible to human beings. How do we know this? Mbiti says that there are many folk tales that speak about the human forms and activities of the spirits.[113] In reality, however, spirits are no longer counted as the living-dead or ancestors because the Akan believe that the spirits pass from that level into another level where they are no longer recognized, and have no family relationships or personal ties with human beings. Because of this, Mbiti maintains that, for the Akan, the spirits at this point are now strangers, foreigners, outsiders, and are even in the category of 'things.'

Viewed anthropocentrically, Mbiti has this to say:

> The ontological mode of the spirits is a depersonalization and not a completion or maturation of the individual. Therefore, death is a loss, and the spirit mode of existence means the withering of the individual, so that his personality evaporates, his name disappears and he becomes less and not more of a person; a thing, spirit and not a man anymore.

Thus, the depersonalization of the individual automatically causes such individual to become a spirit. For this reason, Mbiti states emphatically that humankind need not hope to become a spirit for he or she will inevitably become one. Mbiti further raises an issue concerning the sprits which is worth considering for the sake of the argument. He points out that as a group; spirits have more power than human beings. Yet, in some ways human beings are better off, and the right human specialists can manipulate or control the spirits as they wish. The specialist here referred to are the medicine-men. They are the men or women in the society with the eyes to see and those who can handle all spiritual issues. They also have the power to heal the sick and exorcise those who are bound or are in spiritual shackles. More will be said about the medicine-man in a subsequent section.

The dwelling places of the spirits are identified as the underground, the netherworld, or the subterranean regions, though, in Mbiti's thought some are situated in the land of the spirits above the earth, in the air, the sun, the moon or stars. However, both Mbiti and Idowu claim that the

112. Ibid., 78.

113. Ibid.

"majority of the people hold that the spirits dwell in the woods, bush, forest, rivers, mountains, or just around the villages."[114] Does this mean that the spirits probably live in the same geographical location with humans? Mbiti defends such a claim with this assertion: "It is partly the result of human self-protection and partly because man may not want to imagine himself in an entirely strange environment when he or she becomes spirit."[115] There are two issues in this statement that are of interest to this dissertation.

The first reveals a sense of imagination of the African to determine where he or she would be in the hereafter. The second relates to the question of protection against evil forces. The former may be beyond the scope of our study, but the latter is, because it can be argued that self-protection is indeed needed against the work of evil spirits that are represented in witchcraft, sorcery, magic and other unseen forces which are believed to bring disaster to the society and to individuals. It is to be noted that the Bible is not silent on these evil forces. Paul, in his letter to the Ephesian church, speaks of a spiritual warfare between humanity and evil spiritual forces: "For we wrestle not against flesh and blood but against principalities, against powers, against the rulers of the darkness of this world, against spiritual wickedness in high places."[116]

Mbiti clarifies the world of the spirit from that of humankind to reveal a salient point. He assesses the world of the spirit as a radically different entity from the human world. He points out that:

> The world of the spirit is invisible to the eyes of men; people only know or believe that it is there but do not actually 'see' it with their physical eyes. But more important, even if the spirits may be the depersonalized residue of individual human beings, they are ontologically 'nearer to God'; not ethically, but in terms of communication with him. It is believed that whereas men use or require intermediaries, the spirits do not, since they can communicate directly with God.[117]

The belief that the spirits are nearer to God and communicate with him has become the one important factor in the use of the ancestors to designate a meaningful Christology for Africa. Note that the reference is not

114. Ibid., 79 and Idowu, *African Traditional Religion*, 175.

115. Mbiti, *African Religions and Philosophy*, 79.

116. Ephesians 6:12, Dake's Annotated Reference Bible-Authorized King James Version.

117. Mbiti, *African Religions and Philosophy*, 79.

on the divinities as such, for obvious reasons, some of which have been stated above. The section on ancestors and subsequent sections attempts to shed light on these concerns. However, for now, it is sufficient to say that in the Akan belief system, the spirits and the living-dead act as intermediaries who convey human sacrifices or prayers to God on behalf of the Akan religious believer.

There is, yet, another aspect to the Akan belief system related to the spirit:

> God has servants or agents whom he employs to carry out his intentions in the universe. The spirits fill up the ontological region of the *Zamani (the period of the past, present and future—the period of the big time including eternity)* between God and man's *Sasa (the period of immediate concern for the people-the period of existence)*. The ontological transcendence of God is bridged by the spirit mode of existence. Man is forever a creature, but he does not remain forever man, and these are his two polarities of existence.[118]

This point is intriguing and needs to be assessed thoroughly for our concerns in this dissertation. This servant-hood belief give credence to the earlier thought that some of the divinities play the role of ministers of God. It is such attitude of being servants or ministers, together with the kind of intentions they carry out in the universe that we seek to grasp. When we consider Christology, is it God himself who comes to the Akan in his own Being (another mode of Being) or do we look to the form of divinities (could it be the *abosom* or the *Orinsa-nla*) or to a particular ancestor? The responses to such questions will be probed in the research and discussion of this study.

It is also to be noted from Mbiti that becoming a spirit is a social elevation and for this reason Africans show respect and high regard for their living-dead and for some of the important spirits. But, it does not mean that Africans worship spirits or the living-dead (the ancestors) rather, they show reverence to them. Another reason why Africans revere the spirits is that they are older than human beings. This is because they have moved from the period of *Sasa* into the *Zamani* period and are also nearer to God and communicate with him. Thus, their elevation is far beyond that of the human being. They are offered the respect needed just as in Africa the young ones must necessarily respect the older ones, whether or not they

118. Ibid.

are in their immediate family. Thus, spirits or ancestors are not worshipped but are held in much respect.

According to Mbiti, "Spirits do not appear to human beings as often as do the living-dead . . . . they can act in malicious ways, as well as in a benevolent manner."[119] Are humans, therefore afraid of them? Some really fear them, but generally they are not necessarily feared. It is their strangeness that makes human beings fear them more than the belief that they offer rewards and punishments. According to Idowu, spirits can be controlled or handled by the specialists in the community. The question here is whether these spirits are seen since they are supposed to be invisible and ubiquitous. To this question, African writers provide a common response. Mbiti captures below what the response of the Akan and, for that matter, for most Africans:

> They are said to have a shadowy form, though they may assume different shapes like human, animal, plant forms or inanimate objects. People report that they see the spirits in ponds, caves, groves, mountains or outside their villages, dancing, singing, herding cattle, working in their fields or nursing their children. Some spirits appear in people's dreams, especially the diviners, priests, medicine-men and rain makers to impart some information.[120]

The descriptions indicate the experiences reported by many Africans. Amazingly, African people of all backgrounds, of various social strata, and intellectual capacities have countless experiences with spirits and the living-dead. Therefore, it may not necessarily be that it is only priests or priestesses, prophets or prophetesses or diviners, medicine-men or other specialists who want to play on the ignorance of the poor Akan rather it is the Akan himself or herself who has the experience as well—an intriguing experience. Are these people so wonderful and different? Do Westerners have such experiences across the board? Kwame Bediako suggests that the differences in this regard may explain the inability of the Western mind to grasp the spiritual thought of the Akan.

These reported experiences, nonetheless, offer us empathy in understanding even more easily the issue of spirit possession. Mbiti points out that these spirits are unpredictable so the African would not desire their frequent appearance. In connection with their ability to possess a human being Mbiti comments: "The spirits possess men, and are blamed for forms

119. Ibid., 80.

120. Ibid.

of illness like madness and epilepsy. Spirit possession occurs in one form or another in practically every African society."[121] How difficult would it be for an educated African or even more so a Westerner to accept that fact that spirits can cause madness or epilepsy? It is important to note that the difficulty may stem from the gap that exists in the understandings of the concept of a spiritual universe, and what belief in such a universe entails for an indigenous Ghanaian or African.

In African thought, there can be two ways of spirit possession—natural and artificial. By the natural, we mean the one that comes intuitively without any machinations; and by the artificial, we mean by inducing it through special dancing amidst heavy and charmed drumming. Mbiti observes the following about the latter:

> People induce it through special dancing and drumming until the person concerned experiences spirit possession during which he may even collapse. When the person is thus possessed, the spirit may speak through him or her, so that he or she now plays the role of a medium, and the messages he or she relays are received with expectation by those to whom they are addressed. But on the whole, spirit possessions, especially unsolicited ones, result in bad effects.[122]

What then are these bad effects? Mbiti points out the following: "Severe torment on the possessed person; the spirit may drive him or her away from home (into the forest or elsewhere); it may cause him or her to jump into the fire and get burnt, to torture the body with sharp instruments, or even to do harm to other people."[123] He also asserts that at a high level of possession, the individual in effect loses his own personality and acts in the context of the 'personality' of the spirit possessing him or her. Such a possessed person becomes restless, lacks proper sleeping habits, and may even lose his or her good health and vitality. This is what gives room for the prevalence of exorcism in most African villages.

Mbiti concurs with the statement that "exorcism is one of the major functions of the traditional doctors (medicine-men) and diviners."[124] Is this type of exorcism similar to what Jesus Christ encountered with the demon-possessed in the Gospel narratives? It could be the same. Nonetheless, the

121. Ibid.

122. Ibid.

123. Ibid.

124. Ibid., 81.

effects could be the same but the methodologies and sources of power for the deliverance may not necessarily be the same. This is true because even with Jesus' exorcism, the native people questioned the source of his power, thinking of another source other than the power Jesus, himself, had.

Apart from spirit possession, Mbiti also speaks of real, active, and powerful relationships, especially with the spirits of those who have recently died—the living-dead. He points out that various rites such as the "placing of food and other articles, or the pouring of the libation of beer, milk, water, alcohol or even tea or coffee(for the spirits who have been modernized) in order to keep this contact."[125] Sometimes words may or may not follow such offerings in the form of prayers, invocations or instructions to the departed. These words, for Mbiti, as it is for Idowu, are the bridges of communion. Africans indeed recognize the departed to be alive. Again, Mbiti posits that failure to observe these acts means in effect that human beings have neglected their departed ones and for that matter broken the relationship. What will happen if such a thing occurs?

According to both Mbiti and Idowu, it is dangerous for the individual and the community as a whole, especially, if the neglected dead individual happens to be a chief of the people. Any calamity and misfortune that happens, unless it had been caused by witchcraft and magic, will be seen as the result of the neglect of the spirits.

There are also community shrines with priests or priestesses who receive the offerings for the spirits and the departed on behalf of the community. The spirit of the earth, of the forests, of water and others are all offered what is due to them. For example, for any development in a new area, the Spirit of the Earth is offered a drink in order to clear the way for the development to take place. For a new path to be constructed through a particular forest, the Spirit of the forest must be consulted.

The Akan Concept of Spirit of the Earth

There is a host of divinities as we have noted above. One of them, as she is known among the Akan is the mother Earth. The Earth is known among Africans as a spirit and a god among the pantheon of Akan divinities. Mbiti observes that "the Ashanti consider the Earth to be a female divinity second to God and observe Thursday as her day."[126] Similarly, Kofi Asare notes that

125. Ibid.

126. Ibid., 76.

in Akan society, "she ranks after God and is second in deity to be offered a drink at libations."[127] However she is not worshipped. She is known as *Asaase Yaa* (*Asaase* means Earth; and *Yaa* is the name given to female born on Thursday) in Ashanti and other Akan areas and *Asase Efua* (*Efua* is female born on Friday) among the *Fante*. She is also sometimes referred to as *Aberewa* (old woman/mother). Some days are designated as sacred in her honor and on those days, no work is done in certain areas. Kofi Asare explains that in the areas where she is called *Asaase Yaa* (*Yaa* is the name given to a female born on Thursday) the day of rest is Thursday. Similarly, in the areas where she is called *Asase Efua* (*Efua* is the name for a female born on Friday) the day of rest is Friday. It is important that inhabitants of these neighborhoods observe these special days and avoid land-tilling or going to the stream or river to fetch water. It is a taboo to farm, hunt, go to the river, side or visit certain reserved areas on those days.

It is believed that anyone who disobeys these laws brings a curse not only to himself or herself, but to the entire family or clan. Kofi Asare asserts that there are no priests or priestesses, shrines or temples associated with *Asase Yaa*. However, like other deities, the Spirit of the Earth receives offerings and sacrifices, especially at the beginning of the farming season. Farmers sacrifice fowls to her and sprinkle their blood on the ground.

The Akan Concept of Spirits of Water

Kofi Asare lifts up another facet of the Spirits—the Spirit of water. He mentions a belief that spans the whole of the West African community in deities inhabiting the waters, great and small. He explains that these spirits ruled over the sea, rivers, lakes and lagoons. Worship is offered to some of the water divinities at shrines with priests and priestesses who perform rituals. It is this belief that leads some Akans to worship the gods of the sea, of the lake, of the river, or of the lagoon, all in the pretense of giving worship through them to the Supreme Deity—God.

The Akan Concept of Ancestors

According to Rev. Dr. Abraham Akrong, another research fellow at the University of Ghana, Institute of African Studies, Accra, Ghana, the study of the beliefs and practices of the African peoples leads to the theological

127. Opoku, *West African Traditional Religion*, 55ff.

observation that African traditional religion is a religion of salvation and wholeness (salvation in the sense of protection from evil forces believed to be causal agents of retrogression). Earlier on in this chapter, we pointed out that the Akan seeks spiritual protection from the forces of evil that can affect the society, individual lives, businesses and other meaningful endeavors. Akrong maintains that a careful analysis shows an emphasis on 'this-worldly salvation and wholeness as the *raison d'etre* of African traditional religion."[128]

This wholeness must be understood from the view point regarding the African way of life, which is characterized by a great sense of communality and relationship with one another here and in the hereafter. This communality is witnessed from one's commitment to community living. This is in line with Akrong's study that Africans believe that life is a complex web of relationships and that it may be enhanced and preserved or diminished and destroyed. The goal of religion is to maintain those relationships that protect and preserve life. Akrong emphatically states that "it is the harmony and stability provided by these relationships, both spiritual and material, that create the conditions for well-being and wholeness."[129]

Akrong also observes that the African seeks salvation because there is constant threat to life both physical and spiritual. He thus captures the thought that "the threat is so near and real because, for the African, life is a continuum of power points that are transformed into being and life is constantly under threat from evil forces."[130] It is this threat that enshrines the African world view that life in both the phenomenal and the noumenal realms are inter-related like a family. Mbiti captures this relational metaphysics succinctly in the dictum: "I am because we are and because we are therefore I am."[131] The life of the individual comes into fruition through the social ritual rites of passage. These rites are the process that can help the individual to attain the goals of his or her destiny, given at birth by God. Those who successfully go through the rites of passage become candidates for ancestor-hood, which is the goal of the ideal life.

In this subdivision, we shall begin to disentangle the facts about ancestors with regard to who they are, where they are, their status, how effective and how powerful and whether they continue to have authority over

128. Akrong, "Introduction to African Traditional Religion."

129. Ibid., 1.

130. Ibid., 2

131. Ibid., 34

the living and their relationship and connection with the Supreme Being. The explanations offered in this subcategory will give us the insight for a thorough engagement and to critically analyze the works of Samuel Pobee and Kwame Bediako both of whom have constructed Akan Christology based on the concept of ancestor-hood.

For the African, ancestors are much more than the dead parents of the living. They are the embodiment of what it means to live the full life that is contained in one's destiny. The Akan, like the rest of the numerous ethnic groups in the West African sub-region, have long held the belief that after death the departed soul enters into "a spiritual state of existence."[132] The departed ones are generally referred to as ancestors. Their continued existence and influence over the living are outlined in the works of a Senegalese poet, as quoted by Kofi Asare:

> Those who are dead are never gone:
> They are there in the thickening shadow.
> The dead are not under the earth:
> They are in the tree that rustles,
> They are in the wood that groans,
> They are in the water that runs,
> They are in the hut; they are in the crowd,
> The dead are not dead.
>
> Those who are dead are never gone:
> They are in the breast of the woman;
> They are in the child who is wailing;
> And in the fire brand that flames.
>
> The dead are not under the earth:
> They are in the fire that is dying,
> They are in the grasses that weep;
> They are in the whimpering rocks,
> They are in the forest; they are in the house,
> The dead are not dead.[133]

132. Ibid.

133. Ibid., 35. A quotation from Jahn, *Muntu*, 108.

Kofi Asare supports this poet by stating that the dead are believed to be everywhere, at any time; they continue to live but in another kind of existence. This does not mean that the spirit of the dead or the living-dead possess the attributes of omnipresence and omniscience. Rather, as spirit, they can be anywhere but not anywhere at the same time. The fact of their existence is one of the pillars of the truths of African Traditional Religion. Kofi points out that the ancestors are always revered and held in high esteem. He maintains that after God, who is the final authority in all matters and pre-eminent in all things, the ancestors come next in importance. This claim is given credence in the manner that African chiefs and their subjects celebrate festivals to honor ancestors. Kofi asserts that the ancestors "live in the land of the spirits if they had fulfilled certain conditions in their previous life."[134] Although we all have a destiny of becoming spirits as already indicated above, not all spirits are recognized as qualified ancestors.

Kofi Asare's point seems problematic as if the ancestors rank higher than the spirits and divinities. In terms of hierarchy, one can admit that after God, the Supreme Being, the divinities are the next, followed by the spirits, then the Ancestors who are also called the living-dead. Then the last is the living person. However, Kofi's point can be understood on the basis that all Africans are concerned about the ancestors, but not all Africans are concern about the divinities. The living person approaches God through prayer via an ancestor because that particular ancestor is, first of all, a beloved relative in memory; further, he or she has the closest link to God in his or her new existence after the life on earth.

According to Mbiti, "the departed of up to five generations are in a different category from ordinary spirits. They are considered to be in the state of personal immortality, and their process of dying is not yet complete."[135] Mbiti also maintains that some of the things said about the spirits apply also to the living-dead. But for the living–dead, he remarks:

> They are bilingual; they speak the language of men, with whom they lived until 'recently'; and they speak the language of the spirits and of God, to whom they are drawing nearer ontologically.These are the 'spirits' with which the Africans are most concerned: it is through the living-dead that the spirit world becomes personal to men. They are still part of their human families, and people have personal memories of them . . . . The living-dead are still 'people,'

134. Opoku, *West African Traditional Religion*, 36.

135. Mbiti, *African Religions and Philosophy*, 81–82.

> and have not yet become 'things,' 'spirits' or 'its'. They return to their human families from time to time, and share meals with them, however symbolically.[136]

Moreover, Mbiti points out that the ancestors know and have interest in what is going on in the family. When they appear, they are recognized by the oldest members of the household, they are recognized by name. He also asserts that they inquire about family affairs, and may even warn of impending danger or rebuke those who have failed to follow their special instructions. To sum up the numerous duties of the ancestors as Mbiti observes: "They are the guardians of family affairs, traditions, ethics, activities and finally act as the invisible police of the families and communities."[137]

Mbiti points out that because they are still 'people', "the living dead are the closest link between men and God; they know the needs of men for they have recently been here with us."[138] For the African, as it is for the Akan, it may not matter whether the 'closest link to God' is ontological or not. What matters is that a qualified ancestor is the passage from earth into the 'spirit world' in general. This is probably the reason why the African leans more about the ancestors to reach God, and also why so many African theologians are quick to construct African Christologies around the concept of the ancestor, sometimes without sufficient critical and analytical inquiry into the appropriateness of the concept.

How one becomes an ancestor is very important for our theological inquiry. It is true that one cannot assume ancestor-ship until one dies. This means that the passage from life to death is entry into ancestral life. It is, however, a commonly held view that not every dead person can be considered an ancestor. There are criteria for determining who an ancestor is. There are three important things that ushers the dead into the revered group of ancestors who constitute the backbone of society. These include the character or conduct of the person, whether he or she had children, and the manner of his or her death. According to Kofi Asare, "in Yoruba society too, a person who dies childless is not acknowledged as an ancestor."[139]

Both Kofi Asare and Quarcoopome acknowledge that to become an ancestor in Akan society "one must have died a good death, that is, one's death must not have been due to accident, suicide, or any form of violence;

136. Ibid., 82.

137. Ibid.

138. Ibid.

139. Opoku, *West African Traditional Religion*, 36.

one's death must also not be caused by such 'unclean' diseases as lunacy, dropsy, leprosy and epilepsy."[140] Kofi Asare again explains that "exception can be made in the case of heroic death in defense of one's community, but if it is found that one died while running way from battle or retreating ignominiously from the enemy, then one is obliterated from historical memory."[141] These criteria for determining who a revered ancestor must be among Akans will be an intriguing factor in our eventual critical analysis of the theological implications of Jesus Christ being considered our ancestor.

> Kofi Asare says:
>
> In conformity with West African culture, in which old age has a touch of venerability, the ancestors are respected because they are our elders and our predecessors who have trodden the path of life which we, the living, are now treading. It is also believed that the ancestors enter into a spiritual state of existence after death. They have their feet planted in both the world of the living and the world of spirits.[142]

Asare is not alone in expressing such ideas. Quarcoopome maintains that the ancestors are "the heroes and heroines of the various tribes."[143] He claims that they are believed to have acquired extra-human powers in the after-life and with these powers they are able to intervene in the lives of the living members of the society."[144] Again, Kofi Asare also points out that "the *Mende* of Sierra Leone believe that their ancestors go to rest in *Ngewo's* (God's) Bosom, and the *Kokomba* of Northern Ghana have it that theirs go to *Uumbwardo,* God's House, where they enjoy a large measure of divine favor, and are even believed to form part of the Being of God."[145]

Quarcoopome does not mention anything in relation to the ancestors forming part of the being of God. Rather, he points out that "they act as intermediaries between God or divinities and humankind."[146] Furthermore, Quarcoopome explicates the point that the ancestors are the unseen presidents (facilitators or leaders) at family and or tribal meetings and

140. Ibid.

141. Ibid.

142. Ibid.

143. Quarcoopome, *West African Traditional Religion,* 43.

144. Ibid.

145. Ibid., 36 and 37.

146. Ibid, 43.

perform the duties of guardians and policemen of public morality. According to him, the ancestors punish people when they disobey the norms of society with disease, crop failure, and other natural disasters. At the same time, they reward those who conform to the moral and social orders. Such people, he points out, secure good health, good harvest, and prosperity. The ancestors are venerated but this comes close to worship. They are remembered periodically and at annual festivals when supplications are made to them to ensure procreation, peace, and prosperity.

Similarly, J. B. Danquah says of the Akan ancestor: "They act as friends at court to intervene between humankind and the Supreme Being and to get prayers and petitions answered more quickly and effectively."[147] Kofi Asare maintains that the belief that the ancestors have such intimate relationship with God led to the practice of offering libations: "The specialized method of communicating with the ancestors and ultimately to God."[148] This is the direct and most acceptable form of getting prayers to the Supreme Being, and does not require any assistance from the spirits or divinities.

The Akan Concept of Humankind

Like all West Africans, Akans too believe that the nature of humankind is both "physical and spiritual."[149] The human being is composed of material and immaterial parts making up the body, which is tangible, and the spirit aspect which is intangible. Accordingly, Quarcoopome and Kofi Asare maintain that the physical part is determined by the human being's ancestry and right of inheritance whilst the spiritual dimension is from the Supreme Being, referred to as *Onyankopong* in Akan thought. Quarcoopome delineates the two ways in which the African thinking on this differs from the more general scientific understanding of the human.

Firstly, Quarcoopome points out that science classifies humankind as an animal because human beings are "little separable from arthropods."[150] In West African Traditional Religion, he asserts, "there is a clear distinction between humankind and animal and it is both disparaging and degrading to call humankind an animal."[151] Secondly, he demarcates science's percep-

147. Ibid. 37.

148. Ibid. 37.

149. Ibid., 98 and 105.

150. Ibid., 98.

151. Ibid.

tion of humankind as flesh and blood, whereas the African traditional view, like many other religions, maintains that humankind is both material and immaterial—that is, both biological and spiritual. This important demarcation will be discussed further in the next chapter, especially in relation to the work of Samuel Pobee.

It must be clarified that the physical part of humankind is understood according to different views of inheritance among West Africans. Quarcoopome points out that if the society follows the patrilineal system of inheritance, then, the belief is that the physical part, which is blood, is transmitted through the male. On the other hand, when the blood is understood to be transmitted through the female line, it creates a matrilineal system of inheritance in that particular society (e.g. most Akans of Ghana and the Igbo of Nigeria). Thus, Quarcoopome asserts that "the blood provides the connection between one generation and another and also between a person and his or her lineage, clan and tribe."[152] This means that the blood of a person determines his or her citizenship or membership of a society as well as his or her inheritance.

Again, generally speaking, among West Africans, the spiritual part of humankind is represented by the soul *(Kra)*. The soul and spirit are both very close to "Greek" philo-anthropology and culture. Both Kofi Asare and Quarcoopome denote it as "the vital force which makes a person a living being."[153] They assert that it accompanies humankind in life and, unlike the body which decays in the ground; the soul leaves the body at death. The soul is the immortal part of humankind with permanent individual existence. The spiritual part, which Quarcoopome clarifies as the "link with one's destiny, is determined from spiritual sources and at the same time unchangeable."[154]

According to Quarcoopome and Kofi Asare, the Akan believe that the physical or the biological nature of humankind is made up of the blood *(Mogya)* while the spiritual part is denoted by three entities—the spirit (Sunsum) the father's spirit *(Ntoro)* and the Soul *(Kra)*. As indicated above, for Akan, the blood, which is the biological part of the body is transmitted by the mother. It must be pointed out that there is no indication of a gendered hierarchy. The provision of the substances of one's personality

152. Ibid., 99.

153. Ibid.; Opoku, *West African Traditional Religion*, 37.

154. Quarcoopome, *West African Traditional Religion*, 99.

does not make any of the parents more important than the other. At best, it determines the blood lineage of the offspring as stated.

It can also make the mother-child connection a very unique one in that it identifies the person with a particular family line, clan, tribe and ethnicity. A generational link is thus through the female line for most Akan ethnic groups. Most Akan tribes inherit generally through the matrilineal system where a man's inheritance passes to his sisters' children rather than his own. The sister is thought to have the family blood in her and, therefore, in her children. This practice has changed in recent times, since most men now make sure that their own children become the recipients of their inheritance.

The entity of the spiritual side of humankind, spirit, is termed *Sunsum* in Akan. This, according to Quarcoopome, is the ego and accounts for the character *(Suban)* disposition, and intelligence of a person. He maintains that "the ego is subject to change."[155] It is believed that *Sunsum* can leave the body during sleep and may be attacked by witches or overpowered by another person with evil thoughts, causing a person to become ill.

According to Quarcoopome, from the father, humankind is thought to have received his or her personality and the life force or spirit or *Ntoro*, identified with the male sperm. He postulates that the *ntoro*, therefore, accounts for the inherited characteristics often displayed by the offspring. It may not be easy to tell the difference between the *ntoro* and *sunsum* just as it is with the soul and spirit in western philosophical thought. The father-child (both male and female) bond is therefore spiritual. The last immaterial or spiritual constituent explained by Quarcoopome is the soul *(Kra)*. He writes "the soul *(Okra or Kra)* is the vitalizing force of human beings. It is given directly by God."[156]

The soul, however, is the eternal part of human personality. It is the part that has its direct source in the creator of the universe. It is also the part of the human which makes it the living being. With its departure the body dies. Kofi Asare maintains that the continuous existence of the *Okra* is expressed in the Akan maxim: *"Onyame nwu na mawu"* or *"Onyame bewu na mawu,"* literally meaning, *Onyame* (God) does not die therefore I shall not die, or, If *Onyame* dies then I will die, but since *Onyame* does not die, I shall not die. These Akan idiomatic expressions point to the immortality and the destiny of the soul *(Okra)* after the demise of the person.

155. Ibid.

156. Ibid., 105–6.

The destiny of humankind on earth is connected to the soul *(Okra)*. According to Quarcoopome, the soul is given its destiny before it leaves God to inhabit the body. He asserts that what the Akan call destiny, *Nkrabea,* comes from the two words—*Kra* (meaning to bid farewell or take leave of) and Bea (meaning the way or manner of doing something). Literally, he points out that *Nkrabea* means the way or manner in which the soul *(Okra)* bids farewell to *Onyame* before its departure into this world. Both Quarcoopome and Kofi Asare assert that destiny *(Nkrabea)* decides the soul's *(Okra's)* place or lot in this world.

Quarcoopome and Kofi Asare posit that God determines humankind's destiny *(Nkrabea)* and that once given, it is unalterable. Thus Quarcoopome writes: "The destiny given to humankind cannot be changed."[157] He points to a saying of the Akans that "the order God has settled, no living person can alter"[158] and "if God does not kill you, even if a human being kills you, you will not die."[159] God does not determine who becomes an ancestor. It is determined at the family and clan level. Therefore, one's destiny from God has nothing to do with his or her ancestral status. However, the fact remains for the Akan that God or *Onyankopong* is the Supreme Being and he alone has what it takes to create and to destroy. Thus, if God has not determined your demise or the demise of your vision or ambition, no one on earth has the power to alter it. Absolute power belongs to the Supreme Being.

The Akan view of how one receives his or her *Nkrabea* from God is interesting and, at the same time, quite thoughtful. Quarcoopome indicates two views. In the first view, the *Okra* appears before the Supreme Being and receives his or her destiny. In the other view, he postulates that the *Okra* approaches God and obtains leave from him to come to the world during which he or she asks for his or her destiny from God, which will become his or her mission on earth. Here, reference is being made to the fact that the Akan believe that humankind has the capacity and the will to ask for anything, even though they may not always know what the particular request entails. It is also believed that one has the right to object to a particular package and go in for another one.

It is believed that the approval he or she receives from God is final and binding. The Akan also believe that even though *Nkrabea* is irrevocable, it can be affected by evil forces such as witchcraft, magic and sorcery as

157. Ibid., 106.

158. Ibid.

159. Ibid.

well as by one's own character or unforeseen circumstances like accidents and misfortunes. Akans, therefore, believe, according to Quarcoopome and Kofi Asare, that a situation like an accident that causes premature death only postpones one's destiny until the person is reincarnated to fulfill it. This is the reason Akans believe in reincarnation.

Our next subsection will explore the works of such mystical forces in the spiritual universe of the African. These spiritual forces are manipulated by some human beings who have the spiritual ability to conjure their selfish advantage and disadvantages of both individuals and the society. It is the threat from such spiritual realities that Akan Christology must endeavor to address.

The Concepts of Witchcraft

What are the operations of supernatural or mystical forces in the lives of individuals and the societies in which they live? Belief in the activities of mystical forces is not confined to Africa. Recently, a women vying for a parliamentary position in a powerful western country confessed to having dabbled in witchcraft in her high school days. In an effort to regain her public image, she had to advertise this statement on international television networks: "I am not a witch."[160] In this subsection, we will attempt to discuss who a witch is, where they are found, how they operate, which classes of people are involved in it, who they affect, and how their activities can be halted. The answers to these questions will enlighten us on the reality of the spiritual universe of the Akan for a better engagement with the Christological proposals of the selected Akan theologians— Samuel Pobee and Kwame Bediako.

What definition can be given to a witch? Quarcoopome gives a comprehensive statement that defines who a witch is: "A witch is a person who is believed to be possessed by a witch spirit. This witch can be sent out on errands and is thought to be capable of causing harm to people, and to a lesser extent, do well to others."[161] Thus the point here is that apart from the *Kra* and *Sunsum* of the person, one or more *Sunsum* have the capacity to seize upon some other *sunsum* and possess them and use them for the good or bad of others. Are witches found in every place in this world? Kofi Asare

160. Christine O'Donnell in an effort to regain her public image made a series of televised adverts on Cable News Network.

161. Quarcoopome, *West African Traditional Religion*, 150.

Opoku gives a cautious answer in this way: "Belief in witchcraft is found in most human communities around the world, although there are a few societies in which it is absent— the Bushmen of the Kalahari in Namibia and South West Africa, and the Australian aborigines."[162]

Witchcraft activities are reported in almost every African community. Though most of the activities of witchcraft are considered evil, a few of them are regarded as good. This fact is captured by Kofi Asare Opoku, the author of *West African Traditional Religion*, in the following statement:

> The Akan people of Ghana recognize that there is good witchcraft, *bayi pa,* as well as bad witchcraft, *bayi boro.* The *Tiv* of Nigeria describes witchcraft, *tsav,* as a substance which grows on the heart or liver of the witch. This substance is also of two kinds: the one which is rounded at the edges is good *tsav* (good witchcraft) while the other, which has notches at the edges, is bad *tsav* (bad witchcraft)."[163]

Who cares about good witchcraft? It is the prevalent use of this mysterious power for evil that we wish to expound in order to develop a Christology that can counteract its effects. Among Ghanaians, the terminology is used loosely in a song of one of the great songwriters and musicians, A. B. Crentsil, which says that "the White man's witchcraft is a good one because it has been used to manufacture the airplanes whereas the black man's witchcraft is a bad one because it is being used to destroy humankind."[164]

Among the Akan people there is the belief that many of the misfortunes, disasters, sicknesses, diseases, premature deaths, lack of prosperity, retrogression, failures of crops and businesses, madness that falls on promising students and elites of society, and other numerous evils that plague the society are caused by the activities of witches. This is the reason why, in the Akan Community, when a dangerous disease affects somebody or when there is a loss of a dear one, no one asks the question as to what killed or what caused the disease, but who might have caused this to happen? The question of 'who' in such unfortunate situations is always in reference to a witch in that particular family.

Witchcraft is a very frightening and evil supernatural force that has truly left its imprint on the mind of every Akan. Quarcoopome remarks: "To the African the issue is not, whether witchcraft exists or not, but how to

162. Opoku, *West African Traditional Religion,* 140.

163. Ibid., 141.

164. It has been taken from a song written by the musician A. B. Crentsil of Ghana.

combat or neutralize its anti-social activities or take advantage of its positive potential in improving the lot of man on earth."[165]

It is a fact that some people have categorically denied the existence of witchcraft. For instance, E. E. Evans-Pritchard, the author of *Witchcraft, Oracles and Magic among the Azande,* wrote: "Witchcraft is an imaginary offence because it is impossible. A witch cannot do what she is supposed to do and has in fact no real existence."[166] It is such ideas that led to Evans-Pritchard[167] not being hired by any university because he faced the sharp criticism of one of the most influential pioneers of Social Anthropology—Bronislav Malinowski.[168]

According to Asare Opoku, among the Ghanaian ethnic groups witches are believed to leave their bodies during sleep and to go on nocturnal visitations in the company of other witches and then return to their bodies. He points out that "It is the *Sunsum* (Spirit) of the witch which takes leave of the body, so that one may find the person (witch) fast asleep, while her *sunsum* (spirit) is miles away."[169] What is the nocturnal visitation about?

165. Quarcoopome, *West African Traditional Religion,* 141.

166. Evans-Pritchard, *Witchcraft, Oracles, and Magic among the Azande.*

167. Born in Sussex, England, on September 21, 1902, Sir Edward Evan Evans-Pritchard studied history at Oxford and anthropology at the London School of Economics and Political Science (LCE). He then became familiar with the work of Bronislaw Malinowski. In 1926 Evans-Pritchard began his fieldwork on the upper Nile among the Azande people. His first book, published in 1937, entitled *Witchcraft, Oracles, and Magic Among the Azande,* came out of that experience. That book became a classic in the anthropology field. Evans-Pritchard was not able to acquire a teaching position because Malinowski was very much in disagreement with the contents of *Witchcraft, Oracles, and Magic Among the Azande.* Due to Malinowski's academic reputation and wide circle of influence, it was not until after his death in 1942, that Evans-Pritchard, with the assistance of Radcliffe-Brown, was able to secure a teaching position. (http://www.newworldencyclopedia.org/entry/Edward_E._Evans-Pritchard).

168. Bronslaw Malinowski was born in Krakow, Poland on April 7, 1884. He received his PhD in Philosophy, Physics, and Mathematics from the University of Krakow in 1908 and lectured at the London School of Economics where he earned his PhD in Science in 1916. It was there that he read *The Golden Bough* by Sir James Frazer that sparked his interest in anthropology. Malinowski founded the field of Social Anthropology known as Functionalism. He believed that all components of society interlock to form a well-balanced system. He emphasized characteristics of beliefs, ceremonies, customs, institutions, religion, ritual and sexual taboos. His *New York Times* obituary named him an "integrator of ten thousand cultural characteristics" (Parker, 118). He died a very influential British anthropologist. (http://www.newworldencyclopedia.org/Bronislaw_Malinowski).

169. Opoku, *West African Traditional Religion,* 142.

Throughout Africa, and particularly Ghana, it is believed that the meeting is simply to feast on human beings or to work out plans to destroy their victims, who are normally found dead the next day after their meeting.

Margaret Field observed the following in her field work among the Ga people of Ghana, where there had been admissions of being witches and confessions of their feasting on the souls of human beings to kill them:

"It is the victim's *kla* (soul in Ga Language) which is stolen and eaten . . . the physical body is never injured except by the ravages of disease—and there is no evidence that it is ever disturbed after burial."[170] Thus the evidence is there, in the form of confessions, that witches are believed to eat the souls of their victims. This makes them a very dangerous mystical force in the Akan Cosmos, as they continuously cause havoc in all walks of their victims' lives.

According to Kofi Asare Opoku, the meetings of the witches are believed to "take place at night on top of such trees as the silk-cotton, *baobab* or *iroko*. After leaving their bodies, the witches turn themselves into animals, insects or birds and travel to their destinations."[171] It is also believed that some witches use medications to rub their bodies in order to fly naked, unseen by anyone. Asare Opoku maintains that Animals such as dogs, black cats, toads, rats, or birds are used for riding as airplanes. He also points out that other witches change their bodies into snakes, leopards or antelopes as well as produce flames from their eyes, nose, mouth, ears, and armpits and may walk with their heads on the ground and their feet up. Regarding how witches in other West African tribes travel to their destinations, Kofi Asare Opoku remarks:"The Mende also believe that witches travel on spiders' webs when they are on land, in groundnut shells on water, or on birds or winnowing fans in the air."[172]

Concerning witchcraft in Nigeria, Kofi Asare Opoku shares a similar thought about the Yoruba and the Igbo. He asserts: "The Yoruba of Nigeria, however, believe that witches get to their destinations by means of birds spirits, while the Igbo believe that witches turn themselves into night birds, owls, lizards, or small insects."[173] This is an indication that almost all of the West African tribes share similar stories of witchcraft activities.

170. Field, *Religion and Medicine of the Ga People*, 135.

171. Opoku, *West African Traditional Religion*, 142.

172. Opoku, quoted in Harris and Sawyerr, *Springs of Mende Belief and Conduct*, 74.

173. Opoku, *West African Traditional Religion*, 142.

How then does one become a witch? Humans are created spirit, soul, and blood or body as we have discussed above. There was nothing in the discussion with regard to how a created being acquires a spirit as destructive and evil as this mystical or supernatural force.

According to Quarcoopome,

> A witch spirit can be inherited with a witch mother passing down the witchcraft to her daughter, but not her son. Some girls confess to having been given the witch spirit by either their aunts or close female relations. The women are usually thought to be witches, especially old women. Some are believed to be born witches; others buy or acquire witchcraft intentionally. In parts of Ghana for example, it is held that witchcraft may be bought for a small sum or can be obtained from demons or the dead; others think it is an infection that can be taken with food swallowed accidently.[174]

This quote augments our earlier statement that females have the inclination towards witchcraft. A male in this category will be called a wizard. They are believed to be more dangerous and also more interested in magical arts of wizardry. In polygamous families and societies such as the Akan, witchcraft activities are predominant because of jealousies and enmities among the wives. They are said to affect people of all walks of life, and are considered a menace; a real threat to society. Kofi Asare Opoku comments: "When I speak of witchcraft, I am referring to that which is very disturbingly real as to affect the lives of Africans in every walk of life."[175]

Which classes of people could be exempted or unaffected by these demonic activities? In a long quote from an article *The Challenge of Witchcraft,* Kofi Asare Opoku opines the following:

> . . . by Africans I mean not only the illiterates who carry on with their traditional customs intact, almost as they were received from their forbears; I mean also 'educated' men and women in the civil service, in the mercantile houses, well-known politicians, university professors, university graduates and undergraduates, medical doctors, Imams, Alhajis, Archbishops or Bishops and a host of Christian Ministers, Muslims and Christians. To most of the persons in these categories, witchcraft is an urgent and very harassing reality; it is a diabolical, soul-enslaving presence . . . they are real as

174. Quarcoopome, *West African Traditional Religion,* 150.

175. Opoku, *West African Traditional Religion,* 141.

> murderers, poisoners, and other categories of evil workers, overt and surreptitious.[176]

This list we presume can go on and on to affect every person in the African or the Akan society. No one is left out. Everyone is said to be vulnerable as far as these nefarious activities of the evil witches are concerned. It is intriguing that even church leaders are not exempted from the list. Does it mean they are not sufficiently spiritually fortified? What are the appropriate channels for fighting against the works of these evil doers? Before we deal with the methods of counteracting the evils of the witchcraft, it is important to cite an example of a story involving a witchcraft activity. This account is a quote found in Asare Opoku's book, *West African Traditional Religion*, and is given by D. E. Idoniboye. It is the experience of a witch who turned herself into a fly. Though it is a long quote it is worth stating:

> When I was a small boy in my first year at the Grammar School, great sensation was caused one day in the village where I had gone to spend my holidays with my parents when a fly, the common house fly, trapped in a stopped bottle, was presented as a jilted lover who was found sleeping soundly for three days. No amount of shaking could wake her; a douche of cold water was equally ineffectual. The story is of how a young lady could not renew her affair with her lover who no longer had any interest in her. She pestered him with gifts and entreaties but her blandishments of love rang hollow and he remained intransigent. So the young lady threatened that she would make him unable to sleep until he relented and took her back. It was no idle boast. Any time the lover went to bed and tried to sleep a fly would buzz in his ears and prevent his falling asleep. The only time he could sleep at all was during the day when his jilted lover was unaware that he might want to sleep. This was no good because he could not afford the time to make his siesta long enough to be refreshing. So he consulted a 'traditional doctor' who made it possible for him to catch the ever elusive fly and bottle it up. It was at the intervention of the relations of the jilted lover whom they had missed three days but found sleeping soundly in her bed that the fly was released and the sleeper awoke. The jilted lover could not stand the shame. She was a witch. She had been found out. The following morning she could nowhere be found. She had fled the town.[177]

176. Opoku, "Challenge of Witchcraft," 3ff.

177. Opoku, "Idea of an African Philosopher."

In Ghana there is a saying: "They will not kill you, but can spoil you."[178] Thus it is believed that the power of witchcraft can conceive and effect many things to disturb people, rob them of their peace, and leave some of them in perpetual misery. In much the same way, as pointed out in the above quote, there are experts who can devise spiritual means to counteract every witchcraft power. However, these experts, mostly the 'traditional doctor' or the medicine-man, cannot be trusted because of the limits of their powers. They seem to be powerful only over the witches but, most of the time, they fail to deliver. For instance, if the witch happens to also seek a traditional doctor who is more powerful, the reverse effect can happen. The only power that is believed to effectively neutralize all these powers is the one from *Onyankopong*, the Supreme Being.

Some people have developed a number of theories to explain the witchcraft phenomenon. According to Kofi Asare Opoku, there is a theory called "causation."[179] It explains why certain events happen, but others remain unexplainable. This means that when there is premature death of young ones, an epidemic, a low yield of crops, or disasters, witchcraft is used to explain the misfortune. However, he points out that it may be well-accepted that a person fell sick because he imbibed a contaminated food or drink or that the property was destroyed because of a tornado, or that the crops failed because of a protracted drought.

It is a fact that protracted drought, tornados, hurricanes and all other natural results or events of the weather can cause drastic devastation. However, in Africa, as in other places subjected to natural disasters, there are places that are left untouched while others are destroyed. Can one explain, it is asked, why a swarm of locusts destroyed thousands of acres of farm land except the land of a particular farmer whose fields of grain remained intact because he had some 'medicine' dug in the field? What then is the explanation? Did it occur naturally or spiritually? Could it be the work of evil or spiritual forces? Such concerns need to be addressed when one endeavors to construct Christology for the Akan.

The Concept of Magic and Sorcery

We have noted that there are forces in nature that try to control and determine the course of human life, either for better or for worse. In our

178. A Ghanaian statement used for people believed to practice witchcraft.

179. Opoku, *West African Traditional Religion*, 145.

explanations above, we have noted key mystical forces that are manipulated through witchcraft activities. In this subsection, attention is focused on other means that the Akan employ in order to bring the forces of nature into their control for their own benefit.

According to Kofi Asare Opoku, in order achieve their desires, humankind resorts to the use of "spells and incantations, and sometimes ceremonies and rites, or even sacrifices."[180] He points out that *suman,* or man-made objects such as charms, mascots, amulets (*juju, mana, aduru* or *ogun*) come under the broad category of magic because they aid occult forces into action. The concern here is that these forces are used for both good and evil intentions. For instance, those who practice good magic use their power for the benefit of the society in terms of healing disease and offering protection against the power of witchcraft to individuals or the community.

According to John Mbiti, sorcery also takes the form of spells, poisoning, or other physical injury done secretly by someone against someone else or his property.[181] In his view, in every African community, there are endless stories about the use of magic, sorcery and witchcraft. Moreover, in the African community, witches, evil magicians and sorcerers are the most hated and often feared persons in the community. People fear to relate to them whether they are family members, friends, neighbors, colleagues, school mates, community leaders or whatever other social status they carry.[182] They pose a threat to the progress of individuals and the entire community.

Responding to the machinations of these evil forces of nature many Africans converted to Christianity for the purpose of protection from them. These were deep concerns not only for ancient Africa but they continue even among modern and postmodern Africans. The need to eradicate completely or render their nefarious activities ineffective is the preeminent concern of every African, whether that African resides in the West, East or other parts of the African world. It is to such dreadful experiences that we want to engage the Christological methodologies of our selected Akan theologians and to find alternative methods of developing a Christology that can effectively control or demolish the works of cosmic forces.

180. Ibid., 147.

181. Mbiti, *African Religions and Philosophy,* 82.

182. Ibid. 82.

The Concept of the Medicine-Man

The origin, development, and dependence on medicine in Africa have close relations to African religion. As previously discussed, religion permeates every fabric of African society. Therefore, matters related to methods of restoration of health and longevity cannot be left out of religious considerations. In this subcategory, we shall explicate the use of medicine and the work of the medicine-man. We seek to search for an understanding of how the medicine-men depend on religious elements in the cure of diseases as well as in the protection and preservation of people against witchcraft, magic and sorcery. By doing so, a deeper insight into the spiritual universe of the Akan will be accomplished and, more importantly, we will be able to engage the current indigenous Christological endeavors.

In the thought of the Akan, there is always a spiritual cause for every incident. Thus, apart from the orthodox causes of illnesses which are recognized and accepted, the Akan seeks the traditional or spiritual explanations as well. This attitude of the Akan gives significance to the work of the medicine-men, since they are the experts who determine the causality of the incident. According to Kofi Asare Opoku, the reasons for the traditional explanations are: "Metaphysical explanations such as punishment meted out by offended ancestors, the result of witchcraft or sorcery, fore-ordained destiny, or the consequence of anti-social behavior by the sufferer."[183] Metaphysical explanations cannot be handled by anybody except the medicine-men. They are referred to as the friends of the village, the traditional doctor, witchdoctor, healers and in a more modern sense, exorcists.

One of the key issues that arise here is the punishment effected by offended ancestors. It is believed that ancestors become irritated when the living fails to keep relationship with them. Just as we must keep our relationship with the living for a healthy and harmonious life, we must also keep relationship with the forces and powers that control the universe. Broken relationships always result in catastrophes such as famine and epidemics. Normally, ritual cleansing and the offering of sacrifices are used to restore the relationship and thereby halt ongoing devastation.

According to Kofi Asare Opoku, the treatment of diseases calls for both the orthodox as well as the traditional or spiritual methods. He explains that in African societies, it is believed that human personality is made up of both "material and immaterial substances which make the maintenance of

183. Ibid, 149.

a balance between the spiritual and material in man a condition for sound health."[184] This suggests to us that anything that is made for the total Akan person must necessarily satisfy the two entities of the spiritual and physical. How is the medicine-man able to fulfill such a need? According to Asare Opoku, "the practice of medicine is considered to be a gift of the Creator and is dispensed through the agency of the divinities."[185]

Here lies the key to further enlightenment on the place and work of the divinities. It is important to note that the medicine-man is considered the same as the town or the area herbalist. In Akan society, according to Asare Opoku, all herbalists acknowledge God as the Great Physician and Healer.[186] Usually, these herbalists depend on their deities for any healing method to be employed. It is a common saying that "if God has given you the disease, he will definitely provide the cure."[187] Now Asare Opoku points out that "when devotees are ill they go to their priests who are not only ministers of the deities but also herbalists who know the remedies of particular deities."[188]

Thus the herbalist is the same person who works as the priest and minister of the particular lesser god or lesser deity or divinity. Here is where the problem lies for the development of any Christological endeavor. One of the reasons why the Akan respects and reveres the ancestors, far more than the divinities, is that the former had lived among them and is believed to be on the other side of life where the soul of humankind goes to the owner of its creation. In the case of the latter, no one knows which kind of spirit is involved or who is behind the various cures. Sometimes it is assumed that the source of witchcraft power is a result of the healing performed by the herbalist. Also, some herbalists raise shrines for their divinities. In this case, the divinity assumes the role of a god and in most cases, acts on behalf of the Supreme Being. Such practices make Akan religion assume a polytheistic tendency.

For example, Kofi Asare Opoku makes mention of the Yoruba and Igbo special deities, *Osanyin* and *Agwu* respectively, who are recognized as the guardians of medicine. These deities are believed to call people to become herbalists and doctors and all healing takes place under their

184. Ibid.

185. Ibid.

186. Ibid.

187. Ibid.

188. Ibid.

guardianship. It is, therefore, possible that *Osanyin* and *Agwu* have shrines and priests in much the same way the *Akonnedi* of Larteh, Ghana, possess. Thus, the medicine-man must possess certain spiritual powers just as witches do and sometimes even more than they do. It is interesting that in the Gospel narratives, Jesus was confronted with the charge that he was exorcising demons by the power of Belzebub, the chief of the demons. However, in contemporary societies, the powers of the medicine-men are limited and they are not able to always deliver the victims of witchcraft, magic or sorcery.

It is believed that some witchcraft and magical powers are more dangerous than those of the medicine-man. If these are the deep concerns within the spiritual universe of the Akan, then what kind of Christology should one develop to address the issues faced by the Akan? Can a Christology based on ancestral categories, as Pobee and Bediako have done; really deal with the issues raised here? With these in mind, we explore the sources of Akan religion in the next subcategory. This exposition helps to identify some of the categories that would be useful in developing an Akan Christology.

Sources of Akan Religious Knowledge

The ongoing engagement with Akan cosmology and praxis calls into question the sources of Akan religious knowledge. Is it revelatory as is the claim for the Christian and Jewish beliefs? Does *Onyame* make himself or his truth known to Akans, and if so how has He done it? Again, if so, who gets to know His will and who does not? On the issue of the sources of African religion in general, Bọlaji Idowu has undertaken extensive and thoughtful research that provide important insights into some of the sources of African or Akan religion. Can the Akan religion make claims to some level of revelation?

The Human Link with *Onyame*

Idowu considers the story of creation in the Book of Genesis to make a case for indigenous African religious thought, and subsequently to argue for humankind's inner link with *Onyame*. He comments:

> The author of the first chapter of Genesis describes the pre-cosmic situation as dark chaos indescribable; he presents us with a picture

> of non-existence. Then appears the Spirit of God; God in creative activity. The Spirit like a mother-bird sat upon the dark chaos and, in consequence of God's creative energy, there was cohesion, order, life, and meaning. Thus, from the point of creation, in the very act of creation, the seal of the Maker, the seal of god's self-disclosure, has been stamped all over the face of the created order.

Genesis 1:26 and 2:7 say that "God made man in his own image" and that "The LORD God formed man of dust from the ground and breathed into his nostrils the breath of life; and man became a living being." Dwelling on these verses, Idowu maintains that "man is made a rational being, intelligent, equipped with will, and a sense of purpose; there is something of the divine in him which makes him addressable and responsible... and therefore, there exist; in him the possibility of his spirit being in communion with the Divine Spirit."[189]

Idowu points out that the same fact is expressed in several African concepts of humankind. He says: "the Yoruba believe that whereas an arch-divinity may be commissioned to mold man's physical parts, only Deity has the eternal prerogative of 'putting' the essence of being into man."[190] He also says that for the Igbo as well as the Yoruba: "The designations of the essence of being, *ori* and *chi*, derive directly from the name of Deity: ORISE (Ori-se) CHUKWU (Chi-ukwu); and this by implication means that the essence of man's being derives directly from Deity."[191] Thus for Idowu, humankind's creation is deeply connected with the being of the Deity.

The pertinent point here for Idowu is that revelation presupposes personal communication between the living being who reveals and the living person to whom revelation is made. For Idowu, it would appear that man is a necessity in this situation; for, without a personal mind to appreciate and apprehend revelation, the whole process will prove futile. Idowu thus posits that in the two points of reference, the created order and humankind's inner link with the Deity, revelation or theophany is evidenced.[192]

Idowu admits that erroneous impressions about African religious traditions have resulted because of various misrepresentations and deliberate misjudgments on the part of many of the foreign witnesses of African thought and praxis. On this issue, he writes:

189. Idowu, *African Traditional Religion*, 55.
190. Ibid., 55.
191. Ibid.
192. Ibid.

> In the past, casual observations about African traditional religion were made by the outsiders—European travelers, explorers, civil servants and missionaries. Then anthropologists and ethnographers became interested in the field, and began to present the Western world with written information about Africa. To almost all of these categories of observers or investigators, religion was just one of the elements in Africa's widely varied range of activities. Naturally Western investigators, by and large, had looked at the religion of Africa from the general European point of view; and then each investigator or observer according to his own specialist's line of interest. The travelers had their tales to tell, and a curious religious habit would naturally lend spice to the tale. If the explorers could add to his reports something about the ritual practices of 'the primitives', it would certainly make his report less boring, . . .The missionary had no use for the religion which he had prejudged, before he left home, to be an expression of benightedness, something that he came out to fight and kill; that set the limit to his interest in the religion and, therefore, whatever he said about it was in condemnation.[193]

Having made this important point which still lingers in the mind and heart of some who come into contact with even modern African traditional thought, Idowu asserts, however, that it is out of these researchers, some of whom were genuinely interested and truly appreciated and objectively wrote about African religious thought, that the first accurate information of African Religion emerged to the outside world. He points out that "there came a time when there were missionaries who began to feel that knowledge of the Africans from the inside was necessary for the success of their work of evangelism."[194] It is to this knowledge of the African from inside that we hope to elicit some of the sources of religious knowledge. Our approach will be distinct from European-American or Western resercher's thought as the yardstick for African religious sources.

Oral Tradition

The first source of African religion that Idowu considers is oral tradition. He categorically and definitively states "this is all we have and we have to make the best of it."[195] He maintains that an understanding of the oral

193. Ibid., 85–86.
194. Ibid.
195. Ibid.

traditions will enable the scholar to see and to know the religion from inside. Again, he admits that "Africa, in her every locality, is rich in mythology and folktales."[196] Thus in the Akan locality, as it is in Yoruba or every locality on the African landmass, our thoughts and ancient historical, religious, and theological facts have been transmitted through mythological findings and folktales from one generation to another. He points of that the use of myth for oral tradition should regard the original meaning of myth rather than the later development and modern unfortunate misleading meaning perpetrated by *The Pocket Oxford Dictionary.*[197]

Liturgy

The next source of Akan religious heritage is obtained from liturgy, which Idowu points out, is the pattern and subject-matter of worship and that only experiential participation will be of benefit to the researcher.[198] In his view, liturgical expressions, the invocations and prayers make the participant involved in the calling of and asking of divine assistance. Here the calling of the names and attributes leads to learning and experiencing what each name represents.

Singing

Idowu also calls for the use of songs which constitutes a rich heritage of Africa. Africans are always singing and in their singing and poetry they express themselves; all the joys and sorrows of their hearts and their hopes and fears about the future find outlet. Idowu maintains that just as liturgy is a vehicle for communication singing is always a vehicle conveying certain sentiments or truth.[199] During rituals or sacrifices singing portray the faith of the worshippers in the Deity, belief in the divinities, ancestors, and the

196. Ibid.

197. The *Pocket Oxford Dictionary* gives a definition of the word 'myth,' which is misleading, unfortunately. It defines "myth" as a "primitive tale imaginatively describing or accounting for natural phenomena . . . . tale of gods or demi-gods, old wives' tale, prevalent but false belief, person or things falsely supposed to exist"; and "mythical" as "imaginary, not really existent." The original meaning of myth, however, from the word *muthos* is "anything delivered by word of mouth," "speech," "conversation implying the subject of the conversation," "the matter itself."

198. Idowu, *African Traditional Religion,* 86.

199. Ibid.

spirits. Thus, through singing, the Akan elucidates from the heart their experiences in these spiritual entities.

Epigrammatic Sayings, Proverbs, and Adages

Finally, according to Idowu, Africans have epigrammatic "sayings, proverbs and adages which are the sine qua non of African speech."[200] African wise and concise statements which are full of great substance are in abundance everywhere. He maintains that the wealth of African religious thought found within these sayings is astonishing. John Samuel Pobee, one of the theologians to be engaged in the next chapter, develops his Akan Christology on some of the rich Akan religious traditional proverbs and wise sayings. Though, one can agree that much information can be obtained in these proverbial statements it is necessary to examine whether they provide adequate resources for the Christological projects he embarks on.

On the whole, we agree with Idowu that these "oral traditions constitute the scriptures as well as the breviaries of African Traditional Religion."[201] These represent concrete thought and are of real value in terms of understanding life experiences and challenges. Even though African traditional religion does not have sacred scriptures this valuable information has been preserved over generations through oral traditions. Myths, folktales, trickster stories, music, dance, poetry, art, historical events, stories of rulers and their kingdoms, the thoughts and actions of humankind have been preserved through the oral tradition. However problematic it may be for outsiders, as Idowu pointed out, it is still the greatest, unquestionable source of African religious thought.[202]

Throughout this chapter, we have discussed the concept of *Onyankopong*— the Supreme Being as the creator, owner and controller of the universe, including all spiritual and physical elements. Akan cosmology has been elucidated through the plethora of spiritual beings, spirits and spirits of nature, divinities, ancestors, mystical powers, and their usage for both diabolical and benevolent acts through witchcraft, magic and sorcery.

In addition, we have explored the work of medicine-men in relation to counteracting some the nefarious activities of the use of mystical powers. Finally, we have pointed to the oral traditions of mythology, folktales, wise

200. Ibid.

201. Ibid.

202. Ibid.

sayings, proverbs, adages, dirges, songs and liturgical expressions etc. as source of the articulation of African traditional religion.

In the subsequent sections we will explore and evaluate how the selected theologians have used some of these categories to construct Christology for Africans, especially for the Akan. Of crucial interest will be the role of the ancestors and the relationship, authority, and power they wield in the life of the living, in contrast to the divinities, some of whom are claimed to have divine son-ship either through creation or derivations. These investigations will be pursued by engaging the Christological projects of John Samuel Pobee and Kwame Bediako, who developed Akan Christology, based on ancestral, chieftaincy and *Okyeame* (linguist) categories.

We will seek to point out that given the plethora of spiritual entities that the Akan is supposed to deal with, the ancestral and chieftaincy categories as well as the divinities are insufficient in the provision of a Christology that will be able to militate against the mystical forces at work in the Akan spiritual universe and to provide a vibrant militant church among the Akan ethnic group in Ghana.

2

Akan Christologies—
John Samuel Pobee and Kwame Bediako

Introduction

IN CHAPTER ONE WE attempted to offer the key concepts that defines the spiritual universe of the Akan Society. The study explored some of the main ideas of Akan cosmology elucidating the concept of God and creation. We noted that the Akan believed in a God or Supreme Being, who is the creator of the universe, both celestial and terrestrial. Subordinate to God are the spirit-beings which are made of lesser deities or gods and the ancestral spirits. We also noted that the extra-terrestrial universe is also made up of certain other spiritual beings that can be manipulated by human beings to the advantage and disadvantage of other living beings. Thus, the Akan society lives in a complex spiritual universe.

It is in this environment that the missionaries propagated the Good News of Christianity, which has thrived and continues to gain ground in Africa and among the Akan. However, there are questions about how it has been established and how it is rooted in the lives of the people. Of special interest is also the question of how Jesus Christ has inhabited the spiritual universe of the Akan. It is assumed that although the message of the Gospel was communicated, it was done without any reference to the cultural heritage of the Akan. Therefore, attempts have been made by some Akan theologians to construct theologies that will incorporate some of the indigenous and traditional categories in understanding the faith, and especially of the significance of Christ to the Akan people. Of interest for us are the works of two Ghanaian (Akan) scholars and theologians, John Samuel Pobee and the late Kwame Bediako.

Both of these theologians have endeavored to construct Akan Christologies by integrating the ancestral/linguists and ancestral categories respectively. While Pobee sought to convert the biblical themes into genuine Akan categories, Bediako questioned the incorporation of some of those categories as methodologically ineffective and inadequate for Christological development. Bediako himself offered some alternate proposals which also need close scrutiny. The goal of this chapter is to engage a detailed study of the Christologies of Pobee and Bediako. In the subsequent chapter we will seek to facilitate conversation between these two theologies and the theology of Karl Barth in order to bring out some of the biblical and theological issues in "doing theologies" in relation to cultures. On the basis of these objectives, we hope to make some proposals towards a Christology for the Akan which we hope will remedy what we consider to be weaknesses in the proposals made by Pobee and Bediako.

The Akan Christology of John Samuel Pobee

As noted in the introductory chapter, the Christian theology that was promoted in the African continent was the theology that came with the missionaries. This was natural, because the missionaries carried with them the interpretation of the Gospel that they had received in their own cultural context. However, there was increasing realization among some of the African theologians that indigenous churches need to have an indigenous theology that is drawn from and speaks to the African context. John Samuel Pobee is among the earliest proponents of the ancestral image as key to appropriating indigenous African categories for the construction of an African Christology. In this section, therefore, as we undertake a comprehensive exploration of Pobee's Akan Christological endeavor, we also seek to elucidate his method for developing an Akan Christology. In so doing we hope to bring out the strengths and weaknesses of this endeavor and examine the appropriateness of the use of the ancestral paradigm and proverbs as primary cultural elements in the exploration of an Akan Christology.

In his introductory note on *Toward Christology in African Theology*, Pobee points out that "at the heart of the encounter between Christianity and African culture is the subject of Christology (doctrine of the person and work of Christ)"[1] The Christian *Kerygma,* according to Pobee, is the proclamation of the good news of Jesus of Nazareth as a bridge of reconciliation between God and humankind and that through him, God has redeemed humankind from their sins. For Pobee, "the heart of the *Kerygma* is Jesus Christ."[2] Therefore, he holds that an evangelistic encounter between the gospel and an African or an Akan would raise the following questions: "Who is Jesus Christ? What manner of man is he? How does he affect my life? Why should an Akan relate to Jesus of Nazareth who does not belong to his clan, family, tribe, and nation?"[3] Answers to these enquiries, for Pobee, would determine to some extent, the rooting of Christianity in the African setting.

Sources, Authority, and Approach to Akan Christology

Pobee points out that the Christological discussions continue to be referenced to the Nicene Creed because "it was ratified and expanded by the Council of Constantinople as the plumb line of orthodoxy."[4] For him, however, the Creed was an attempt of a predominantly Hellenistic society to articulate its belief in Jesus in its own language and concepts. He maintains that whether we are Americans, Africans or Europeans, most of the ideas and idioms of the Nicene Creed are unfamiliar to us today, especially in the context of modern languages and thought forms that have developed since the formulation of the creeds. Therefore, without questioning the faith that stood behind the creeds, he poses challenging questions about the language and concepts that were deliberated by the Councils to express their convictions:

> Who today, theologian and philosopher included, normally uses terms such as 'substance' or 'person' or 'hypostasis' in their technical Chalcedonian sense? The Creed was, indeed, an attempt to 'translate' the biblical faith into contemporary language and thought forms. In other words, so far as it concerns us, the issue is

1. Pobee, *Toward Christology in African Theology,* 81.
2. Ibid.
3. Ibid.
4. Ibid.

> to get behind the Creed to the biblical faith. And so, whatever we evolve should be tested against the plumb line of the biblical faith.[5]

On the basis of this attitude regarding the creedal formulations, Pobee proceeds to construct a Christology with concepts drawn from the local culture which, in his view, are also faithful to biblical thought. Pobee's difficulty with the classical theology is that it is heavily dependent on the use of metaphysics for the discussion of Christology.[6]

He asserts that the tendency to discuss Christology in metaphysical concepts comes from classical theology's heavy indebtedness to Greco-Roman culture. For him, the biblical approach to the discussion of Christology needs to be very different. He comments:

> Metaphysical speculations about the relations within the Godhead are absent (in the bible). Even the Fourth Gospel, which declared 'The Word was God,' nowhere speculates on how the Word was God. Indeed, it soon leaves the heavenlies and comes down to earth with the tremendous affirmation: 'The Word became flesh and dwelt among us, full of grace and truth; we beheld his glory[7] (John 1:14 RSV).

If metaphysical speculations on Christology are absent in the bible, what approach does he find in the Bible? Pobee holds categorically that "in the biblical faith, Christology was expressed in functional terms, expressing impressions of Jesus in terms of his activity."[8] It is such an approach that Pobee wants to pursue in the development of Christology for Africa. He chooses this method because he sees it as congruent with Akan society which also prefers concreteness of expressions to abstractions. How is this achievable? What medium of communication in Akan society exhibits concreteness?

Pobee finds that the Akan reflect on matters of life in the form of proverbs, which play a very important function in directing human life and interactions. He declares that "the use of proverbs even in very serious discussions in the Akan society confirms that a functional approach to the discussion of Christology will be the most apt approach to take towards an

5. Ibid., 82.

6. Ibid.

7. Ibid.

8. Ibid.

Akan Christology."[9] Therefore, for Pobee, proverbs must necessarily replace Western philosophical abstraction in the discussion of Christology for Akans. He will have more to say on the use of proverbs and give examples as to how it helps in the formulation of indigenous Christology. Though, we share his critique that philosophical abstraction in the discussion of Christology may not be effective, it is necessary to examine whether the use of proverbs, only, would be sufficient for any Christological endeavor for Akans. To this we will return later in the chapter.

Pobee holds that the 'the process of philosophical abstraction that has been the chief trend of Western theology" has to be seen in "the context of certain views of the semantic nature of abstractions, concrete language, and mythological/metaphoric language, and the different ways in which they relate to thought and language" within Western thought.[10] He does not, however, engage in more detailed discussion of what is meant by this criticism, but having rejected abstractions for Christology, he goes into a discussion of the different kinds of Christologies that are present in the New Testament. He uses this diversity to buttress his own new methodology for doing Christology.

Within the diversity of Christologies in the New Testament, Pobee identifies two major trends, namely, "Judeo-Christian and Hellenistic-Christian."[11] He also highlights the teachings on the Cosmic Christ as found in the Captivity Epistles, and the Priestly conception found in the Book of Hebrews. Pobee welcomes this plurality of Christologies in the New Testament and adds that even though these do not exhaust the list, such plurality must be expected because theological formulations spring out of people's experiences and culture.

We see here some key words gradually emerging to form the guiding principles for Pobee's Akan Christology: functionality, concreteness, activity, Akan proverbs, experiences and culture. Nonetheless, Pobee maintains strongly that all the diversities of Christologies in the New Testament converge on two points: "Jesus Christ is truly man and at the same time truly divine."[12] For him, all Christological endeavors, whether African, American, European, Akan, Yoruba, or Igbo must capture these two ideas, even if the

9. Ibid.

10. Ibid.

11. Ibid.

12. Ibid., 83.

actual terminologies or imageries may be different: "The humanity and the divinity of Jesus are two non-negotiables in any authentic Christology."[13]

Even though Pobee's Christology hangs on the full humanity and divinity of Christ, he does not discuss these two Christological titles in terms of the Nicean or Chalcedonian creeds because of his interest in moving away from philosophical abstraction to concreteness and functionality by using proverbs and other Akan thought forms. To achieve this, Pobee first discusses the question of what it means for Jesus to be human in the Akan context.

Proverbs as a Concrete or Functional Method in the Presentation of the Humanity of Jesus Christ in the Thought of John Pobee

Pobee begins to explore the meaning of Christ's humanity to the Akan with the following question: "What manner of person is he [Jesus Christ] to the Akan, his family, clan, tribe and nation?" Pobee believes that the Akan can easily absorb the idea of Christ's humanity in terms of the Akan anthropological thought. In this subsection, we expound on his attempt to understanding of the humanity of Jesus with Akan proverbs and anthropology.

To begin with, Pobee gives his understanding of Christ's humanity as he discerns it in the New Testament:

> The humanity of Jesus is one aspect of New Testament Christology which the attempt to construct a Christology in an African theology cannot skirt. The evidences for Jesus' humanity settle down to his anthropological make up of being spirit, flesh, and body; his finitude in terms of his knowledge and power; and his deep consciousness of total dependence on God.[14]

Pobee asserts that whiles Descartes proclaimed *Cogito ergo sum,* the Akan society rather argues *Cognatus ergo sum*—that is, "I belong by blood relationship, and therefore I am." He explains that in the Akan society, a human being fully realizes himself or herself as a human being only because he or she belongs to a family, a clan, and a tribe. Does it mean that since Christ does not belong to the Akan society by blood, he cannot have anything to do with them? Rather, he wants to find a way of getting Akans, and for that matter all Africans, to relate to Jesus like a real relative.

13. Ibid.

14. Ibid., 84.

According to Pobee, in Akan anthropology "a person is *mogya* (blood) *sunsum* (spirit) and *kra* (soul)."[15] He points out that *mogya* is a material substance one receives from one's mother. *Mogya* makes one a human being at the biological or physical level; it gives the person lineage ties and membership in the mother's family or ancestral line as well as rights and obligations as citizen. *Sunsum*, also known as *ntoro*, obtained from the father, is the spirit of the person; it determines one's character and individuality and places the person as a member of the father's kinship group. The third, which is the vitalizing power of the human being, is the *Kra*, which is obtained from God with its destiny; it goes back to God at death. With this summary of Akan Anthropology, Pobee begins to find a place for Jesus in Akan thought and develops his Akan Christology to some extent from the Akan family resources of clanship and lineage.

He asserts:

> Since belonging to a kinship group is a mark of a man, our attempt at constructing an African Christology would emphasize the kinship of Jesus. His identity as a man was well demonstrated by his relationship to Mary, which gave him status and membership in a lineage and clan. And precisely because that fact was too clear to the people of Nazareth, underscoring his humanity, they found it difficult to believe that there was anything else to him than being a man, living among his kith and kin.[16]

For further explication, Pobee uses some biblical statements that affirm the humanity of Jesus, as for instance the statement by the people of Nazareth that he was the carpenter's son and that Joseph was his father: "Is not this the carpenter, the son of Mary . . . ?"[17] (Mark 6:3 RSV). He also points out that having Joseph as his father gave him a lineal descent from David (Luke 2:4 cf. Matt. 1:16). Pobee maintains that Jesus' group belonging is further advanced with the references to his siblings: "Jesus had brothers, some of them known by name as James, Joses, Judas, and Simon (Mark 6:3). He also had sisters, whose names are not preserved for us by the New Testament (Mark 6:3)."[18] To buttress his point of Jesus' belonging to kinship and having real family ties, Pobee points out that even Jesus' leadership after

15. Ibid., 88.
16. Ibid.
17. Ibid.
18. Ibid., 88–89.

his death soon passed into the hands of "James the Just, the brother of our Lord, as happens in Akan society."[19]

Jesus' siblings are significant for Pobee, because in the Akan society fullness of life requires that one is part of a family. According to Pobee, the proverb that matches with it is—"*Akonam ye yaw*, meaning, "it is a pain and curse to be alone." The fullness of man's humanity is understood by the relationships he has; this truth is at the heart of the extended family system of Africa."[20]

Another point that Pobee uses to articulate the humanity of Jesus Christ is his circumcision on the eight day, as reported in Luke's Gospel chapter 2:21. Pobee argues that in the same way circumcision makes a child belong to the People of God in Judaism (Gen. 17:10–11) so in Akan society it is practiced to incorporate a child into a kinship group with its manifold implications. Thus, for Pobee; "in Akan context, the circumcision of Jesus would underline Jesus' belonging to a kinship group and therefore demonstrate his humanity."[21] Pobee acknowledges his awareness that there are differences between the Akan and Judaic views of circumcision. The former is primarily an act of incorporation into a kinship group, but the latter is for both kinship and an entry into a covenant relationship with God. Kinship, however, plays a key role in both cases.

Pobee also uses the baptism of Jesus to argue for his humanity from the Akan perspective. He maintains that "baptism was not only to wash away sins, but also to show his identification with the rest of mankind." Thus for Pobee, whatever else Jesus' baptism was, in addition it was also a rite of solidarity which went into the making of "the man, Jesus" in the African sense. From the Akan perspective, through baptism he was declared a man, because by that rite he was declared a member of the group— *cognatus ergo sum*.

Moreover, Pobee contends on the death of Jesus Christ as another meaningful way of giving expression to his humanity and his identification to the Akan. Here he will depend on some of the Akan proverbs to elucidate his point. He argues that "in Akan society, death is the lot of every mortal being. Akan sayings and proverbs eloquently express this: "'*Obiara bo wu*'—meaning, 'everyone will die.'"[22] Another proverb used by Pobee on

19. Ibid., 89.

20. Ibid.

21. Ibid.

22. Ibid.,

death is: "'*Onyimpa ba, obra tware wu*'—meaning, 'For man that is born of woman, life should end in death.'"[23]

For further clarification on this point Pobee gives another traditional saying: "'*Atwenetwem di nda; dee beba mmba da. Owuo beba nso wose odeba beba, a, ommba da*'—meaning, 'The long awaited arrives late; what is most expected to happen has been delayed. Death will come, but often it does not come when eagerly awaited.'"[24] Thus for Pobee, death is the eventual end and is an essential part of being human. Jesus yielded to it, and so exhibited his humanity and finitude. Pobee also gives significance to Matt. 27:50, which says that "Jesus . . . yielded up his spirit." He argues that Jesus' yielding to his spirit is reminiscent of the Akan anthropology, where *Kra* (Spirit) returns to God at the point of a person's death. Jesus' spirit returned to God thus proving his humanity.

Pobee also points to another aspect of humanity that relates to death in Akan thought. He argues that even though in Akan thought death is the lot of everyone, it is also dreaded. This dread of death is demonstrated in the final days of Jesus' life on earth. Pobee uses the following proverbs to demonstrate this thought: "'*Owu ye yaw*— 'it is painful to die.'"[25] Again: "'*Owuo Kwaaku, abo-abusua-dom ntoro a osinkete hye dom*'— 'beware, beware, for death is alive; there he is, there he is, he who is a member of the *Abusua* (clan) and belongs to *Ntoro* (lineage) and who delights in wanton destruction of the many.'"[26] Pobee argues that Jesus demonstrated his humanity once again by the expression of some form of fear of death in the Garden of Gethsemane. Therefore, he declares: "so the death of Jesus in its various facets is a way of referring to the humanity of Jesus in both the biblical faith and Akan Christology."[27]

Pobee further points out that the Akan is also conscious of the limits of human knowledge. One of the proverbs says, '*Obi nnyim adzekyee mu*'— "a man does not know what the next day has in store for him.'"[28] Pobee uses Jesus' claim about his lack of knowledge concerning the Parousia to argue that such a limitation in knowledge serves to impress the Akan. He points

23. Ibid.,

24. Ibid.,

25. Ibid., 90.

26. Ibid.

27. Ibid.

28. Ibid.

out that this thought will "challenge the (false) doctrines of the omniscience of Jesus which has obscured the humanity of Jesus in traditional belief."[29]

Akans hold that human beings show dependence on some power beyond themselves. Pobee says that "Prayers typically symbolize that dependence because prayers in Akan society are addressed to the determiner of destiny, God, even if praying is done through the mediation of ancestors and /or gods."[30] Pobee therefore contends that Jesus' prayers demonstrate in concrete terms his dependence on God and shows his humanity in much the same way as it is for the Akans.

Finally, Pobee points to Jesus' Abba relationship to the Father, to whose will he was devoted. This relationship, in Pobee's view, shows both his humanity and divinity. He says that "unlike him, all other men have become less than human by following sin, which marred the *imago Dei* (the image of God) in man. But Jesus by his sinless-ness is more truly human than the rest of us."[31]

So far, we have outlined how Pobee used some of the Akan thought forms related to anthropology, kinship and proverbial sayings to elucidate Jesus' true humanity as may be perceived by the Akan. Throughout the argument Pobee demonstrated in positive ways "how the Akan and biblical ways of expressing humanity are very similar if not identical."[32] In the next

29. Ibid.

30. Ibid., 91.

31. Ibid., 91.

32. Ibid., 91. On this issue, Pobee points outs that Joshua Kudadjie, a Ghanaian theologian at the University of Ghana, has raised a question of methodology with regard to expressing Jesus' humanity by way of pointing the similarities between Jewish view of humanity and the Akan. It seems to him that the approach should be: "What does the Akan understand the person of Jesus to be? He need not accept the conclusion of the Greco-Hellenistic-European theologians that Jesus is human-divine, and then see whether the Akan also sees Jesus thus." He is "advocating for a radically different approach—as if the Akan were the first to work out a Christology. How would he do it, from his knowledge of Jesus in the Gospels." First, let us say we are unable to accept that Akan man has any choice about Jesus being human-divine. That is the nonnegotiable affirmation of the church whether Judeo-Christian or Hellenistic Christian. Surely this was what the Christological controversies of the first four centuries were about and to which the councils responded. So that is the given affirmation of the church. One cannot repudiate it without coming close to heresy. Again, the suggestion that the Akan person must behave as though he were the first is impossibility. For as a matter of fact, he cannot do otherwise. That suggestion is only raising the much more difficult problem of the facts about Jesus, whom the Akan person did not see. That approach seems to us to be wild goose chasing. Third, we ourselves are persuaded of the similarities between the Akan world view and the Semitic and biblical world view. At least the evidence adduced in

subsection, we will demonstrate Pobee's thought on the divinity of Jesus Christ as perceived in Akan thought.

Proverbs as a Concrete or Functional Method in the Exploration of the Divinity of Jesus Christ in the Thought of John Pobee

Having looked at Pobee's discussion of the humanity of Jesus in relation to biblical and Akan thought, we now turn to his divinity. In this subsection, attention is given to exploring Pobee's understanding of the divinity of Jesus with Akan proverbs and anthropology. While explicating his divinity, we will also attempt to show how he communicates these basic ideas to Akan society. The discussion of Jesus' divinity relates to his sinless-ness, the power he wielded in his acts of healing and the authority he had over nature etc. Pobee comments:

> The divinity of Jesus Christ is to some extent mirrored through his humanity. In Jesus the disciples saw what man is meant to be, that is Jesus is the *imago dei.* The determinative theological moment came when the disciples were compelled to say: 'What I see in this Man commands my worship. What I see in him changes my concept of God, What I have seen in terms of his Manhood I now recognize as Divinity, my Lord and my God.[33]

He begins his exploration of the divinity of Jesus with a discussion of his sinless-ness. He puts it simply: "Jesus was sinless."[34] He acknowledges that "the Gospels record Jesus' temptations to sin. That is, soon after his baptism, he was tempted to use wrong methods for God's purposes. His obedience to the will of God was tested at many points, but with all of these, Jesus turned away from sin, and remained faithful to his calling even to the point of death on the cross."[35] Pobee introduces a key point which sums his search for the divinity, which at the same times also attests his humanity: "But perhaps the quaint language of Hebrews 4:15 is unbeatable: Jesus is

this section is an argument in favor of that view, not to mention the works of Kwesi A. Dickson, J. B. Danquah, Modupe Oduyoye, even if we take some of the linguistic arguments *cum grano salis*. In view of these arguments we feel it more fruitful to proceed by discussing the similarities between Akan and Jewish views of humanity.

33. Ibid., 85.

34. Ibid.

35. Ibid.

'one who in every respect has been tempted as we are, yet without sin.'"[36] He points out that this message affirms both the humanity of Jesus "as one potentially capable of sinning, and his divinity, because he did not yield to temptation and remained sinless."[37] For Pobee, sinless-ness is an important aspect of Jesus' divinity. In support, he points out to a reference in Mark 10. 18: "No one is good but God alone."[38] With this saying Pobee stresses that the divinity of Jesus is expressed in his total devotion to the will of God. He also claims that thereby Jesus kept intact and to the fullest the *imago Dei*.[39] Explaining further the issue of the *imago Dei*, Pobee points out:

> When God created man, man was 'in the image and likeness of God.' He was as God. What marred the *imago Dei* was sin, man's egocentricity and disobedience. Unlike the rest of humanity, Jesus shunned sin and consequently continued to be as God. He is the authentic man bearing the *imago Dei*. It was as man that he achieved sinless-ness and thus came to be seen as divine.[40]

Interestingly, Pobee is very focused on the sinless-ness of Jesus and argues it to the point of almost undermining his humanity. He admits that the elucidation of Jesus' divinity into basic Akan thought is much more difficult than his humanity. His idea of Jesus' sinless-ness is also challenged by what F. B. Welbourn, a European researcher on African thought, has written in his book, *Some Problems of African Christianity: Guilt and Shame in Christianity in Tropical Africa*. In this volume Welbourn comments that "it has often been alleged that the Akan, like other Africans traditionally had no idea of sin before the advent of Christianity."[41] Confronted with this challenge Pobee first points out the evidence adduced for that view comes from two realities: "First, the apparent unconcern of God with private and perhaps public morality. And second, it is argued that Akan society is apparently a 'shame' culture rather than a 'guilt' culture because respect for public opinion seems to be the moral force."[42]

Pobee argues that such an impression is erroneous. To buttress his point, he turns to two Ghanaian theologians, Elizabeth Amoah and J. B.

36. Ibid., 86.
37. Ibid.
38. Ibid..
39. Ibid.
40. Ibid.
41. Ibid., 91. A quotation from Welbourn, "Some Problems of African Christianity."
42. Ibid., 91.

Danquah. In an article on, *Moral and Social Significance of Proverbs,* Elizabeth Amoahmaintains that Akans have a clear concept of sin.[43] Similarly, J. B. Danquah, in an article on *Obligation in Akan Society,* indicates that "the proverbs of Akan society amply demonstrate God's concern with and dislike of evil and sin."[44] Pobee then gives example of proverbs that support his point, such as, *"Onyame mmpe bone"—"God is opposed to, indeed hates evil/sin."*[45] With such proverbial statements, Pobee maintains that "sin is a factual contradiction of established order and that there is a belief of rendering of account of all that each person has done in the afterlife to the ancestors and the Supreme Being by the spirit of the deceased."[46] Thus, for Pobee, sin is not alien to traditional African society.

Further, Pobee argues that in Akan society, sin such as jealousy, murder, rape, incest is considered as ill-will towards other persons that causes harm to them. He maintains that such anti-social behavior "fractures the interpersonal relationships centered on the ego."[47] The Akan proverb for this assertion according to Pobee is: "'*eku obi sunsum*'—'to kill or destroy the individual personality of man.'"[48] Sin, therefore becomes uncleanness, destruction, and the breaking of a covenantal relationship. In contrast, the good life, expressed in Akan language (not proverbial) is "'*adoye*'—a loving life, to love the other man or woman, who alone produces the harmony, peace and cohesion of society."[49]

With these in view, Pobee discusses the sinless-ness of Jesus in two ways:

> First, Jesus strove and endeavored not to destroy the individual personality of any man—'*Iesu hye ne ho do, ma oannku obiara ne sunsum.*' This, so to speak, looks at sin from the human angle. But the second, we propose to express the idea of sinless-ness from the divine angle, namely *Iesu ne bra ye adoye*—'Jesus' life was one story of perfect loving of fellow men.[50]

43. Ibid.
44. Ibid.
45. Ibid., 92.
46. Ibid.
47. Ibid.
48. Ibid.
49. Ibid.
50. Ibid.

This life of love, according to Pobee can be illustrated with concrete examples from Jesus' life. Here Pobee thinks of Jesus' concern for the oppressed in any form and his efforts to relieve their pain and suffering. He argues that this pattern of life in Akan society is what pleases the spirit-world and is the characteristic of the Supreme Being as well as the ancestors.

In the endnotes, Pobee points out that "a third way of referring to the sinless-ness of Jesus and therefore his divinity would be through the noumenal or ethical sense of his being pure, and holy."[51] However, he is not sure that these two words do justice to the biblical conception. He thus suggests that it may be good to add words such as *koronkoron* (sanctity) and *hotewee* (cleanliness). Also, he admits that one is not sure how *mysterium tremendum* may be interpreted into Akan. But he also maintains a belief that they are all covered in the communication of the sinless-ness of Jesus.

The authority and power Jesus wielded is the second subject of discussion on Jesus' divinity. Here Pobee compares the sources of power of the medicine-man and that of Jesus Christ. He points out that healing and all manner of cures are attributed to the Supreme Being in Akan society. Here is how he puts it in his words:

> A healer, before performing a cure, does two things. First, he looks up to the skies in acknowledgment of his dependence on the Supreme Being for the power to heal. Second, he specifically addresses a prayer to the Supreme Being for his blessings on the venture. Thus the good miracles performed by Jesus would be a concrete way of expressing his power and divinity. *'Jesus wo Nyame ne tum'—'Jesus has the power of God and wields it.'* He could not have wielded that power unless he had been 'en-souled' with God.[52]

Pobee realizes such a comparison can create confusion. Therefore, to minimize the potential for conflict and confusion, he asserts that "some confusion may arise out of the fact that both the healer and Jesus look up to heaven acknowledging their power from God."[53] He admits that they do that to show "their dependence on God and their humanity."[54] Therefore, Pobee points out that it does not argue for the divinity of either the healer or Jesus. Rather, for him, the final product and what the Akan believes is the source of such a product are the important issues. Thus Pobee writes,

51. Ibid.
52. Ibid. 92.
53. Ibid., 93.
54. Ibid.

"The concern is with the end product, the actual healing or act of power which in the thinking of traditional society is impossible unless the Spirit-Being does it."[55]

Pobee concedes that in preparation for a cure, the traditional healer, unlike Jesus requires some form of ritual. Pobee writes, ". . . . before a cure the traditional healer goes through ritual motions so as to be sinless and in a state of holiness, so to speak. At the moment of cure, the healer is not his normal self, but only the vehicle of the Spirit-Being to effect a cure. This is what we mean by being 'en-souled' with God."[56] But though the traditional healer enters into some form of purity and state of sinless-ness, it is but for a moment and does not compare with the kind of sinless-ness Jesus Christ is endowed with. In this case, there must be a difference in the level of being en-souled with God. On this note, Pobee shows a striking difference:

> The difference between Jesus and the healers would be the unprecedented scale on which he was 'en-souled' with God: Jesus was in a perpetual state of holiness, perpetually 'en-souled' with God so much so that the divine power was like a continuously flowing electric power in him, unlike the traditional healer, who has the occasional experience of it.[57]

Quite apart from this unique experience of Jesus which has no parallel in Akan thought, for Pobee there is yet another point that relates to the miracles of Jesus. Pobee admits that "Jesus' miracles related to the idea of Creator."[58] Again, Pobee attempts another comparison in relation to Akan prayers for cures. This is how he addresses the issue: "In Akan prayers at healings the Supreme Being is regularly addressed as *"Oboadee,"* i.e., Creator. In order words, cures and miracles were evidence that God is creator."[59] For Pobee, the Akan is thus informed on the basis of Jesus' miracles that he too shared in the power of God as Creator and that through his activity the Akan know of the love and power of God expressed in his willingness to heal, deliver or exorcise, and to save.

In this analysis, Pobee does not bring in the medicine-man or the traditional healer in that for him, "the idea of creator should not be limited

55. Ibid.
56. Ibid.
57. Ibid.
58. Ibid.
59. Ibid.

to the cures in the ministry of Jesus."[60] He points out that the role of creator for Jesus goes back to his pre-existence as an agent of creation. Indeed, Pobee admits that "that will be the distinctively Christian claim which has no parallel in Akan religion: the claim that the power of Jesus predates the creation of the world. That in itself would mean that Jesus was a peculiar personality who shared divinity with God."[61]

To give more emphasis on the power of Jesus as Creator, Pobee turns to one of the Akan expressions that throw more light on the issue: *"Iesu ne kra ye dur.*"[62] This literally means that Jesus has a heavy *kra* (soul). Pobee explains as has already been done in some of the above sections that "the *kra* is the mark of the Creator, the vitalizing power of the Creator within him. Therefore to say that the miracles of Jesus are evidence of a heavy *kra* is to assert that Jesus retained unimpaired and in double dose that authority and power of the Creator."[63]

There is yet another distinction Pobee draws in relation to the Akan and Jesus Christ. He points out that "in Akan society every man is a child of God. That is *'Obiara ye Onyame ba*— all people are God's children; none is the earth's child." For Pobee this saying emphasizes the vitalizing power of the Creator in everyone. However, for him, it is precisely here that the difference between the rest of humankind and Jesus emerges. Pobee returns to the subject of sin and sinless-ness of Jesus to show the distinction. He writes: "Whereas in the case of the rest of mankind that vitalizing power has been impaired by sin, Jesus retained it intact and to the fullest by remaining sinless. Consequently, his ability to perform the great acts of power which other men could not do."[64]

Finally, Pobee concludes this section with another aspect of Jesus' authority and power as judge of the deeds of humankind. He asserts that "in

60. Ibid.

61. Ibid.

62. Ibid., 93. Pobee quotes from Williamson, *Akan Religion and the Christian Faith,* 92. Kudadjie has questioned our understanding of heavy *kra.* He comments, "One is said to have a heavy *kra* not because he performs some wonders, but because he is unconquerable by evil spirits, accidents etc." We are unhappy about contrasting the performance of wonders and unconquerable-ness by evil spirits. For in traditional society, the latter is proved by the former, since all evil is attributed to personal forces of evil. Consequently, to cure amounts to sharing greater power than the evil spirits that caused the original havoc.

63. Pobee, *Toward Christology in African Theology,* 92–94

64. Ibid., 94.

Akan society the Supreme Being and the ancestors provide the sanctions for the good life and punish evil. And the ancestors hold that authority as ministers of the Supreme Being."[65] Thus, for Pobee, ancestors have a great task to perform on behalf of the Supreme Being. With these arguments, Pobee emphatically points out: "Our approach would be to look on Jesus as the Great and Greatest Ancestor—in Akan language, *Nana*."[66] According to Pobee, with that go the power and authority to judge the deeds of humankind.

But Pobee is cautious in this application, in that the ancestor position assigned to Jesus may create potential for serious theological problems. Again in his own effort to minimize the confusion he posits the following: "In our context we shall seek to emphasize that even if Jesus is *Nana* like other illustrious ancestors, he is a nonpareil of a Judge; he is superior to other ancestors by virtue of being closest to God and as God. As *Nana* he has authority over not only the world of humankind but also of all spirit beings, namely the cosmic powers and the ancestors."[67] This explanation, though limits the potential for confusion, does not actually draw the curtain on the issues Pobee raises.

Thus, based on the discussions above, Pobee articulated his Christological thoughts on the divinity of Jesus Christ as it might be understood within the cultural elements of Akan society. Most of the issues were based on comparative studies to which we will return in our evaluation of his Akan Christology, especially on the issue of Jesus as ancestor, which we think is problematic. In the next subsection, Pobee seeks to clinch his argument and discussion with the illustration of the court of the royal house in Akan society. Here, Pobee seeks to use the elements of Chieftaincy to describe the sacral and priestly role of Jesus Christ to both the living and for the departed ones—ancestors. To this dimension of his Christology, we now turn.

Akan Christology—Court of the Royal House in Akan Society

In the previous section, Pobee argued for the approach to look on Jesus as the Great and Greatest Ancestor to whom the title *Nana* was assigned. For Pobee, this kind of assignment is reminiscent of the court of the Royal

65. Ibid.
66. Ibid.
67. Ibid.

House in Akan society. Therefore he turns to establish Jesus as *Nana* in true Akan fashion, using the chieftaincy categories. Pobee relies on the work of a Ghanaian sociologist, Kofi Abrefa Busia, to bring out what he really wants for his Christology from the royal house in Akan society. Of the institution of chieftaincy, the sociologist has written:

> The pervasive influence of religion spread into the political system of the Ashanti. The most important aspect of Ashanti chieftaincy was undoubtedly the religious one. An Ashanti chief filled the sacral role. His stool, the symbol of his office, was a sacred emblem. It represented the community, their solidarity, their permanence, their continuity. The chief was the link between the living and the dead and his highest role was when he officiated in the public religious rites which gave expression to the community values. He then acted as the representative of the community whose members are believed to include those who are alive, and those who are either dead or are still unborn. The sacral aspect of the chief's role was a powerful sanction of his authority.[68]

Pobee argues that the chief is "at once a judge, a commander-in-chief, a legislator, and the executive and administrative head of the community."[69] However, Busia argued that this must not be seen as "many offices, but a simple composite office to which various duties and activities, rights and obligations were attached."[70]

Pobee finds a similar thought in Akan religion, for which he relies on the work of Antubam on *Ghana's Heritage of Culture*: In Akan religion, the Supreme Being is perceived as a great paramount chief who is 'so big' that he has to be approached through sub-chiefs and his official spokesman, called *okyeame*, who in public matters is as the chief and exercises royal authority, even if it is subordinated to that of the paramount chief.[71]

Pobee holds that every chief in Akan society has *okyeame* who serves the chief in several capacities. He believes that there are some similarities between the Akan religion and the biblical faith with regard to the kingship of God:

68. Ibid., 94–95. A quotation from Busia, *Africa in Search of Democracy*, 26; Busia, *Position of the Chief in the Modern Political System of Ashanti*, 23.

69. Pobee, *Toward Christology in African Theology*, 95.

70. Ibid.

71. Ibid. A quotation from Antobam, *Ghana's Heritage of Culture*, 93.

> In the Bible, God is King. As Psalm 10:16 puts it, "The Lord is king forever and ever" (cf. Ps. 44:4; 47:7). Similarly, in the New Testament, God is described as king—Matthew 5:35; I Timothy 1:17; 6:15. On the other hand, Jesus is also described as king, as, for example, the parable of the sheep and goats makes clear (Matthew 25:32; cf. Rev. 17:14; 19:16). Indeed, his charge had been that he claimed to be king of the Jews (Matthew 27:37; Mark 15:26; Luke 23:38; John 19:19). Thus both Jesus and God are kings. But as the earliest Christians would have said, Jesus shares in the kingship of God and holds his kingship under God (I Corinthians 15:24, 25, 28).[72]

With this understanding of kingship in the Bible and based on the Akan chieftaincy system, Pobee, in search of Akan Christology, looks to the *okyeame* of the royal house. To him, Jesus is the king of a type that fits the *okyeame* of the royal house, who serves the paramount chief just the same way that Jesus serves the Great Supreme Being. Therefore, Pobee proposes to think of "Jesus as the *okyeame,* or linguist, who in all public matters was as the Chief, God, and is the first officer of the state, in this case, the world."[73]

For Pobee this explanation captures something of the Johannine portrait of Jesus as the *Logos,* being at one and the same time, divine, and yet, subordinate to God. But even with this Johannine thought, Pobee still turns to speak of Jesus' humanity. In his words: "Jesus as chief is human and shares common humanity with the rest of mankind. He is totally depended on God."[74] On this dependency on God, Pobee shares an Akan view in his endnotes, which uses one of the proverbial sayings to buttress the Akan belief in the necessity for a hierarchy of power in the rank. The saying is: '*Dibere nyinaa nnse; bi da bi akyir*'— '*all ranks are not equal; they vary in importance.*' Some are more important than others. The powerful symbol of this hierarchy is the state umbrella called '*Bidabiakyir,*' which literally means, '*one will be behind another.*'"[75]

72. Pobee, *Toward Christology in African Theology,* 95.

73. Ibid. Pobee writes in the endnotes that there are two types of *Okyeame*: the first one is known as *Ahenkyeame,* who is also a chief, and that is hereditary. The second one is the common linguist who is appointed by the Chief because he was judged to be responsible and reliable and was generally capable of fulfilling the roles of an *Okyeame.*

74. Ibid.

75. Ibid., 95 and 167.

In a further explanation to his point that Jesus is chief of a sort because he identifies him with the linguists, Pobee draws out the duties of the chief to clarify the duty of Jesus in relation to humanity and God. Here is how he puts it: "Just as the Chief exercises a sacral and priestly role as well, so too does Jesus exercise a sacral and priestly function between God and men."[76] Yet, for Pobee, as it is to the author of the Book of Hebrews, "Jesus' priesthood is exercised not only on the earth but also in the heavens."[77] Based on the arguments in the Book of Hebrews, Pobee asserts that Jesus is able to mediate the salvation and forgiveness of sins for humankind in his capacity as both a priest and a former victim.

In addition, Pobee asserts that "as a chief he is head of a community, namely the church."[78] Here one immediately perceives that Pobee is referring to the paramount chief. This is because it is the paramount chief who is the head of the community and not the linguist or the chief of the linguists in the court of the royal house. But, despite the discrepancy, Pobee stays with the image because for him, at this point the supreme chief should be viewed to be Jesus Christ because he is making a comparative analysis with the head of the church. Here is the full text:

> The chief not only represents the community, but also in him the community coheres. He is the soul of the nation, symbolizing a people's identity, unity and community. And that community owes allegiance to him. For the same reason he is their judge and exercises authority over them and their lives. All these apply to Jesus' chief-ship (chieftaincy). But there is one new element in the case of Jesus—the community over which Jesus is King cuts across tribal and political boundaries and, indeed, embraces all mankind.[79]

76. Ibid. 95. This assignment for Jesus at this point is quite confusing in that Jesus has not been assigned the role of the Chief. At best, Pobee assigns him a subordinate position of a linguist in the court of the royal house. Even if he is the chief of the linguists, which may seem to the ordinary person as a chief in his own capacity, it is never so. That position does not assume the sacral and priestly role of the paramount chief that Pobee compared with God. Jesus cannot fulfill such function unless he becomes an ancestor something on which Pobee has deliberated. So why does Pobee not remain in the ancestral categories to elucidate the priestly and mediatorial functions of Jesus? We hope to discuss these issues at length in the next section.

77. Ibid., 95–96.

78. Ibid., 96.

79. Ibid.

Thus we see here that Pobee has projected Jesus Christ unto the throne of the King. So, we grasp the understanding that as Jesus Christ is for the church so is he also for the community. This community for Pobee is not just one clan or two tribes. It covers the whole universe. Thus, Pobee has rightly given Jesus Christ the status he deserves. However, the ambiguity he creates becomes problematic for effective elucidation of Akan Christology. To this and other related issues, we will turn in the next section.

In fact, in the course of expounding his Christology, Pobee employs a number of honorific titles designated for Paramount Chiefs in Akan traditional societies, which he perceives capture aspects of the New Testament Christology of Jesus Christ. They include but are not limited to the following: "*Osuodumgya, Kasapreko, Katamanto, Osagyefo, and odomankoma.*"[80] For instance, the title *Osuodumgya* literally means water that extinguishes fire— fire being the symbol of pain, suffering and disaster.

According to Pobee, *Osuodumgya* describes the Chief as one who gives a new lease on life by removing all that is inimical to humankind. In his comparative analysis, he points to the statement in the Johannine Gospel about water (John 4:10). He argues that "water is so important in the teaching of Jesus, where it symbolizes life, therefore, Jesus is *Osuodumgya* because he gives life and delivers from the flames of passion, the flames of sin and gives hope."[81] The second Akan title, *Kasapreko,* literally means, he who speaks once and for all and does not foreswear himself. Pobee agrees that it has similar meaning to *Kantamanto*— one who does not break his oath. He points out that "the Chief is a determined soul, one whose yes is his yes, and his nay, is his nay. This honorific title will also capture an aspect of Jesus, his determined devotion to God, serving God to the bitterest end."[82]

The next one is *Osagyefo m*eaning one who saves in battle; therefore, a deliverer. The basic idea is comparable to the judges of the Old Testament, who saved the people from the tyranny of their oppressors. Pobee points out that this honorific title is also applicable to Jesus as the deliverer, but still with a difference. He points out that "in the case of Jesus it is not deliverance through a literal battle but, rather a figurative one. It is deliverance from the inimical forces of legalism, self-sufficiency, and the cosmic

80. Ibid.

81. Ibid.

82. Ibid.

forces."[83] Deliverance from 'cosmic forces' is one of the major concerns in Akan thinking.

Finally, Pobee also uses a traditional title for Christ that is never used for any Akan chief but is taken from biblical sources. This is the title, *Asomdweehene*, meaning the Prince of Peace. Pobee argues that "this title was never used in traditional society as an honorific title of the Chief, though the Chief's role included ensuring peace and harmony in society."[84] A similar statement is found in the Old Testament messianic passages (Isaiah 9). Pobee holds that this title for Jesus has the biblical origin and conceives a kingship which is not necessarily for war but for the peace which leads the people to their salvation and to a covenant relationship with God.

We are able to infer from the overall argument that Pobee finds a location for Jesus within the chieftaincy categories in the Akan traditional court of the Royal House. He says: "It seems to us, therefore, that among the African tribe of the Akan of Ghana a royal priestly Christology aptly speaks to our situation. However, every image is bound to be partial and a half-truth."[85] This brings us to the conclusion of the synopsis of John Samuel Pobee's Akan Christology. As outlined, Pobee's methodology of functionality through concrete expressions with proverbial sayings is well argued. We also note that in his arguments he has not only depended on proverbs but more on resources from Akan anthropology and chieftaincy. On these assumptions, he arrives at three points for his Akan Christology.

First, he proposes to think of Jesus as the Great and Greatest Ancestor with the title—Nana. Secondly, whiles delving into the court of the Royal House and deliberating on the characteristics of chieftaincy, he proposes to think of Jesus as *Okyeame*—the linguist with well-defined appellations and titles of paramount chief bestowed on him. This led Pobee to finally declare that a royal priestly Christology for the Akan society maybe the best way forward. How far are these proposals adequate for an Akan Christology? What are some of the problems they present? It is to these questions we turn in the next section.

83. Ibid., 96–97

84. Ibid., 97.

85. Ibid., 97.

Comments on John Samuel Pobee's Akan Christology

As noted above, Pobee has articulated his Akan Christological endeavor basically on the humanity and divinity of Jesus Christ. He does this by engaging some of the Akan cultural and traditional resources such as the Akan anthropology, proverbial sayings and its chieftaincy. He has struggled with them to come out as one of the pioneers of this endeavor. As he pointed out himself, the task of elucidating the divinity of Jesus from Akan resources was daunting. Yet, he has presented us with significant comparative research that draws out elements within the Akan culture that can contribute to an African Christology. Notwithstanding the effort, there are also several issues in his exploration that needs closer examination. In this section, we hope to bring out some of our criticisms and the problems identified in the course of the discussion of his work.

On the issue of the humanity of Jesus Christ, Pobee went deep into the meaning of being human, pointing to human finitude, physical and intellectual limitations, and mainly the human susceptibility to sin and evil as marks of being human. His colleague, Joshua Kudadjie, questioned his work on the humanity of Jesus as it related to the understanding of being human in Akan society. The argument that ensued between them is captured here by Pobee:

> My colleague Joshua Kudadjie has suggested to me that in the Akan view of humanity, one important aspect is the unreliability, wickedness, evil, failure, and such characteristics of man. He cites in evidence such sayings as *Suro Onipa* (Akan: Fear men!) or *Gbomo adesa, gbomo adesa ni* (Ga: O man—the deeds of men!). These were uttered when someone does something wrong, and they express not only disapproval of the act but also the view that it has happened as one would expect a mortal man to behave. Kudadjie argues that if this is so, Jesus then, to the Akan, lacks an important attribute of manhood, namely wickedness, unreliability. Therefore, Jesus would not be truly man.[86]

Pobee's answer to this is very intriguing. Instead of answering the question regarding whether Jesus is truly man in the thought of the Akan, Pobee takes on the Akan phrases cited in the formulation of the question. For instance, he holds that the phrases such as "Fear man!" and "O man-the

86. Ibid., 90.

deeds of men!" may not necessarily point only to evil deeds.[87] In any case, Kudadjie's criticism may not be justified because even though committing sin is part of the human predicament, Pobee does not see it as a necessary part of being human. He has argued that Jesus was truly human because, despite the human inclinations to do evil, he remained sinless.

In this encounter, we find that Pobee refutes Kudadjie's criticism by calling on him to first repudiate the Greco-Hellenistic-European method of defining Jesus Christ and using it as a yardstick to measure his ideas of the humanity of Jesus. Pobee claims that he has a radically different approach of developing a Christology based only on the gospel narratives. But, as seen in our discussions, Pobee does not rely on the Gospels alone to develop his ideas of the humanity of Jesus, but is also influenced by Akan traditional thought on being human. In some places, the parallels he draws appear to be somewhat superficial."[88]

This is most evident in Pobee's silence about the biblical accounts of Jesus' resurrection and ascension and the many passages in the Bible that assert his divinity. Even though Pobee begins by asserting that the Bible should be the plumb line for Christian theology, he resorts to using one set of arguments from the Bible to assert the humanity of Jesus to the neglect of many other passages that would challenge some of his propositions. When he argues for the humanity of Jesus from the Bible it appears that the Bible knows nothing of his divinity. His silence on the biblical witness to resurrection is the most glaring example of this. Having established Jesus' humanity, he makes a new entry point in the Bible to argue for his divinity.

Kwame Bediako has also questioned Pobee's methodology. Bediako is in agreement with Pobee's position on the application of the ancestral category for the formulation of Akan Christology. His reservation, however, as stated earlier, is that Pobee has built his argument for this on a very shallow foundation by looking to the proverbs for support. In his view, "Pobee approaches the issue largely through Akan wisdom sayings and proverbs, and so does not deal sufficiently with the religious nature of the question and underestimates the potential for conflict."[89]

What kind of conflict is Kwame Bediako referring to? For Bediako, if we claim the Greatest Ancestor as one who, at the superficial level, does not belong to his clan, family, tribe, and nation, the Akan non-Christian might

87. Ibid., 166.

88. Ibid.

89. Bediako, *Jesus in Africa*, 24.

well feel that the very grounds of his identity and personality are taken away from him.[90] This being the case, one needs to go well beyond proverbs to provide religious and spiritual reasons for why an outsider like Jesus could become one's ancestor. Akan wisdom sayings and proverbs are idiomatic expressions that speak to various issues regarding life, work, ethics, and relationships. They are not necessarily intended to inform the society about its spiritual universe, though some of them may give statements that may inform the Akan about how to behave in relation to the myriad of spirits.

The argument for Bediako with Pobee, however, is solely on methodology but not the end product— Jesus Christ as the Greatest Ancestor. There is a reason for that because, as we shall see later, Bediako, himself develops his Akan Christology on the same category but with an entirely different methodology. There is the larger question we have in regard to the work of both Pobee and Bediako as to whether the ancestor category is an appropriate concept from which to build an Akan Christology. This question is addressed in the final chapter of this study.

Returning to Pobee, another difficulty relates to his analysis concerning Jesus as a linguist/chief. First, we note that just as every Akan has the potential of becoming an ancestor, the linguist is also very likely to become one in the afterlife. According to Pobee's thinking, however, we note that he assigns chieftaincy status to Jesus Christ. Thus, Jesus becomes the chief of the linguists in Pobee's thought so that he can be viewed as performing his duty as priest of the dead and the living. But, the assignment for a linguist is very different from that of the chief. No linguist in Akan society performs the sacral role of priesthood. They are not even considered the assistants to the paramount chief. The fact that they are spokespersons does not mean they are the same as the chief they serve. Yet, Pobee makes Jesus Christ, the linguist, and at the same time, endows him with all the attributes that are reserved only for the paramount chief.

Pobee also interprets some of the other Akan traditions for his Christology in ways which are at variance with the understanding within Akan thought. In Akan traditional thought, for instance, male circumcision is not just a ritual but a celebration of life. It is, however, not understood as an invitation to belong to a kinship group. Today, many adhere to the practice for hygienic reasons but, in the past, the practice was a serious abomination for the people of the royal house, especially for the would-be chiefs. The chief in Akan thought is never to be touched with a knife. Thus,

90. Ibid.

circumcising a person of royalty is a disgrace, a humiliation, and degradation to the body of the would-be ruler. It is an abomination and a taboo. A circumcised royal, therefore, is an unqualified candidate to the position of a chief. Pobee, somewhat uncritically, applies the Jewish practice of circumcision as incorporation into the community to the Akan context. In reality, it would automatically disqualify one as a candidate for the position of a chief among the Akans. In a similar manner, Pobee uses Jesus' power of healing and his capacity to perform miracles as arguments for his divinity, whereas these powers within the Akan do not carry such meaning. In fact, Pobee was himself, aware that some of the parallels he was drawing might lead to confusion.[91]

All these show that there were some methodological problems in Pobee's attempt to develop an Akan Christology. There is no doubt, however, that Pobee made a significant contribution to African theology by taking the Christological question head on and making some bold moves, both by setting aside the tradition received during the missionary era and by his attempt to interpret the significance of Jesus to the Akan with their own traditional categories. He also provided the inspiration and courage needed for other African theologians to also enter this venture.

One of these was Kwame Bediako, who followed Pobee in his desire to develop an Akan Christology around the concept of the ancestor but with a different methodological approach. In the section that follows, the efforts of Bediakoto construct Akan Christology on the basis of ancestor-mediator category are outlined. The two theologians will then be engaged in conversation with Karl Barth who was also struggling to develop an adequate Christology for the European cultural context, specifically in reaction against Protestant Liberalism and German Christianity before and after the nineteenth century. Finally, based on the lessons learned, some of the new directions in which one might move in developing a Christology for the Akan, are pointed out.

Akan Christology of Kwame Bediako

Pobee's pioneering work on Akan Christology inspired other theologians who were also interested in interpreting the Christian faith from an African cultural perspective. One of the leading figures among them was Bediako, who, too was also interested primarily on the Christological issue.

91. Ibid., 93.

Manasseh Kwame Dakwa Bediako (July 7, 1945–June 8, 2008) was the Rector and Co-founder of Akrofi-Christaller Institute for Theology, Mission and Culture in Akropong, Ghana. His Christological works are found mainly in two of his books, *Jesus in Africa: The Christian Gospel in African History and Experience* and *Jesus and the Gospel in Africa: History and Experience.* Kwame Bediako began his contribution to the discussion with his critical observations on the historical, cultural, and theological developments of the Christian missionary encounter in Africa.

From this critical analysis, he claims that his own understanding of Jesus Christ arises in the light of "the quality of contact between Christian proclamation and the traditional religious life."[92] For Kwame Bediako, this quality of contact did not help the Western missionary enterprise to achieve a genuine encounter between the Christian Faith and the world view of his own people.[93] For him, the missionaries failed because they did not understand the world view of the Akan that led to a lack of genuine contact with their life and culture.

We shall seek to explore the Akan Christological contribution of Bediako with the aim of investigating how he resolved this problem. In dealing with this issue, we shall do a detailed study of Bediako's Akan Christology from the perspective of the way he utilized three features of Akan religio-traditional heritage— sacrifice, priestly mediation, and ancestral functions. Each of these factors contributed to defining his methodology and the criteria for doing indigenous theology. In doing so, we shall also attempt to determine how successful he had been in the application of his methodology and in developing an indigenous Christology. The study also assesses the ways biblical resources and the concept of the ancestor has been used to expound his Christology as well as examine the strengths and weaknesses of his proposals.

Kwame Bediako's Akan Christological Background

Some work on Christology had been done by other African scholars before Kwame Bediako began his work. Even though they had also attempted to use "genuine African categories and thought forms" in doing theology, Bediako found their methodologies inadequate for the task before them. [94]

92. Ibid., 20.

93. Ibid.

94. Pobee, *Toward Christology in African Theology,* 81.

Thus, his Christological investigations still attempt to answer the re-stated question of John Taylor:

> Christ has been presented as the answer to a question a white man would ask, the solution to the needs that western man would feel, the Savior of the world of European world view, the object of the adoration and prayer of historic Christendom. But if Christ were to appear as the answer to the questions that Africans are asking, what would he look like?[95]

It is this statement that Kwame Bediako seeks to address. He feels that the work that had been done to that point had adequately addressed the issue. Thus, in reaction to both the teachings of the Western missionaries and attempted works of African theologians, he postulates the following:

> This telling commentary (by John Taylor, quoted above) on the presentation of the Gospel of Jesus Christ in Africa was made by one of the more perceptive missionaries of Africa of our time and describes the general character of western missionary preaching and teaching in Africa since the arrival of missionaries on our continent during the 19th century. It raises a question that must be faced by African churches and African Christians today who are convinced that Jesus Christ, as Universal Savior, is the Savior of the African world, and who feel that the teaching they have so far received is inadequate.[96]

So, unlike Pobee, who critically assessed why an Akan should relate to Jesus Christ who is not from his clan, tribe, or nation, Bediako is not perturbed by who Jesus is to the Akan. Rather, Bediako concentrated on the inadequacies of the gospel message presented to the Akan people by Western missionaries. These inadequacies, according to Bediako, were interwoven with the generally negative attitude missionaries adopted toward the Akan world view. Akan Christian worship was, therefore, restricted to models from Christian traditions of Europe.

Bediako thus raises a question pertinent to the general character of the Western Christian missionary enterprise that pointed to the total disregard of African-ness: "Must we become other than African in order to be truly Christian?"[97] In answer to the question, he asserts that the Western

95. Bediako, *Jesus in Africa*, 20.

96. Ibid.

97. Bediako, "Biblical Christologies in the Context of African Traditional Religions," 125.

missionary enterprise did not achieve a genuine encounter between the Christian faith and the world view of his own people. For this reason, he posits that "Christ could not inhabit the spiritual universe of the African consciousness except, in essence, as a stranger."[98]

Nonetheless, Bediako finds good reasons for not focusing much on the undesirable side of the Western missionary endeavor. First, he explains that "the vitality of our Christian communities bear witness to the fact that the Gospel really was communicated, however inadequate we may now consider that communication to have been."[99] Bediako gains support for this assertion from John Taylor's statement that "There is always more to the 'hearing' of the Word of God than can be contained in the actual preaching of it by the human agents."[100] He also agrees with the commonly held view that "the Holy Spirit is also present to interpret the Word of God directly to the hearers' whiles the mercy and providence of God override human shortcomings."[101]

However, Bediako acknowledges the Pauline defense of Gentile Christians' freedom from the Jewish Christian attempt to impose the regulations of the Jewish Law (Acts 15; Galatians). He points out that:

> Paul grasped firmly the universality of the Gospel of Jesus the Messiah, insisting that the Gospel includes all people without reserve. He gave Gentile Christians the essential tools for assessing their own cultural heritage, for making their own contribution to Christian life and thought and for testing the genuineness and Christian character of that contribution.[102]

With this argument, Bediako believes that African theological thinkers now share in the inheritance of the Gospel as the Apostle Paul proclaimed. They have also been given the right and authority to delve into their own cultural heritage and make their own contribution to Christian life and thought. From the works of Bolaji Idowu, John Mbiti and Setiloane, Bediako points out that for many years African theologians have refuted the derogatory assessments and treatments of African religions held by Western Christian missionaries, and that they have shown consistently the continuity of God from the pre-Christian African past into the Christian present. Bediako

98. Ibid., 125.

99. Bediako, *Jesus in African Culture*, 20.

100. Ibid.

101. Ibid.

102. Ibid., 21.

thus posits emphatically: "They have, therefore, like the Apostle Paul, handed to us the assurance that with our Christian conversion we are not introduced to a new God unrelated to the traditions of our past, but to one who brings to fulfillment all the highest religious and cultural aspirations of our heritage."[103] With this understanding, he argues that the flaws of the evangelistic endeavor should not hinder the growth of Christian thought and confidence in our churches.

Bediako looks at two divergent views held within Western missionary thinking on the relationship between the Christian message and the African Traditional religions. The first is that of W. H. T. Gairdner, a theologian of the early twentieth century, whoseworks held the view that "traditional religious beliefs are more or less backward and degraded peoples all over the world and it held no preparation for Christianity."[104]

Disregarding this statement, Bediako makes reference to an alternate view put forward by Andrew Walls, Director of the Oxford Center for Missions Studies, which holds that "Christianity has spread most rapidly in societies with primal religious systems."[105] These according to Bediako, include religious systems akin to African Traditional Religion. The argument points in the direction of such societies like the Mediterranean world of the early Christian centuries, the ancient peoples of Northern Europe, and modern Primal Religious adherents of Africa, Asia, South America, and Oceania.

This fact, according to Bediako, has led to the question whether there might be "affinities between the Christian and primal traditions."[106] W. H. Turner, author of *The Primal Religions of the World and their Study*, states that "it shows clearly that the form of religion once held to be the farthest removed from the Christian faith has had a closer relationship with it than any other."[107] Turner points further to Andrew Walls' contention that it is because the primal religions are the 'most fertile soil for the Gospel' that the vast majority of Christians of all ages and all nations are drawn from this background."[108] One more support for his assertion stems from a reference

103. Ibid.

104. Gairdner, *An Account and Interpretation of the World Missionary Conference*, quoted in Bediako, *Jesus in African Culture*, 21.

105. Walls, "African and Christian Identity," 21.

106. Bediako, *Jesus in African Culture*, 21.

107. Turner, "Primal Religions of the World and their Study"; quoted in Bediako, *Jesus in African Culture*, 21.

108. Walls, "African and Christian Identity," 11–13; quoted in Bediako, *Jesus in*

from John Mbiti that "Africa's 'old' religions have been a crucial factor in the rapid spread of Christianity among African peoples."[109] On the bases of all these supporting arguments, Kwame Bediako points out that the African traditional religions were "vital preparation for the Gospel."[110]

Unlike Pobee, Bediako spends more time dealing with the Christian missionary enterprise because, for him, it presents a pertinent challenge to the African theologians to find alternatives and "opens the way for a fresh approach as to how we may relate Jesus as Lord and Savior to the spiritual realities of our context."[111]

Kwame Bediako's Akan Christological Foreground

We have gathered from the discussions above that the way to relate Jesus Christ to the spiritual realities of the Akan is relevant to any evangelistic encounter. To this end, Bediako explores the issues within the Akan spiritual universe that inform the Akan of the need for a savior like Jesus Christ. From John Mbiti's articles on the African Independent Churches, Bediako offers two main issues that are characteristics of an African understanding of Christ.

First,Bediako points out that in Africa, "Jesus is seen above all else as the *Christus Victor* (Christ as supreme ruler over every other spiritual rule and authority)."[112] For Bediako, "this perception arises from Africans' keen awareness of forces and powers at work in the world that threaten the interests of life and harmony. Jesus is victorious over the spiritual realm and particularly over evil forces. Thus he meets the need of the Africans for a powerful protector."[113] The reality of these evil forces in the thought of the Akan cannot be overemphasized. In African thinking, their evil machinations have been demonstrated in almost every city, town, village, cottage, home, work place, and the church.

Second, Bediako states that "for African Christians the term 'our Savior' can refer also to God and to the Holy Spirit. Jesus, as our Savior, brings

African Culture, 21.

109. Mbiti, "Encounter between Christianity and African Religion"; quoted in Bediako, *Jesus in African Culture*, 21.

110. Bediako, *Jesus in African Culture*, 21.

111. Ibid.

112. Ibid., 22; quoted from Mbiti, "Our Savior as an African Experience."

113. Ibid., 22. quoted from Mbiti, "Our Savior as an African Experience."

near and makes universal the almightiness of God."[114] Bediako, therefore, holds that Christ, in this sense, is "able to do all things, to save in all situations, to protect against all enemies, and is available whenever those who believe may call upon him."[115] Thus, Bediako believes that the humanity of Jesus and his atoning work on the Cross are in the background and Jesus is taken to belong essentially to the more powerful realm of divinity, the realm of spirit-power. In Bediako's view, these considerations "bring us near the heart of the problem of understanding Christ authentically in the African world."[116]

Kwame Bediako's Method for an Akan Christological Formulation

This background of the nature of the spiritual expectations of the Akan plays an important methodological role in Bediako's Christology. He seeks to move toward a method of Christological formulation that brings into focus the functions of the 'spirit fathers' (another name for ancestors) to the center. For Africans to believe in a supernatural deity, that deity must be supreme and powerful enough to conquer every spiritual or evil force known in the African world that incessantly plagues individuals and communities. Bediako says:

> Accepting Jesus as our savior always involves making him at home in our spiritual universe and in terms of our religious needs and longings. So an understanding of Christ in relation to spirit-power in the African context is not necessarily less accurate than any other perceptions of Jesus. The question is whether such an understanding faithfully reflects biblical revelation and is rooted in true Christian experience. [117]

On the question of biblical revelation, Bediako makes it clear that the Bible points to who Jesus is and what he can do. He states: "Jesus is who he is (Savior) because of what he has done and can do (save) and also that he was able to do what he did on the Cross because of who he is (God the son) (Colossians 2:15ff)."[118] Thus we observe here that the issue of humanity

114. Ibid.
115. Ibid.
116. Ibid.
117. Ibid.
118. Ibid.

and divinity of Jesus Christ is not problematic for Bediako's Christological exploration.

For him, it may not necessarily matter what one conceives Jesus Christ to be; but whatever that conception may be, it should speak to the realm of the Akan worldview. He is convinced that Jesus as the spirit-father (ancestor) may be the best articulation that would meet this need:

> Since 'salvation' in the traditional African world involves a certain view of the realm of spirit-power and its effects upon the physical and spiritual dimensions of human existence, our reflection about Christ must speak to the questions posed by such a world view. The needs of the African world require a view of Christ that meets those needs. And so who Jesus is in the African spiritual universe must not be separated from what he does and can do in that world. The way in which Jesus relates to the importance and function of the 'spirit-fathers' or ancestors is crucial.[119]

So Bediako believes that the most meaningful way of accepting Jesus Christ in the Akan world is to accept him in relation to the spirit-fathers or ancestors. How does Bediako perceive this relationship?

Similar to Mbiti, Quarcoopome, Asare and others, Bediako teaches that the Akans' spirit world primarily involves God, the Supreme Spirit Being *(Onyame)* Creator and Sustainer of the universe. Subordinate to God, with delegated authority from God, are the 'gods' (*abosom*) sometimes referred to as children of God (*Nyame mma*) and the ancestors or 'spirit fathers' (*Nsamanfor*). He points out that "the ancestors are essentially clan or lineage ancestors."[120] Thus, for him, the ancestors have authority within their respective clans and families or even communities, but not "with a system of religion." [121]

Yet, the religious functions and duties that relate to ancestors become binding on all those within that particular group who share common ancestors. Quoting Samuel Pobee, Bediako asserts:

> By virtue of being the part of the clan gone ahead to the house of God, they are believed to be powerful in the sense that they maintain the course of life here and now and influence it for good or ill. They . . . provide the sanctions for the moral life of the nation

119. Ibid.

120. Ibid., 23.

121. Ibid., 23.

> and accordingly punish, exonerate or reward the living as the case may be.[122]

If the ancestors have this primary role to play within the society, Bediako thinks that Pobee was right in raising the question, "Why should an Akan relate to Jesus of Nazareth who does not belong to his clan, family, tribe and nation."[123] Bediako, holds that the churches have avoided such questions and presented the gospel as unrelated to issues that are pertinent to Akan life. Such unasked questions have clouded the crucial issues and therefore left certain terrorizing and fearful traditional experiences unexplained. He says,

> As a result, many people are uncertain about how the Jesus of the Church's preaching saves them from the terrors and fears that they experience in their traditional worldview. This shows how important it is to relate Christian understanding and experience to the realm of the ancestors. If this is not done, many African Christians will continue to be men and women 'living at two levels,' half African and half European, but never belonging properly to either. We need to meet God in the Lord Jesus Christ speaking immediately to us in our particular circumstances, in a way that assures us that we can be authentic Africans and true Christians.[124]

If we are to relate our Christian thought and issues to the realm of the ancestors, is Bediako in agreement with Pobee? Regarding Pobee's utilization of the ancestor category, Bediako comments, as follows:

> Pobee suggests that we look on Jesus as the Great and Greatest Ancestor, since in Akan society the Supreme Being and the ancestors provide the sanctions for good life and the ancestors hold that authority as ministers of the Supreme Being. However he approaches the issue largely through Akan wisdom sayings and proverbs, and so does not deal sufficiently with the religious nature of the question and underestimate the potential for conflict.[125]

According to Bediako, if we claim as the Greatest Ancestor someone who, at least at the superficial level, does not belong to his clan, family, tribe and nation, the Akan non-Christian might well feel that the very grounds

122. Ibid. Also quoted from Pobee, *Toward an African Theology*, 83.

123. Ibid., 23. Also quoted from Pobee, *Toward an African Theology*, 81.

124. Ibid., 23.

125. Ibid., 24.

of his identity and personality are taken away from him. This is an essential fact that differentiates what he is doing from whatever Pobee has done. Bediako is convinced that in dealing with the ancestor category, to understand Christ we must not turn to proverbs but must deal with the fears and anxieties of the Akan and the meaning and intentions of the allegiances that they have in relation to the spiritual world.[126]

Bediako's proposal to elicit a new thought about Christ's relationship with the ancestors begins with the assumption that "Jesus is not a stranger to our heritage."[127] Secondly, he thinks there is the need to read the Scriptures with "Akan traditional piety well in view," so that we can see its meaning to their spiritual life.[128] Even though he does not mention Jesus' pre-incarnational existence as the Word, he elucidates the history of Jesus from the perspective of his universality rather than his particularity as a Jew, and affirms that "the Incarnation of Christ was the incarnation of the Savior of all people, of all nations and of all times."[129] This for Bediako does not reduce the incarnation to a mere accident of history. Rather, he affirms that "we hold on to his incarnation as a Jew because by faith in him, we too share in the divine promises given to the patriarchs through the history of ancient Israel (Ephesians 2:11–22)."[130] He asserts that even though according to John, "salvation is from the Jews' (John 4:22) it is not thereby Jewish. "To make Jesus little more than a typical Jew is to distort the truth."[131]

What counts for Bediako is one's response to Jesus Christ. He maintains that our true humanity as men and women made in the image of God is not to be understood primarily in terms of racial, cultural, national or lineage categories but, in Jesus Christ, himself.[132] He holds that as long as we put our faith in Jesus Christ, we become the true children of Abraham in the same way that Abraham trusted God and was received on that basis (Romans 4:11–12). In this manner, and in agreement with Andrew Walls, Bediako writes: "Consequently, we have not merely our natural past; through faith in Jesus Christ, we have also an 'adoptive' past, the past of

126. Ibid.

127. Ibid.

128. Ibid.

129. Ibid.

130. Ibid.

131. Ibid.

132. Ibid., 24.

God, reaching into biblical history itself, aptly described as the 'Abrahamic link.'"[133]

Thus, Bediako affirms that all humanity, and therefore also the Akan, shares a common heritage with Jesus Christ who is the image of the Father and has become one of us. "It is within this human heritage that he finds us and speaks to us in terms of its questions and puzzles, and challenges us to turn to him and participate in the new humanity for which he has come, died been raised and glorified"[134]

Bediako argues that if this way of perceiving Jesus Christ is accepted, there will be no need to make special attempts to accommodate the Gospel in our culture; "The Gospel becomes our story."[135] Bediako is convinced that some of the biblical teachings resonate with the above argument. He reflects on this point as follows:

> Our Lord has been from the beginning the Word of God for us as for and all people everywhere. He has been the source of our life and illuminator of our path in life, though, like all people everywhere, we also failed to understand him aright. But now he has made himself known by becoming one of us, one like us. By acknowledging him for who he is and giving him our allegiance, we become what we are truly intended to be, by his gift, the children of God. Our response to him is crucial since becoming children of God does not stem from, nor is it limited by, the accidents of birth, race, culture, lineage or even 'religious' tradition. It comes to us by grace through faith.[136]

For Bediako, once the Akan grasps these facts, it makes it easier for further understanding and appreciation of "the close association of our creation and redemption as found in the readings of the early verses of Johannine's Gospel that echo the verses of Genesis chapter one." For Bediako, both creation and redemption have been achieved *in* and *through* Jesus Christ. He holds that in the very act of creation, God has revealed himself to us and has made a covenant with us."[137] With this understanding, Bediako points out emphatically that it was "in the creation of the universe

133. Walls, "African and Christian Identity," 11–13, also quoted in Bediako, *Jesus in African Culture*, 21 and 24.

134. Ibid.

135. Ibid.

136. Ibid.

137. Ibid.

and especially of man that God first revealed his Kingship to our ancestors and called them to freely obey him."[138]

Arguably, for Bediako, once we work from this understanding, it enables people of primal traditions to have a biblical basis for discovering God as the creator and sustainer that is deeply rooted in their traditional heritage. What is more important here for Bediako is not just the discovery of God and what he does in creation, but also how meaningful such revelation is to the primal traditional believer to come to terms with his or her humanity. He claims, "We are enabled to discover ourselves in Adam (Acts 17:26) and come out of the isolation which the closed system of clan, lineage, and family impose, so that we can rediscover universal horizon."[139]

Bediako sees the solidarity of the primal traditions with Adam not only in creation but also in the sin that followed. Adam sinned and lost his place in the garden.[140] Comparatively, he points out that whereas the biblical account speaks of the expulsion of man (Genesis 3) African myths of origins talk of the withdrawal of God from humankind. This withdrawal of God in the African myths means that God was nowhere to be found in their daily activities; but he is continually there in people's thoughts. In the light of this reality, Bediako asserts that "the experience of ambiguity that comes from regarding lesser deities and ancestral spirits as both beneficent and malevolent can only be resolved in a genuine incarnation of the Savior from the realm beyond."[141] Bediako also believes that this conviction should still be held within the Trinitarian faith, because the "God who has become so deeply and actively involved in our condition is the Son (John 1:18) whom to see is to 'see' the Father (John 14:15ff; Acts 2:38f) and this is made possible through the Holy Spirit (John 14:23)."[142] This quick exposition of Trinitarian thought by Bediako is of interest and relevant for this study, but this issue will be discussed in a later chapter. In the meantime, it is important to take a detailed look at Bediako's use of the category of the ancestor for his Christology.

138. Ibid.

139. Ibid.

140. Ibid.

141. Ibid.

142. Ibid.

God's Son (Jesus Christ)—Ancestor and Sole Mediator in the Thought of Kwame Bediako

Based on the previous analysis, we turn now to Bediako's exploration of Jesus Christ as the Ancestor and the sole mediator. He begins with his assertion that there is a dichotomy in Akan spiritual experience between an intense awareness of the existence of God and the sense of remoteness from him. Bediako holds that this experience of remoteness from God in African Traditional Religion is dealt with by Jesus Christ alone, because "there has been a death which sets people free from the wrongs they did while the first covenant was in force."[143] Intriguingly, however, the interest here for Bediako is not only the kind of salvation that this death produces but also how this death is related to the story of the Akan people and, particularly, to their natural 'spirit-fathers' or the ancestors."[144]

Bediako asserts that often there is no adequate understanding of the views of sin and morality within the Akan society, and therefore the solutions offered in terms of the assurance of forgiveness and moral transformation are also inadequate. In his view, the problem of sin among the Akan is one of "soiled consciousness" that results from wrongdoing which requires purification rites and sacrificial offerings to restore social harmony. The problem for the Akan is that the traditional purification rites and sacrificial offerings have been ineffectual."[145] Bediako also notes that since sins committed against another person in society are also against God, the remedy needs to deal with the fuller reality.

Bediako points out that such an understanding is seen in the Book of Hebrews as the writer expounds on the significance of the sacrificial death of Jesus Christ:

> Our Savior has not become one of us; he has died for us. It is a death with eternal sacrificial significance. It deals with our moral failures and infringements of social relationships. It heals our wounded and soiled conscience and overcomes once and for all and at their roots, all that in our heritage and somewhat melancholy history brings us grief, guilt, shame and bitterness.[146]

143. Ibid., 26.

144. Ibid.

145. Ibid.

146. Ibid.

In relation to the Akan society, therefore, Bediako argues that such a savior, within traditional thought, would first of all become "brother." He thus postulates that "our savior is our Elder Brother who has shared in our African experience in every respect, except our sin and alienation from God, an alienation with which our myths of origins make us only too familiar."[147] Why should our savior, who Bediako describes as God's Son, become our Elder Brother? For Bediako there is a good reason for such an exposition. He holds that "being our true Elder Brother now in the presence of his Father and our Father, he displaces the mediatorial function of our natural 'spirit-fathers.'"[148] This, fundamentally, is Bediako's Akan Christology.

For him, Jesus Christ has to take up such function because the ancestors themselves need salvation from him because they have originated from us. He argues from Christian missionary history that one of the first actions of the new converts was to pray for their ancestors who had passed on before the Gospel was proclaimed. He says that "this important testimony speaks to the depth of their understanding of Jesus as sole Lord and Savior."[149] Further, he holds that Jesus Christ, 'the second Adam' from heaven (I Corinthians 15:47) becomes for us the only mediator between God and ourselves (cf. 1 Timothy 2:5). Additionally, according to Bediako, Jesus Christ is the mediator of a new covenant (Hebrews 8:6) relating our human destiny directly to God, which also makes him truly our high priest who meets our needs to the full.

He further explicates that on the basis of Akan cosmology, the resurrection and ascension of Jesus also account for the fact that "Jesus has now returned to the realm of ancestor spirits and the 'gods.'"[150] In Akan thought, the realm of the ancestor spirits and the gods are the sources of power and resources for living as well as for the terrors and misfortunes which could threaten and destroy life. With this in view, he expounds on the thinking on what Jesus is capable of doing to cosmic forces that would sit well within the Akan worldview:

> But if Jesus has gone to the realm of 'spirits and the gods,' so to speak, he had gone there as Lord over them in the same way that he is Lord over us. He is Lord over the living and the dead, and over the 'living-dead,' as ancestors are also called. He is supreme

147. Ibid.

148. Ibid.

149. Ibid.

150. Ibid., 26–27.

> over all gods and authorities in the realm of spirit, summing up in him all their powers and cancelling any terrorizing influence they might be assumed to have upon us.[151]

Having shown who Jesus Christ is and what he is capable of effecting in the spiritual universe of the Akan, Bediako turns to the work of the Holy Spirit. He points out that "the guarantee that Jesus is Lord also in the realm of spirits is that he has sent us his own Spirit, the Holy Spirit, to dwell with us and be our protector, as well as Revealer of Truth and Sanctifier."[152]

He also asserts that Jesus' statement that he is "going to the Father" in John 16:7ff includes the idea of his lordship and also the protection and guidance that the Holy Spirit he sends will provide for his followers. "The Holy Spirit is sent to convict the world of its sin in rejecting Jesus, and to demonstrate, to the shame of unbelievers, the true righteousness which is in Jesus and available only in him."[153] Another aspect of the work of the Spirit, in Bediako's thinking, is that the Spirit will "reveal the spiritual significance of God's judgment upon the devil, which deceives the world about its sin, and blinds people to the perfect righteousness in Christ."[154]

Thus, according to Bediako, upon entering the region of the spirit, Jesus sent the Holy Spirit to his followers to give them understanding of the realities in the realm of the spirits. For him, therefore, the close association of the defeat and overthrow of the devil ('ruler of this world') through the death, resurrection and exaltation of Jesus (John 12:31) is significant; and of equal importance in the protection of his followers from the 'evil one.' These are some of the main themes of Jesus' prayer in John 17, described as his 'high priestly' prayer.[155] It is this high priestly function of Jesus Christ that Bediako begins to explore in his concluding thoughts. Bediako sees these sacrificial, mediatory, and priestly functions of Christ as ancestral in character among the Akan and sees them as the basis for his interpretation of Jesus Christ as ancestor and mediator.

Turning to the Epistle to the Hebrews, Bediako claims that the view of Jesus Christ in the epistle involves making room within the tradition of priestly mediation for someone who, within the Jewish tradition, was an outsider to it. In this way, he seeks to address Pobee's Christological

151. Ibid., 27.

152. Ibid.

153. Ibid.

154. Ibid.

155. Ibid.

questions regarding why an Akan should relate to Jesus of Nazareth who does not belong to his clan, family, tribe and nation[156] Bediako points out that a similar question might have occurred to some Hebrews at the time the epistle was written.

According to Bediako, the writer's approach was to translate "the meaning of the death and resurrection of Jesus into the biblical tradition of sacrifice and high priestly mediation."[157] Thus, Bediako claims that the belief in the incarnation and the universality of the work of Christ were the basis on which the Hebrew people were called upon to accept him as the Savior and mediator. The writer of the Epistle to the Hebrews "shows that the High Priesthood of Jesus is not after the order of Aaron, the first Hebrew High Priest, but rather after the enigmatic non-Hebrew, and greater priest-king, Melchizedek (Hebrews 7 and 8)."[158]

Since the claim of the priesthood of Jesus Christ is beyond the Hebrew tribe, family, Aaronic priesthood and other Jewish traditional sources, Bediako holds, as the writer of the Epistle to the Hebrews does, that the mediation and salvation that Jesus Christ offers to all humankind belong to an entirely different category. Bediako, therefore, argues that the quality of the achievement and ministry of Jesus Christ, for and on behalf of all, together with who he is, reveal his absolute supremacy. This supremacy makes his sacrifice speak to every culture in every context. Thus, it goes beyond the Hebrew or Jewish context. He notes:

> As one who is fully divine, he nonetheless took on human nature in order to offer himself in death as sacrifice for human sin. Jesus Christ is unique not because he stands apart from us but because no one has identified so profoundly with the human predicament as he has, in order to transform it. The uniqueness of Jesus Christ is rooted in his radical and direct significance for every human person, every human context and every human culture.[159]

Thus Bediako had turned to the presentation of Jesus Christ in the Epistle to the Hebrews to demonstrate the relevance of Jesus, and what he had done to every human person, context, and culture, including the Akan tradition with its deep rituals and customs relating to sacrifice, priestly mediation,

156. Ibid. 28; a quotation from Pobee, *Toward an African Theology*, 81.

157. Ibid.

158. Ibid.

159. Ibid.

and ancestral function. Bediako then moves to a more detailed exploration of these three aspects he builds his Christology.

The Rite of Sacrifice

According to Bediako, in Ghanaian society, the rite of sacrifice is "a way of ensuring a harmonious relationship between the human community and the realm of divine and mystical power."[160] Thus, for the Ghanaian community, sacrifice is a common practice in everyday life and pertains to building relationships, communities, and the nation as a whole. However, Bediako points out that though the Akan may assume that the mere performance of the rite of sacrifice, with its attendant ritual and practices, is sufficient, the real problem is whether sacrifice, in itself, achieves its objectives. The complaints about the rite of sacrifice not fulfilling its intended purposes may stem from the nature of the sacrifice that is offered. He points out that the Epistle to the Hebrews gives its insight on the issue: "Since it is human sin and wrong-doing that sacrifice seeks to purge and atone for, no animal or subhuman victim or sinful human being can stand in for human beings."[161]

Using Hebrews 9.12, Bediako holds that only the action of Jesus Christ, who is himself divine, sinless, and incarnated to willingly lay down his life for all humanity, fulfills perfectly the end that all sacrifices seek to achieve. Thus, for him, the one perfect sacrifice effected by Jesus Christ, of himself, for all time, and for all people, everywhere, can never be compared to any number of animals or other victims offered at any number of shrines. One cannot, therefore, reject such worthy sacrifice of Jesus Christ on the grounds of race, ethnicity, and cultural tradition. Such rejection, according to Bediako, is to "act against better knowledge, distort religious truth, and walk into a blind alley". In the words of Hebrews, it is to court "the fearful prospect of judgment and the fierce fire which will destroy those who oppose God" (Hebrews 10:27).[162] Thus, Bediako looks at Jesus' sacrifice on the cross as an all-sufficient sacrifice that would speak meaningfully with the Akan culture.

We now turn to the second feature of Akan traditional heritage.

160. Ibid.

161. Ibid.

162. Ibid., 29.

The Rite of Priestly Mediation

On the role of Jesus as the mediator, Bediako argues that "if the quality of Jesus' self-offering in death sets his sacrifice above all others and achieves perfect atonement, so also his priestly mediation surpasses all others."[163] In keeping with Hebrews 7.14, and 8.4, Bediako points out that Jesus had no human hereditary claim to priesthood. He, therefore, turns to the beliefs in incarnation and the doctrine of the humanity and divinity of Jesus Christ as the basis for the assertion of Jesus' priesthood. He writes:

> His taking of human nature enabled him to share the human predicament and so qualifies him to act for humanity. His divine origin ensures that he is able to mediate between the human community and the divine realm in a way no human priest can. As himself God-man, Jesus bridges the gulf between the Holy God and sinful humanity, achieving for humanity the harmonious fellowship with God that all human priestly mediations only approximate.[164]

On the question of whether Jesus fulfills his priestly ministry on earth, Bediako argues that Jesus priestly ministry does not take place in temples or shrines, but in the realm of the spirit where issues are decided—in the divine presence (Hebrews 9:24). He contends that the priestly ministry of Jesus Christ brings into the divine presence "all who by faith associate themselves with him."[165] This means that for Bediako there is a convergence of the perfect sacrifice and the perfect priestly mediation in the one person, Jesus Christ. He agrees with the writer of the Epistle to the Hebrews that "having identified with humanity in order to taste death on behalf of humanity (Hebrews 2:14–15) he has opened the way for all who identify with him to be with him in the divine presence (Hebrews 10:19–20)."[166]

For Bediako, this accomplishment by Jesus Christ renders all other priestly functions totally obsolete and ineffective. Therefore, he holds that one cannot disregard this awesome priestly ministry of Jesus Christ for all people, everywhere, on the grounds of ethnic priesthood in the name of cultural heritage. According to him, to disregard it points to the human failure to recognize the true meaning of the end of all local priestly

163. Ibid.

164. Ibid.

165. Ibid.

166. Ibid.

mediation, to abdicate from belonging to the one community of humanity, and to clutch the shadow and miss the substance. Having argued for the "perfect sacrifice" and the "perfect priestly mediation," Bediako, then turns to the third aspect of the "ancestral function".

The Ancestral Mediation or Function

The third of the three features of the traditional heritage which Bediako discusses is ancestral mediation or function. Bediako finds it more difficult to relate this function to Jesus, but he believes that it can, indeed, be given a Christological focus. He first deals with the cult of the ancestors from the mythological point of view. He argues that they are the projection of the community which produces them. He holds that, "Strictly speaking, the cult of the ancestors, from the intellectual point of view, belongs to the category of myth, ancestors being the product of the myth-making imagination of the community."[167] The characterization of the cult of ancestors as 'myth,' according to him, does not mean it is unworthy of serious attention. Rather, the terminology for him emphasizes the functional value of the cult of ancestors. Delving further into the question, he describes the value of myth as follows:

> Myth is sacred, enshrining and expressing the most valued elements of a community's self-understanding. Its role ensures social harmony by strengthening the ties that knit together all sections and generations of the community, the present with the past and those as yet unborn.[168]

For him, this is the reason the cult of the ancestors form the core part of the ritual ceremonies that take place during birth, 'outdooring' of a child, initiation into adulthood, marriage, death, installation of a King, and the celebration of harvest.

Further, Bediako points out that the origin of the cult of ancestors, and the myth-making imagination of the community about them, are based mainly on the life that they had lived on earth and what their life has meant to the community, rather than on the reality that they were now in the transcendent realm. It is the same myth-making imagination of the community about their life on earth that also sacralizes them and confers upon them the authority that they exercise in the community. Therefore,

167. Ibid., 30.

168. Ibid.

Bediako says,"The potency of the cult of the ancestors is not the ancestors themselves; the potency of the cult is the potency of myth."[169] For him, once the cult of the ancestors as myth is accepted, it would be easy to see how Jesus Christ fulfills the ancestral role.

In a comparative analysis, Bediako weighs the origins and functions of the cult of ancestors with the life and work of Jesus Christ. He points out that the ancestors lived among the people and brought benefits to them. Jesus did the same, but in a much more profound way: "Jesus Christ, who reflects the brightness of God's glory and the likeness of God's being (Hebrews 1:3) took our flesh and blood, shared our human nature and underwent death for us to set us free from the fear of death (Hebrews 2:14–15)."[170] Jesus had every reason to abandon sinful humans, but he was not ashamed of his brethren (Hebrews 2:11). Further, Bediako says that the ancestors had no barriers to cross in order to live among us and share our experience. But, as for Jesus, "his incarnation implies that he has achieved a far more profound identification with us in our humanity than the mere ethnic solidarity of lineage ancestors can ever do."[171] Bediako believes, therefore, that "by virtue of who he is in himself he surpasses our natural ancestors."[172]

Another revealing fact between Jesus Christ and the ancestors that he explores is that for the ancestors, though they may be described as ancestral spirits, they never change from being human spirits, no matter what benefits they are said to offer to the living community. On this issue, Bediako uses the divinity of Jesus Christ to show a stark difference between him and the spirit of the ancestors. He claims that "Jesus Christ took human nature without loss to his divine nature. Belonging in the eternal realm as Son of the Father, he has taken human nature into himself (Hebrews 10:19) and so, as God-man, he ensures an infinitely more effective ministry to human beings (Hebrews 7:25) than can be said of merely human ancestral spirits."[173]

Bediako also argues that Jesus showed that he possessed an indestructible life through his death and resurrection. This can never be said of any ancestor in the Akan tradition. He points out that the ancestors do not owe their existence in the realm of the spirit through such demonstrable power, as in the case of Jesus Christ, but rather through the myth-making

169. Ibid.

170. Ibid.

171. Ibid., 31.

172. Ibid.

173. Ibid.

imagination indicated above. The belief in benefits claimed to be bestowed on humanity by the ancestors, likewise, originated in the same myth-making imagination, which projects the departed beings into the transcendental realm. Bediako, therefore, comes to the following conclusion: "While not denying that spiritual forces do operate in the traditional realm, we can maintain that ancestral spirits, as human spirits that have not demonstrated any power over death, the final enemy, cannot be presumed to act in the way tradition ascribes to them."[174]

Having arrived at this conclusion, Bediako goes on to declare that, "Since ancestral function, as traditionally understood, is now shown to have no basis in fact, the way is open for appreciating more fully how Jesus Christ is the only real and true Ancestor and Source of life for all humankind, fulfilling and transcending the benefits believed to be bestowed by lineage ancestors."[175] This claim is similar to his earlier statement that Jesus Christ has displaced the mediatorial function of the ancestors and this is the heart of Bediako's Akan Christology.

In addition, Bediako holds that by the atonement he effected through his self-sacrifice, and by the eternal mediation and intercession he makes as God-man in the divine presence, Jesus Christ has secured eternal redemption for everyone who acknowledges who he is and what he has achieved for them (Hebrews 9:12). He further holds that "As mediator of a new and better covenant between God and humanity (Hebrews 8:6; 12:24) Jesus brings the redeemed into the experience of a new identity in which he links their human destinies directly and consciously with the gracious will and purpose of a loving and caring God (Hebrews 12:22–24)."[176]

Therefore, for him, no longer are human horizons limited by lineage, clan, tribe, family or nation; the Akan, indeed, the whole humanity has been redeemed, and the redeemed now belong within the community of the living God in the joyful company of the faithful of all ages and climes. For him, the redeemed are united into a fellowship in Jesus Christ that is infinitely richer than mere social, family, or national bonds that make the stranger a virtual enemy. Therefore, in his theology, the limitations that our lineage imposes on us have been cleared to make way for universal horizons.

174. Ibid.

175. Ibid.

176. Ibid.

So far we have attempted to articulate the Akan Christology of Kwame Bediako which intends to present a Christology that would bring genuine contact between Christianity and the Akan people. We have elucidated the facets of the traditional resources and the biblical themes that he has used to develop his Christology. In the subsection that follows, we will attempt to comment on the strengths and weaknesses in his presentation with the view of learning from them and thus, towards making new proposals for a Christology in the Akan context.

Comments on Kwame Bediako's Akan Christology

As we have pointed out from the onset, Kwame Bediako's Akan Christological endeavor begins with identifying some of the problems he perceived in the articulation of the Christian faith during the Christian missionary encounter with the Akan culture. He also has some reservations on the way some of his own contemporaries were seeking to remedy the situation. His concern was that the Gospel has not been communicated to the Akan in ways it would address the issues and problems that are deeply rooted in the spiritual universe of the Akan culture. What he has attempted to do is to address the inadequacies of the earlier approaches and to make a fresh Christological proposal that he believes speaks more directly to the spiritual needs of the Akan people.

Bediako's endeavor has undoubtedly taken a fresh approach towards a Christological initiative for the Akan society. His call for the universality of the significance of the person and work of Jesus Christ and his interpretation of Jesus as divine ruler of the African spirit world, with the power to overcome the evil powers, resonates very well with the Akan. His identification of Jesus' priestly function with the enigmatic Melchizedek and his dependence on the Epistle to the Hebrews to expound his Christology speak well with the Akan whose faith is rooted in the Bible. Nonetheless, there are some weaknesses and contradictions in this methodological approach we need to make note of at this point.

Let us begin with the application of the ancestral category as a method of Christological endeavor for the Akan. It was John Pobee who first rendered Jesus Christ as "the Great and Greatest Ancestor."[177] Though Pobee attempted to elucidate the humanity and divinity of Jesus Christ and translate it into basic Akan thought, Bediako found Pobee's exposition inadequate

177. Ibid., 94.

on methodological grounds, because he does not consider proverbs an adequate basis on which to develop a Christology. He also questions Pobee's argument that Jesus is unrelated to the Akan lineage. Bediako claims that "If we claim as the Greatest Ancestor one who, at the superficial level, does not belong to his clan, family, tribe or nation, the Akan non-Christian might feel that the very grounds of his personality has been taken from him."[178]

Bediako, therefore, has sought to establish this lineage by re-interpreting the concept of lineage at the wider human level. Why then does Bediako argue for Jesus Christ as our Elder Brother? How would Jesus, as an Elder Brother, displace the mediatorial function of the ancestors? Charles Nyamiti, the Tanzanian Roman Catholic theologian and author of *Christ as our Ancestor*, has also interpreted Jesus as our Elder Brother Ancestor. Attributing to Jesus the status of the elder brother, in itself, does not resolve the problem raised by Pobee because, as Archbishop Emeritus Peter Kwasi Sarpong, a theologian and author of many traditional books, points out, in the Akan understanding, ancestral relations are primarily blood related in a particular kind of lineage.

As pointed out in chapter two on the analysis of the Akan cosmology, in Akan anthropology, lineage is either inherited from the *mogya* (blood) of the mother or the *sunsum* (spirit) of the father, but not through *kra* (soul) which is the vitalizing force obtained from the Supreme Being or *Onyankopong*. For the Akan, without these three connections, one cannot be a human being and without the first two, one cannot become one's brother. Thus, in Akan thought and language, the English word "cousin," does not exist. "*Nua*" means brother and "*Me Nua*" means, my brother. One's cousin is also called "*Nua*" or "*Me Nua*." This is because of the *mogya* and *sunsum* found in the mothers and fathers of a particular people group. Within the system, however, one's brother cannot become one's ancestor.

Because of the extended family system, both among the matrilineal and patrilineal systems of inheritance in Akan thought, the Akan is always connected to myriads of great ancestral spirits in the form of fathers, grandfathers, great grandfathers, mothers, grandmothers, great grandmothers, aunties, grand aunties, great grand aunties, uncles, granduncles, great granduncles and so forth to the third, fourth and fifth generations. Within this system a departed brother cannot take the place as an ancestor and it would, in fact, be a taboo in Akan thought, for such a circumstance

178. Bediako, *Jesus and the Gospel in Africa*, 24.

to occur. The elder brother argument alongside the ancestor argument, therefore, would not sound very meaningful to the Akan.

Another area that needs closer examination in Bediako's thinking is that "Jesus Christ has displaced the mediatorial functions of our 'spirit fathers.'"[179] Since his contention for such displacement is based on Jesus Christ, as Elder Brother, it is also arguably weak and untenable.

Further, Bediako, arguing from the intellectual point of view, says that the ancestral category itself is a myth: "Ancestors being the product of the myth-making imagination of the community."[180] Bediako builds his arguments on this assumption without estimating the potential for the confusion and the conflict it poses. For instance, if one were to deal with the interpretations given to Jesus, both within the Bible and Greco-Roman world, in the form of creedal statements as the myth-making imagination of the community, many of the assumptions on which Bediako builds his Christology can also be seriously questioned. This may be the reason why Pobee cautiously skirts away from metaphysical speculations in his Christology. Bediako applies the concept of myth vigorously to the ancestor category but refrains from doing so when dealing with the assertions about Christ.

Moreover, in the Akan society, no one can become an ancestor unless the person fulfills certain qualities. Some of those qualities are living up to the full age, establishing a family etc. One would quickly see that the manner of Jesus' life and death would disqualify him for the position of an ancestor. We will return to this discussion in our concluding chapter, but this is an important concern in assessing both Pobee's and Bediako's interpretations of Christ. In the concluding chapter, we will examine more closely the fundamental premise on which these Christologies have been built.

In the next chapter, we will attempt to elucidate some aspects of the theology of Karl Barth and put them into conversation with the Christological endeavors of both John Samuel Pobee and Kwame Bediako. Karl Barth is the conversation partner of choice for this theological conversation because Barth also struggled with the cultural challenges of his time and attempted to develop a theology that would respond to the challenges of his time. It is hoped that this conversation will help the African theologians to see their own theologies in the light of some of the wider concerns related to "doing" theology in context.

179. Ibid., 26.

180. Ibid., 30.

3

A Theological Conversation with Karl Barth

Introduction

The task of developing an Akan Christology has so far led us to the study of the customs, traditions and cosmology of the Akan and to the exploration of the theological contributions of two of the leading Ghanaian theologians, John Pobee and Kwame Bediako, both of whom have done pioneering work on indigenous Christology. The former identified some of the concepts and ideas that informed both the spiritual and physical environment of the Akan. He also demonstrated how some of these could be utilized for the purpose of developing a Christology that spoke within their tradition. The latter, using the Epistle to the Hebrews, made a groundbreaking attempt at translating biblical thinking and images into genuine African categories of thought.

The two of them employed the ancestor/linguist and ancestor-mediator paradigms respectively with different methodological approaches. As indicated earlier, there are issues of both substance and methodology when one begins to translate beliefs that are embedded in one culture into another, or when one attempts to make the faith speak to specific contexts. In order to identify and articulate some of the shortfalls of the two Akan theologians in this respect, and to learn from them, in this chapter, a conversation is facilitated between them and nineteenth-twentieth century

Swiss reformed theologian, Karl Barth, who also developed his theology in response to the challenges of his context.

In this chapter we also explore some of the factors that led to the development of Barth's theology and his theology of Revelation and of the Scripture or the Word of God. Of specific interest here is Barth's methodological move to always assert a distinction between God's revelation and natural human knowledge. An attempt is also made to elucidate his concept of the three-fold form of the Word of God in order to show how Barth constructs his concept to affirm the authority of the biblical witnesses. In addition, some of these thoughts in conversation with the methodological concepts of John Pobee and Kwame Bediako are engaged. Finally, the question of whether the ancestral paradigm is appropriate for Akan Christological development is explored. These tasks culminate in the concluding chapter with a discussion of our proposals for doing Akan Christology.

The Theology of Karl Barth

To give a good synopsis to the theology of Karl Barth, which is said to have caused a revolution beginning in 1919, it is equally essential to give a brief historical account of the theological environment that gave rise to his thinking. At this time, two camps, existed, the liberal and the conservative, and the theological faculties in Germany mirrored this division. The universities in Tubingen, Marburg, and Berlin were the proponents of the liberal scholarship.[1] The fact that Barth studied in these three indicates the theological orientation with which he began. Barth began to respond to this liberalism which tended to give importance to natural theology, often in disregard of some of the key biblical teachings, especially because he felt that the move away from the Bible was at the root of some of the serious problems encountered by the society of his time.

Factors that Contributed to the Development of the Theology of Karl Barth

Karl Barth was disillusioned about what he had to proclaim as a preacher in his parish. This disillusioning experience is captured by Herbert Hartwell: "It was the peculiar situation of the preacher who is called to proclaim the

1. James D. Smart, *The Divided Mind of Modern Theology: Karl Barth and Rudolph Bultmann 1908–1933* (Philadelphia: Westminster, 1967) 25.

Word of God but instead was in constant danger of speaking the word of man."[2] The word of man here, for Barth, refers to the European culture of his time. Thus he wanted to distinguish the "Word of God" which, for him, is God's revelation, from the human word.

Karl Barth therefore wrestled with the problem of how he could genuinely digest and present God's revelation and prevent his sermons from being merely his own words. According to Herbert Hartwell, Barth later addresses the issue, which every genuine minister of God must face, in these words: "As ministers we ought to speak of God. We are human, however, and so cannot speak of God. For, to speak of God seriously would mean to speak in the realm of revelation and faith."[3] Thus "revelation" and "faith" became two key words in Barth's theology.[4]

In order to speak from the realm of revelation and faith, Barth began to search for the Word of God; that search, as well as the responsible hearing and expounding of the Word of God, has since then become for him, "the constant motive force and the guiding principle of all his theological labors."[5] Pobee and Bediako were also, well guided by the methodological concept of the Word of God and kept it as a constant underlying factor and guiding principle to elucidate their African theological initiatives. In addition they also saw the need to distinguish between biblical Christianity from European Christianity. Thus, these conversation partners at present have the same premise for performing their theological tasks.

To find the Word of God or God's revelation,Barth had to turn to the Bible. Herbert realized that not only the leading theologians of his time, such as his teachersW. Herrmann and A. V. Harnack, but also Ernest Troeltsch and most of the theologians since the Reformation were of no help in that respect. On the contrary, they had, to a larger or lesser degree, substituted the word of man for the Word of God.[6] What exactly was meant when Barth assumed that the theologians of his time had substituted the word of man for the Word of God?

The word of man refers to the prevailing and pervading thought in the eighteenth century in Europe that saw the revival of the sixteenth century renaissance. According to Barth, this is the century when European thought

2. Hartwell, *Theology of Karl Barth*, 3.

3. Ibid., 4.

4. Ibid.

5. Ibid.

6. Ibid., 4.

that humankind could master life, its problems and riddles, by means of his own understanding. It was designated as the "age of enlightenment;"[7] but Barth referred to the period as "the century of absolute man."[8] Barth defines 'the century of absolute man' as "Man's discovery of his own power and ability, the potentiality dormant in his humanity, that is his human being as such, and looks upon it as the final, the real and absolute."[9]

According to Hartwell, the rationalism dominating that century put human reason on the seat of judgment, and demanded that: "every Christian doctrine must undergo trial in the court of reason."[10] Since this anthropocentricism that marked and changed philosophical and theological thought, culminated in Liberal Protestantism and became the singular most important system of thought, concerned Barth greatly, it is important to give a more detailed account of it so as to have a better appreciation of Barth's theological trajectory.

This anthropocentric thought of humankind during the Enlightenment reached its zenith in the philosophical Idealism of Immanuel Kant, Fichte, Schelling and Hegel. In the field of theology, according to Hartwell, it was found in the Protestant theology of the nineteenth century. Schleiermacher, whose theology dominated the nineteenth century, "made man's feeling of utter dependence, that is, the feeling of his connection with God, in other words, man's religious consciousness the basis, the theme and the criterion of theology."[11] Again, Hartwell points out that in the view of Schleiermacher, "the kingdom of God is identical with the advance of civilization since religion in general, and the Christian, religion in particular, is to him the highest value in life, and civilization without religion, without the Christian religion, is incomplete."[12]

In the same era, Hegel developed a theology that was entirely speculative or metaphysical having its basis in abstract general reasoning. In his theology, according to Hartwell, "religion is man's imaginative response to the universe, and philosophy is the supreme court of appeal also with regard to the Christian Faith and its tenets."[13] For Hegel, Jesus was not the

7. Barth, *Church Dogmatics* I/1, 11ff.

8. Barth, *Church Dogmatics* IV/3, 183ff.

9. Quoted in Wingren, *Theology in Conflict*, 23ff.

10. Hartwell, *Theology of Karl Barth*, 4.

11. Ibid., 5.

12. Ibid.

13. Ibid.

God-man but, rather, the first man to perceive a great (speculative) truth, namely the truth that God and man are one. God had reality only in the minds of those who believe in Him.

Another theologian, Albrecht Ritschl, rejecting both Hegel's speculative rationalism and Schleiermacher's subjectivism, sought to root theology in history, more particularly in the person of Jesus Christ. Hartwell points out: "Ritschl conceives the work of Jesus Christ in history and his person as well as the kingdom of God in essentially intra mundane terms."[14] According to Ritschl, Jesus Christ, because of the work he did for humankind, had for man the value of Godhead. In his view, the kingdom of God essentially served a moral purpose in this world. Hartwell comments:

> Ritschl's historical positivism decisively contributed to the fact that in the second half of the nineteenth century theology became to a large extent the study of the history of religions including the Christian religion, and his rationalistic moralism, his view of Christianity, as an outlook upon life, as morality, and of reconciliation as the realization of the ideal of human life prepared the way for that 'Cultural Protestantism' which, adapting the Christian message to the culture of the nineteenth and the beginning of the twentieth century, became one of the main targets of Barth's early theology.[15]

Furthermore, Hartwell reveals the thought of another person of influence in the century of absolute man, Adolf von Harnack, who happened to be a historian rather than a theologian and also was a teacher of Karl Barth. His position is that "Jesus Christ was not the Son of God who became man, in other words, the incarnate Word of God in the sense of John 1:14, but merely the supreme teacher and revealer of God."[16] For him, the essence of Christianity was seen in the teaching of Jesus Christ, especially in that of the Sermon on the Mount. In von Harnack's thought, it is the Father and not the Son who is part of the Gospel as taught by Jesus.

Hartwell argues that this process of substituting the word of man for the Word of God reached its climax, or rather its rock bottom, in Ernst Troeltsch's theology of scientific religious history. In his thought, according to Hartwell, Christianity was treated as but one religion among the others and Jesus Christ considered as a great religious personality. According to

14. Ibid.

15. Ibid.

16. Ibid.

Hartwell, claiming that "theology as such has no special method of its own but simply applies one common to all forms of mental science, Troeltsch employed the idea of a general evolution in religious history in such a manner as to make a peculiar or exceptional self-revelation of God ...wholly inconceivable."[17]

Again, Hartwell points out that according to Troeltsch "no religion, even Christianity, is valid universally or forever, because each faith is but an individual form of the pure spirit of religion and has power and authority only within the concrete and historical conditions under which it first arose."[18] Hartwell further admits that it was this reduced assertion for Christianity that made Troeltsch conclude that "Christianity could claim validity for the European civilization only, and even that validity was according to his aforesaid proposition only a temporary and a relative one."[19]

In relation to this development of liberal Protestantism from religious, anthropocentric, humanistic lines and, at least partly caused by it, there emerged a third factor which operated as a motive in Barth's theology, namely the failure of the ethics of modern theology in the catastrophe which overtook Europe in 1914 at the outbreak of the First World War. Barth points out that "accidently or not, a significant event took place during that very year. Ernst Troeltsch, the well-known professor of systematic theology and the leader of the then most modern school, gave up his chair in theology for one in philosophy."[20] Barth recorded his own reaction to the tragic events of that time in these telling words:

> One day in early August 1914 stands out in my personal memory as a black day. Ninety-three German intellectuals impressed public opinion by their proclamation in support of the war policy of Wilhelm II and his counselors. Among these intellectuals I discovered to my horror almost all my theological teachers whom I had greatly venerated. In despair over what this indicated about the signs of the time I suddenly realized that I could not any longer follow either their ethics and dogmatics or their understanding of the Bible and of history. For me at least, 19th –century theology no longer held any future.[21]

17. Ibid.

18. Ibid.

19. Ibid., 6–7.

20. Barth, "Evangelical Theology in the 19th Century," in *Humanity of God*, 14.

21. Ibid., 14.

This dissatisfying experience together with the move of Troeltsch from the theology department into philosophy indicated to Barth the shallowness and bankruptcy of liberalism. Thus, from a theological stand point, August 1914 in a sense marked the end of the nineteenth century in Europe. Thus for Barth and for many, 19th century theology no longer was what it had been. In support of this assertion, Barth argues that:

> Nineteenth-century theology was burdened with the heritage of the eighteenth century. There was an all-pervasive rationalism and a retreat of vital or would-be vital Christianity into the undergrounds of many kinds. These factors, coupled with the emergence of obscure forms of religious fanaticism, led to a kind of secularism probably more pointed than the much praised or deplored secularism of today.[22]

In addition, he discloses that "theology was measured against the impressive achievements and personalities of the so-called classical era of German culture, philosophy and poetry."[23]

In the early 1930's, the process was virtually repeated. Germany's hope of economic emancipation was found in Adolf Hitler's National Socialist Party; a large part of the church endorsed this movement seeing it as God's way of working in history. Barth, however, opposed the Nazi government's policies vehemently and, as a result, lost his university teaching position in Germany.[24] With these in view, we now turn to the next section to explore the methodological concept Barth employs for the development of his theology. It is our intention to use the methodological decisions to facilitate a discussion between Barth and the two Ghanaian theologians after this section.

22. Ibid., 15.

23. Ibid. Barth writes: "Against the breathtaking political movements of the war of liberation 1813–15, followed by the years of revolution and restoration, the foundation -laying of the empires, and the subsequent repercussions of all these events down to World War I. . . . Above all, theology was measured against the all-embracing triumph of the natural sciences, of philosophy of history, of modern technology, as well as against Beethoven, Wagner, and Brahms, Gottfried Keller and Theodor Fontane, Ibsen and Sudermann. What did theology have to say to this century—not to speak of the shadow of Goethe, Bismarck and Friedrich Nietzsche?"

24. Erickson, *Christian Theology*, 188.

The Word of God as a Methodological Concept

What then is Barth's theology? What does it entail? How does he approach his theological task? In search of his theology, Barth turned to an intensive study of the Bible particularly, the Pauline epistles. From this study, he identifies some key thoughts that became fundamental to his own theological pursuit. These key thoughts led to a radical position of Barth's theology to the point that almost all the work of theologians as well as the philosophical works within this century and the previous one were subject to discussion. Hartwell comments on the character and impact of Barth's theology:

> Though many theologies have been developed in the course of the history of Christianity, of only a few of them can it be said that they have accomplished a real turning-point in man's theological thinking, let alone, to use another metaphor, have turned the helm through an angle of 180 degrees. This, however, is precisely what Barth has done, taking his stand on a new point of departure for the whole problem of theology, a point of departure diametrically opposed to that of most of the other Protestant theologians since the Reformation, so that his theology may be said to represent a Copernican turn in the history of human thought.[25]

First, Barth discovered that the God of the Bible is entirely different from the God whom his theological teachers and theologians of the last two or three centuries had presented. This led him to also search for a possible theme of the Bible and led him to conclude that "It could not possibly be man's religion and religious ethics but the deity of God, more exactly God's deity—God's independence and particular character, not only in relation to the natural but also the spiritual cosmos; God's absolute unique existence, might and initiative, above all, in His relationship to humankind."[26] Thus for Barth, it is only in this manner were we able to understand the voice of the Old and New Testaments. He points out: "Only with this perspective did we feel we could henceforth be theologians, and in particular, preachers, ministers of the divine Word."[27]

Second, Barth discovered that the theological thought of his century and of a few centuries before his, humankind has been magnified at the expense of God and that nothing less than a radical revolution in humankid's

25. Hartwell, *Theology of Karl Barth*, 1.

26. Barth, *Humanity of God*, 40.

27. Ibid., 41.

thinking was required to reestablish the biblical truth of the Supremacy of God. Thus he set out his theological agenda to:

> demythologize the picture which man had made of himself, man's arrogant idea of being the criterion, the norm, of his and every understanding, and to restore to God and His Word the place in theology and, consequently, in the Church which belongs to them of right according to the witness of the Bible to God's self-revelation in Jesus Christ.[28]

The third point that formed the basis of his theological endeavor is that humankind cannot of itself know God and speak of God. Rather, on the contrary, humankind in that respect is entirely dependent on God's revelation of Himself in the person and work of His Son Jesus Christ, and that this divine self-revelation is moreover an act of the sovereign and free grace of God.

This means that Barth tries not to depend on a system of philosophical idealism, or preconceived abstract general ideas but on revelation. What then is revelation for Barth? For him, revelation is redemptive in nature. As far as Barth is concerned, to know God, or to have correct information about him, begins with a relationship with God in a salvific experience. In opposition to many other theologians, Barth comments that it is not possible to elicit from the Epistle to the Romans 1. 18 -22 any statement regarding a "natural union with God or knowledge of God on the part of man in him."[29] In his debate with Emil Brunner, Barth made this statement: "How can Brunner maintain that a real knowledge of the true God, however imperfect it may be (and what knowledge of God can be considered imperfect?), does not bring salvation."[30] "Ever since about 1916," declares Barth in his reply to Emil Brunner, "When I began to recover noticeably from the effects of my theological studies and the influences of the liberal-political pre-war theology, my opinion concerning the task of our theological generation has been this: we must learn to understand revelation as grace and grace as revelation and therefore turn away from all 'true' or 'false' '*theologia naturalis.*'"[31]

Karl Barth opposes any human capacity to have knowledge of God apart from the revelation received in Christ. For him, such knowledge

28. Ibid., 42.

29. Barth, *Church Dogmatics* II/1, 121.

30. Barth, "No!" 62.

31. Ibid., 71.

would point to the fact that humankind was absolutely capable of knowing the being and the existence of God without having anything to do with his grace and mercy. Human possession of such knowledge, according to Barth, would jeopardize the unity of God as well as his activity.[32] In order not to compromise the principle of grace alone, Barth insists that "revelation is always and only revelation of God in Jesus Christ: the Word become flesh."[33] Thus anything apart from the incarnation carries no revelation.

He also tried to avoid the neo-Kantian concepts, of which he had made use in his earlier works especially in *The Epistle to the Romans,*and also tried to avoid the use of any existential thought he adapted from Soren Kierkegaard. He attempted to make sure that nothing of human origin can gain the position and function, which can be the prerogative of only the Word of God. According to his methodological convictions, Barth contends that:

> Since it is solely the Word of God which determines the thinking and speaking of the theologian, and since that Word arises out of the sovereignty and freedom of God's action and work in the history of mankind, as that action and work is accomplished in the revealed Word of God as the way which God has taken, takes and will take with man in the person of Jesus Christ and through the operation of the Holy Spirit, there is no room for any preconceived, abstract ideas and philosophical speculations.[34]

Barth's theology attempts to begin with the Word of God as spoken by God Himself in his sovereignty and freedom, in and through the person and work of Jesus Christ by the active operation of the Holy Spirit. Thus, for him, theology cannot begin as a system does with man-made abstract general principles. There can be room only for the proper exegesis of Holy Scripture and faithful obedience to the Word of God. Barth points out that such a method is based on grace, as humankind hears the Word of God as attested in the Bible and obeys it.

Consequently, the characteristic features of Barth's theology are easily discernible. There are two main features that recur continually. These are his thorough concentration on Scripture and the absolutely Christological character in his theology. Additionally, three other features must be outlined for a better appreciation and understanding of Barth's work.

32. Barth, *Church Dogmatics* II/1, 93.

33. Ibid.

34. Ibid., 20.

With the movement of Barth's thought one realizes that the Word of God is seen as "the source, the basis and the criterion of his theology."[35] This, according to Barth, is directly in opposition to the theology of Friederick Schleiermacher who rendered man's religious consciousness the basis, theme, and criterion of his theological thought. Barth explicates that the Word of God is not to be seen as a general idea or an abstract thought. For him, there is a unique revelation of God-self and his will for humanity in the person and work of Jesus Christ, who is also the incarnate Word of God. Barth contends that this unique revelation in the person and work of Jesus Christ is a particular event or rather a series of particular events constituting the *Heilsgeschichte*.[36]

This particular event is not to be seen as a past event but that which continues to happen in this world in the course of the history of humankind. Hartwell admits that "Barth's thought constantly starts from that particular fact, from these particular events, and this means that his thought continually moves form the particular to the general."[37] Has Barth reversed the usual way of doing theology? Hartwell maintains that "in his theology the usual movement of thought from the general to the particular is reversed, and this reversal has far-reaching consequences for the whole trend of his theology."[38]

The basic concepts Barth employs in his teachings are throughout derived from that particular event of God's self-revelation in Jesus Christ; they are not abstract concepts; that is, they are not determined and shaped by human speculation nor by existential philosophy but "by the reality of the self-revelation of the Triune God in Jesus Christ and through the Holy Spirit and therefore have a concrete meaning."[39]

As far as Barth is concerned, the issue of the self-revelation of God "is always, first, a question of fact, of reality, on the basis of faith, and that this fact, this reality is the particular event of God's revelation in Jesus Christ."[40] Thus, for Barth, it is always a question of an objective happening that has taken place, takes place or will take place in the world, and therefore in

35. Barth, *Church Dogmatics* I/1, 282ff.

36. Ibid., 284ff.

37. Ibid., 285ff.

38. Ibid.

39. Barth, *Church Dogmatics* II/1, 172ff.

40. Ibid.

history.[41] This means for him "the knowledge of the Christian Faith is based on a historical fact, that is, on Jesus Christ."[42] His *Church Dogmatics* is therefore "concerned with the exposition and interpretation of a story, the story of God's gracious dealing with mankind in Jesus Christ from eternity."[43]

Barth offers a short historical commentary on the first article of the *Theological Declaration* of the Synod of Barmen on May 31st, 1934 to buttress his point. The text is as follows:

> *I am the way, the truth, and the life: no man cometh unto the Father, but by me" (John 14:6). Verily, verily, I say unto you, he that enters not by the door into the sheepfold, but climbs some other way, the same is a thief and a robber . . . . I am the door: by me if any man enter in, he shall be saved" (John 10:1,9).*[44]

Barth comments:

> Jesus Christ, as He is attested to us in Holy Scripture, is the one Word of God, whom we have to hear and whom we have to trust and obey in life and in death. We condemn the false doctrine that the Church can and must recognize as God's revelation other events and powers, forms and truths, apart from and alongside this one Word of God.[45]

This short commentary is indirect reference more to the demand of the government to get the Evangelical Church to follow the dictates of "the God-sent Adolf Hitler, a source of specific new revelation of God, which demanding obedience, and trust, took its place beside the revelation attested in Holy Scripture, claiming that it should be acknowledged by Christian proclamation and theology as equally binding and obligatory."[46] However, it still brings out Barth's attempt to clarify God's revelation as it is witnessed in the Scriptures from any form of philosophical ideas and abstract thoughts.

Barth's theology also alludes to a fact that "The objective fact of a reality outside of humankind, which is neither of man's making nor at his disposal but on the other hand, inescapably affects him and determines

41. Ibid.
42. Ibid.
43. Barth, *Church Dogmatics* I/1, 198ff.
44. Barth, *Church Dogmatics* II/1, 172.
45. Ibid.
46. Ibid., 173ff.

his destiny."[47] He further explains that the objective reality is primarily God Himself, that is, "the sovereign Lord of humankind in the reality both of His inner Trinitarian life as Father, Son and Holy Spirit and of His revelation to man in Jesus through the Holy Spirit."[48] Thus, for Barth this objective reality found in the God-man, Jesus Christ, is connected to his incarnation, the Cross, resurrection, and resurrection-appearances, and is the objective reality of his work of reconciliation, including his prophetic work as the risen Lord. Barth relentlessly insists on the far reaching objective significance that these events in the life of the God-man, Jesus Christ have for humankind. Further, he demonstrates humankind's incapability of bringing about these events by their actions and will and the fact that it is this factor that rather determines and affect humankind's destiny.

The final characteristic feature of Barth's theology points to the essential elements of the Christian Faith such as "the Word of God, the divine revelation, man's faith, love, and hope, the Church and the Christian are represented as existing only in *actu* and therefore as being real and genuine only *in actu*."[49] Thus, according to Barth, these elements of the Christian Faith can only exist as real and genuine as long as they owe their existence to an act of God. He points out that he does not know of any 'es gibt' ('there is') nor of any having or 'possessing' that is independent of God's giving, but only a constant 'giving' and 'receiving.' Thus God continually gives and humankind continually receives.

In Barth's thought, therefore,the Word of God is not something that is given for the complete possession of mankind once for all. Rather, it remains the word of humankind unless God makes it ever again God's own Word by his own action. It must ever again become the Word of God in order to be the Word of God. Thus he explains "it becomes God's Word for us whenever it becomes revelation for us through the work of the Holy Spirit in us, and it does so only 'when and where God pleases.'"[50] Thus, in the thought of Barth, the Word of God and revelation go together.

47. Ibid.

48. Ibid.

49. Ibid., 175ff.

50. Barth, *Church Dogmatics.* Volume I/1, 79.

Karl Barth's Doctrine of the Word of God— The Three-Fold Form of the Word of God

In the previous section, we have dealt with the factors that challenged and caused Barth to make the Word of God the methodological concept of his theology. In this section, we concentrate on his doctrine of the Word of God in its three-fold form. The discussions here will form the core issues that will facilitate an objective and meaningful conversation among Barth, Pobee and Bediako. We anticipate that the deliberations will be helpful as we continue in the final chapter to develop a Christology for the Akan people of Ghana.

It is a known fact that in attempting to develop a theology based solely on the Word of God, Barth insistently and consciously sought to distance himself and all that he wrote from what he perceived to be the interpretations of revelation from Protestant liberalism and Roman Catholicism. We may not want to delve into Barth's critique of what he perceived to be the theological methods, which he refers to variously as liberalism, Cartesianism, neo-Protestantism, modernism or anthropological theology. This is because it is beyond the scope of this thesis. We want, however to quote the following lengthy statement in his lecture on the *Humanity of God* delivered in 1956 on the rationale for his dissatisfaction with this prevalent tradition:

> Evangelical theology almost all along the line, certainly in all its representative forms and tendencies, had become *religionistic, anthropocentric,* and in this sense *humanistic.* What I mean to say is that an external and internal disposition and emotion of man, namely his piety—which might well be Christian piety—had become its object of study and its theme. Around this it revolved and seemed compelled to revolve without release...What did it know and say of the deity of God? For this theology, to think about God meant to think in a scarcely veiled fashion about man, more exactly about the religious, the Christian religious man. To speak about God meant to speak in an exalted tone but once again and more than ever about this man—his revelations and wonders, his faith and works. There is no question about it: here man was made great at the cost of God—the divine God who is someone other than man, who sovereignly confronts him, who immovably and unchangeably stands over against him as the Lord, Creator, and Redeemer.[51]

51. Ibid., 39–40.

In Barth's *Church Dogmatics, Volume I,* parts i and ii, he develops his prolegomena in terms of an exposition of the "The Doctrine of the Word of God." Within this large volume, Barth treats the "Revelation of God," in terms of "The Triune God;" "The Incarnation of the Word;" and "The Outpouring of the Holy Spirit." Barth heavily depends on the Word of God to develop his theology. On the issue of his dependence on the Word of God, and his belief that it should be the criterion of every theologian and theological task, Barth has this to say later in his book, *Evangelical Theology—An Introduction:*

> Before human thought and speech can respond to God's word, they have to be summoned into existence and given reality by the creative act of God's word. Without the precedence of the creative Word, there can be not only no proper theology but, in fact, no evangelical theology at all![52]

Turning to Evangelical theology, he points out that it even depends on the creative act of God, which for him is the reality of the incarnation in the God-man Jesus Christ. But let us read what Barth considers God's Word to be, as it has come to us in the past, present and even the future:

> The Word of God is the Word that God spoke, speaks, and will speak in the midst of all men. Regardless of whether it is heard or not, it is, in itself, directed to all men, and with men. His work is not mute; rather, it speaks with a loud voice. Since only God can do what he does only he can say in his work what he says. And since his work is not divided but single (for all the manifold forms which it assumes along the way from its origin to its goal), his Word is also (for all its exciting richness) simple and single. It is not ambiguous but unambiguous, not obscure but clear. In itself, therefore, it is quite easily understandable to both the wisest and the most foolish. God works, and since he works, he also speaks. His Word goes forth. And if it be widely ignored *de facto,* it can never and in no place be ignored *de jure.* That man who refuses to listen and to obey the Word acts not as a free man but as a slave, for there is no freedom except through God's Word. We are speaking of the God of the Gospel, his work and action, and of the Gospel in which his work and action are at the same time his speech. This is his Word, the Logos in which the theological logia, logic, and language have creative basis and life.[53]

52. Barth, *Evangelical Theology*, 18.

53. Ibid., 18–19.

This avowal offers a clearer picture on how Barth understands, depends, and uses the Word of God. But, more importantly, it also raises questions that are pertinent to our thesis. If God has thus spoken, speaks, and continues to speak to us all, can we argue that Christ is not a member of our clan and therefore, we will not relate to him? Or can we assert, as Bediako pointed out, that Jesus Christ could not inhabit the spiritual universe of the Akan or Africans? We shall return to these questions in later sections. The lengthy quote above, however, gives us the opportunity to understand what Barth really wants to achieve in his overall theological endeavor. In the *Church Dogmatics,* he teaches about the Word of God that is preached; the written Word of God in the Holy Scripture, and finally, the revealed Word of God which, in its fullest sense and form, represents Jesus Christ.

The Preached Word of God or the Proclamation of The Church

In the presentation of the threefold Word, Barth deals with the issue of dealing with "the proclamation of the church" as the Word of God.[54] Barth discussed thoroughly his thought on the preached or proclaimed Word. In this deliberation, one can see that Barth seems to attempt to answer, in part or full, some of the questions that prompted his attention as ayoung Swiss Pastor and Preacher, which later helped him to delve into serious theological studies.

We have noted earlier that Barth's concern was that in his context, the word of humans was displacing the Word of God. Again, as already noted, the word of man here is in reference to German culture, philosophy, and liberal Protestantism of his time, while the Word of God is simply the Holy Scripture.

In the sub-section on the 'Word of God and the Word of Man in Preaching,' Barth points out that preaching or more generally, proclamation, is no less Gods' Word than the revealed or the written Word. For him, God proclaims himself in the proclamation of the church. He thus argues that since we cannot measure or test this pragmatically, we believe and accept it as God's grace in Jesus Christ. He admits: "The human impossibility of speaking of God in such a way that others hear of him cannot alter the fact that God in the freedom of his grace makes good what we do badly, so that the true impossibility can be understood from the reality."[55] It is

54. Barth, *Church Dogmatics* I/2, 744ff.

55. Ibid., 746ff.

further noted that this reality, for Barth, must be explained in the context of the "miracle of God himself in both the speaker and the hearer."[56] In this sense, he points out that the confidence of preachers must be tempered by a sense of their need for forgiveness, as they reflect on how little their own words correspond to what is required.[57]

Two statements from the prolegomena make Barth's position evident. They include: "The language about God to be found in the Church is meant to be proclamation, so far as it is directed towards man in the form of preaching and sacrament, with the claim and in an atmosphere of expectation that in accordance with its commission it has to tell him the Word of God to be heard in faith."[58] The second statement, which is even more revealing, points to the following:

> The Word of God is God Himself in the proclamation of the Church of Jesus Christ. In so far as God gives the Church the commission to speak about Him, and the Church discharges this commission, it is God Himself who declares His revelation in His witnesses. The proclamation of the Church is pure doctrine when the human word spoken in it in confirmation of biblical witness to revelation offers and creates obedience to the Word of God.[59]

Thus, for Barth preaching and sacraments occupy a distinctive place in the manner in which the Church speaks about God. This is because the church has a mandate from Jesus Christ to proclaim the revelation of God through these means. Thus, he defines preaching as "the attempt, essayed by one called thereto in the Church, to express in his own words in the form of an exposition of a portion of the biblical testimony to revelation, and to make comprehensible to men of his day, the promise of God's revelation, reconciliation and calling, as they are to be expected here and now."[60]

Thus, according to Barth, preaching, if it is to be authentic preaching, must be subservient to the Word of God attested to in the Holy Scriptures. He argues that the Roman Catholic Church has customarily relegated preaching to a secondary role because of the primacy of the sacrament as the medium through which God's grace is dispensed to the faithful. He

56. Ibid., 750ff.

57. Ibid., 752ff.

58. Ibid., 100.

59. Ibid., 101.

60. Barth, *Church Dogmatics* I/1, 61.

opposes the traditional Roman Catholic Church's view of the sacrament because "grace neither is nor remains here the personal free Word of God."[61]

On the mistakes of Protestant liberalism, he points out, that it moves in the direction of subjectivism by conceiving preaching to be the unfolding of the piety of the preacher. In this sense by equating preaching with "self-exposition" meant its dissolution. Thus, for him, it also meant that the preacher no longer needs to listen to Scriptures' testimony to God's self-revelation. Liberalism has no conception of preaching becoming the Word of God through God's gracious presence.

Though the preachers are admonished to depend on prayer, Barth cautions that prayer does not eliminate the summons to the serious and honest work undertaken, not in self-confidence, but in the confidence in God which will tolerate neither indolence nor indifference. It would be a serious mistake to conclude from these propositions that Barth identifies the words of the Bible or the Church's proclamation with the Word of God. He makes perfectly clear that both the Bible and the proclamation of the Church are the result of human activities and, on that account are, in themselves, merely the words of man and not the Word of God, being afflicted with all the limitations and weaknesses which are inevitably bound up with anything human.

In this sense, Barth examines the human requirement of our human speaking if it is to be the Word of God. First, he points out that "our human speaking about God must receive a specific goal and rule, and then it must examine it correctness. Next, it must be set under a definite responsibility toward God."[62] For him, doctrines must help to achieve this. But he also points out that "whether or not doctrine achieve this depends finally on God's own speaking in and with our speaking."[63] In other words, God in his good pleasure sanctifies, as it were, the words of his servants so that while remaining human words, at the same time, they become words "in which and through which God himself speaks about Himself."[64]

However, according to Barth, the human preacher must recognize that preaching depends on exposition (biblical theology) and application (practical theology) as well as reflection (dogmatic theology).[65] Yet, Barth

61. Ibid., 75.

62. Barth, *Church Dogmatics* II/1, 758–62.

63. Ibid., 765.

64. Ibid., *Church Dogmatics* I/1, 106.

65. Ibid., *Church Dogmatics* II/1, 766.

assigns a central role to dogmatic theology because he believes that it supervises the transition from exposition to application that has to be made in preaching and teaching. Thus, he maintains: "pure doctrine is dynamic, not static. It is achieved by the gift of the Holy Spirit in the fulfillment of the task of dogmatics."[66] Also, Barth argues that this must be done in order to avoid wandering off into abstraction or falling victim to the invading forces of philosophy and culture.

Again, Barth claims that in proclamation, one must resist the tendency to abandon the proper task. For him, this consists of hearing the word of proclamation, then praying, then asking basic and rigorous questions about what is being said on crucial matters. However, he maintains that such questions must not be asked in judgment or correction but in a process of weighing and testing. He suggests two questions that must always be asked. These are the question of the dogmatic norm, and the question of the use of that norm.

Barth opposes any independent ethics based on general anthropology. His main reason for this is that anthropology will tend to absorb dogmatics and ultimately swallow up biblical and practical theology as well.[67] On this note, we move to explore the second aspect of the threefold Word of God.

The Written Word of God—Holy Scripture

Although, Barth speaks of Jesus Christ as the center of God's revelation, he also admits that the written Word and the preached Word are secondary forms of God's revelation. This leads us to discuss Barth's second form of the Word of God, which is Holy Scripture. In Barth's theology, the Biblical writers of both the Old and New Testaments occupy a place of special authority in the church because they are primary witnesses to God's mighty acts of revelation. He writes: "They are called directly by the Word to be its hearers, and they are appointed for itscommunication and verification to other men."[68] It is through the witnesses of the Bible that posterity learns of God's gracious act of revelation and dealings with humankind.

Barth defines the Bible as: "The concrete medium, by which the Church recalls God's revelation in the past, is called to expect revelation in the

66. Ibid., 768ff.

67. Ibid., 782.

68. Barth, *Evangelical Theology*, 26.

future, and is thereby challenged, empowered, and guided to proclaim."[69] This definition is consistent with Barth's position that the Bible, itself, is not the primary form of revelation but it contains the testimony of the primary witnesses to God's revelation. Therefore, Barth is careful always to distinguish between God in his revelation and the witnesses to that revelation.

How is Barth able to speak of Holy Scripture as the Word of God? How does this human fallible witness of prophets and apostles become the Word of God? As far as the Bible is concerned, Barth's position never wavers. He emphatically writes: "The Bible is God's Word so far as God lets it be His Word; so far as God speaks through it."[70] In later sections of*Church Dogmatics,* Barth acknowledges that "Scripture is holy and the Word of God, because by the Holy Spirit it became and will become to the Church a witness to divine revelation."[71] Further, he points out that since God in His Spirit inspired these witnesses and makes Himself present in their testimony through His Spirit again, we can confess that the Bible is the Word of God.

According to Barth, we must think of the Bible in terms of its divinity and humanity in as much as we confess both in Jesus Christ. In this sense, Barth points out the following:

> If we want to think of the Bible as a real witness of divine revelation, then clearly we have to keep two things constantly before us and give them their due weight; the limitation and the positive element, its distinctiveness from revelation, in so far as it is only a human word about it, and its unity with it, in so far as revelation is the basis, object and content of this word.[72]

Thus, we see clearly that Barth sees the close relationship between Holy Scripture as the written Word of God and the revelation of God to which it points. Here, Barth is in agreement with the doctrine of Holy Scripture developed by the Reformers and held subsequently by Protestant Orthodoxy. Though he is critical of the development of the post-Reformation doctrine of the infallibility of the Scripture in Protestant Orthodoxy, we will not delve into such criticisms since it does not necessarily form part of the scope of this project. We only point out that in as much as Barth reaffirms the primary authority of the Scriptures in the fashion of the reformers, unlike

69. Barth, *Church Dogmatics* I/1, 124–25.

70. Ibid., 123.

71. Barth, *Church Dogmatics* I/2, 457ff.

72. Ibid., 463.

them, he does not want to encourage bibliolatry. As can easily be confirmed throughout his work, Barth's consistent position has been demonstrated on the fact that: "Jesus Christ, as He is attested to us in Holy Scripture, is the one Word of God, whom we have to hear and whom we have to trust and obey in life and in death."[73] With these in mind, we now turn to the revealed Word of God, Jesus Christ.

The Revealed Word of God—Jesus Christ

In his exegesis of the following scriptural texts, John 1.1, 14; Hebrews 1.2 and Revelation 19.13, Barth asserts that the revealed Word of God in its highest expression is identified with Jesus Christ. Thus for him, the Incarnation is the primary form of the Word and, therefore, of revelation. Barth writes: "Revelation in fact does not differ from the Person of Jesus Christ, and again does not differ from the reconciliation that took place in him. To say revelation is to say, 'The Word became flesh.'"[74]

This notion is intended to render a Christian understanding of the revelation of Jesus Christ, the Word made flesh, different from all other forms of revelation. Barth steadily insists and claims the uniqueness of the biblical understanding of revelation and of the God who reveals himself in his revelation. Many of his contemporaries worked with the biblical understanding of revelation but were also open to an understanding of God drawn from abstract conceptions of revelation or of ultimate being. Barth, however, insists on beginning with what he considers to be the actual and concrete self-manifestation of God. It is of interest that Pobee also prefers an indigenous Christology based on concreteness that is devoid of all philosophical abstractions. It will be interesting to compare their respective assertions during the conversations in the next chapter.

This methodology of beginning with the concrete makes Barth oppose any conception of revelation determined by philosophy, metaphysics, or by any other idealist scheme developed by any human being. He insists that:

> Knowledge of revelation does not mean an abstract knowledge of a God confronting an abstract man. Rather, it is a concrete knowledge of the God who has sought man and meets him in his concrete situation and finds him there. Revelation is a concrete

73. Barth, *Church Dogmatics* II/1, 172.

74. Barth, *Church Dogmatics* I/1, 134.

> knowledge of God and man in the event brought about by the initiative of a sovereign God.[75]

For Barth, all attempts at conceiving God's revelations that fail to work out from the actual form by which this revelation takes place in God himself through Jesus Christ and the Word are incorrect. For him, it is only through God alone that God may be known. Therefore, Barth's theology consistently maintains that human being cannot speak and think as though he has the capacity that enabled him to determine what revelation should be in advance of being encountered by God. He claims that "the very definite order of being which Holy Scripture makes manifest, when in its witness of God's revelation it confronts and relates God and man, divine facts and human attitudes, enforces an order of knowing corresponding to it."[76] Our capacity to reveal who God is from any other sources apart from what scripture reveals is an illusion and assumptions that cannot be trusted. Beginning with Jesus Christ, Barth points out that in Christ God is manifested as Lord, through his reconciling self-revelation of God. Thus, for him, Jesus Christ enables sinners to hear God's Word by reconciling them to God.

Barth made the doctrine of the Trinity the key to understanding the Christian conception of revelation and of God. This is pointed out in the telling statement: "God's Word is God Himself in His revelation. For God reveals Himself as the Lord and that according to Scripture signifies for the concept of revelation that God Himself in unimpaired unity yet also in unimpaired difference is Revealer, Revelation and Revealed-ness."[77] For him, this revelation "Is the revelation of Him who is called Yahweh in the Old Testament and *Theos* or concretely *Kurious* in the New Testament."[78]

What then is the concrete concept of this revelation? How has he revealed himself? He points out that "we have to do with the concept of revelation of the God, who according to Scripture and proclamation, is the Father of Jesus Christ, is Jesus Christ Himself, and is the Spirit of this Father and of this Son."[79] For Barth, it is possible also to inquire about other revelations, concepts of revelation, and possibly into general concepts of revelations. However, in such cases, the inquirer would have left dogmatics where it was. For him, it is the "concept of this God and it alone that interest

75. Barth, *God in Action*, 11–12, quoted in Mueller, *Karl Barth*, 62.

76. Mueller, *Makers of Modern Theological Mind*, 62.

77. Barth, *Church Dogmatics* I/1, 339.

78. Ibid.

79. Ibid., 334.

dogmatics."[80] Thus Barth confines his study strictly to the revelation of the Word attested in Holy Scripture.

With this understanding, Barth cautions us about the use of reasoning from analogies of the revelation of God found in nature, culture, history, or human existence. For him, this will be another form of natural theology that unnecessarily leads to the projection of humankind's thought about God. Still on the issue of the revelation of God, Barth's position on the Trinity is of prime importance to our conclusions. Though he does not claim that the doctrine of the Trinity can be found in the Bible, he maintains an explicit stand that investigations of the unity and diversity of the ways in which God reveals himself brings us "up against the problem of the doctrine of the Trinity."[81] Again, Barth postulates that when we are asked who this self-revealing God is, the Bible gives the answer "in such a way that we are impelled to consider the Three-in-oneness of God."[82]

Therefore, in opposition to most of his followers who regarded it as a speculative doctrine, somewhat peripheral in Christian theology, Barth undeniably declared: "It is the doctrine of the Trinity which fundamentally distinguishes the Christian doctrine of God as Christian … in face of all other possible doctrines of God and concepts of revelation."[83] Since there is a great wealth of exegetical and historical material which forms the basis of the development of his doctrine of Trinity, we would only concentrate on those that are pertinent to his view and for our work.

At this point, we need to consider what essential New Testament teachings helped with this development. For Barth, the New Testament

80. Ibid.

81. Ibid., 348.

82. Ibid.

83. Ibid. Barth argues that for that very reason, and also in harmony with the Church Fathers and with the mediaeval Scholastics, and nowhere as insistently as here, they have spoken of the necessity of revelation as the sole source of the knowledge of this mystery which dominates all mysteries. But also there fits most adequately into this the denial which modernist Protestantism, from the days of Servetus and the other anti-Trinitarians of the Reformation period, brought against this very doctrine. As Schleiermacher very rightly saw and declared, it is emphasized above other Christian doctrines because it cannot be made comprehensible as the immediate utterance of the Christian self-consciousness. Or, who would assert that the impression made by the divine in Christ obliges us to conceive such an eternal distinction (in the highest being) as the ground of it (namely, the impression)? We take the actual fact, that this theology declares that, the standpoint of its understanding of revelation; it has no access to this matter, as a sign that this matter should be noted and considered in the first place, at the point where real revelation is involved.

makes us aware that the doctrine of the Trinity was precipitated by the confession of Jesus Christ as Lord in the New Testament. This confession led the Church's acknowledgment of God to be present in Jesus the Son. Thus, God determined to be present in yet another form. In this sense, Barth is in agreement with the early church's affirmation of distinguishing the Son from the Father, simultaneously recognizing that he was one with the Father in terms of his essential nature or essence. In addition, the Church also confirmed that God was present in yet another form in the person of the Holy Spirit. Here, too, the one God was present, yet again.

In the light of scriptural evidence, Barth consistently agrees with the church at least concerning two essential truths about the nature of God's self-revelation in the Son and in the Spirit. First of all, all subordination is totally ruled out.[84] The question of subordination is of prime importance, if not a problematic issue in the development of Akan Christological endeavors. This is because of the application of both ancestral and linguist/chieftaincy categories as methodologies for the determination of who Jesus Christ is among the ethnic Akan and the nature of the relationship posited by the tradition between the ancestor and the Supreme Being. We will return to this in due course.

However, in Barth's thought, neither the Son nor the Spirit is subordinate in rank to the Father. He points out that we are not dealing with some semi-divine beings in the Son and the Spirit. Rather, he contends that the one God confronts us in these different modes of his being. Since categories of divine beings are employed in the African context, it is important to note Barth's insistence that in the various modes of God's being in his self-revelation in history we are met with none other than God himself. We conclude this section with the following quote from Barth:

> We mean by the doctrine of the Trinity, in general and preliminary way, the proposition that He whom the Christian Church calls God and proclaims as God, therefore the God who has revealed Himself according to the witness of Scripture, is the same in unimpaired unity, yet also the same in unimpaired variety thrice in a different way. Or, in the phraseology of the dogma of the Trinity in the Church, the Father, the Son and the Holy Spirit in the Bible's witness to revelation are the one God in the unity of their essence, and the one God in the Bible's witness to revelation is in the variety of His Persons as the Father, the Son, and the Holy Spirit.[85]

84. Ibid., 350ff.

85. Ibid., 353.

Now we should turn to how Barth perceives Jesus Christ's revelation for us. This means we must work with the concrete revelation of God in Jesus Christ as the manner in which God is free for humankind. Since both Pobee and Bediako have no problem with the Incarnation as such, a deeper understanding of the discussion here can help us in our thoughts on Jesus Christ and the Supreme Being.

Barth declares:

> According to Holy Scripture God's revelation takes place in the fact that God's Word became a man and that this man has become God's Word. The incarnation of the eternal Word, Jesus Christ, is God's revelation. In the reality of this event God proves that he is free to be our God.[86]

The main point here for Barth is that Holy Scripture is witness to the fact that God's revelation to humankind is witnessed in the historical person, Jesus Christ, objectively and concretely through his incarnation, life, death and resurrection. For him, from the biblical sources, "The Word or Son of God became a Man and was called Jesus of Nazareth; therefore this Man Jesus of Nazareth was God's Word or God's Son."[87] It is in this sense that Barth affirms the God-man of Jesus Christ which also resonates with the confession of the early church that Jesus Christ is "very God or truly God" and "very man or truly man."[88] This is in keeping with Pobee's contention that thedivinity and humanity of Jesus Christ is settled forever. For him it is non-negotiable. However, the question remains as to whether the concept of the ancestor has the dangers of subordination to the Supreme Being. We shall explore that in later sections.

Barth regards the Johannine confession (John 1:14) as the guide for understanding that Jesus Christ is at the same time, "very God and very man."[89] This Johannine confession or witness, according to Barth, is a key to any Christological formulation. He argues that the possibility of maintaining the deity of Jesus Christ will be lost, if one begins with a preconceived notion of God. He points out that it is Jesus Christ alone who determines what the Incarnation is. In him, "the Word became flesh" (John 1:14). This

86. Barth, *Church Dogmatics* I/2, 1

87. Ibid., 13.

88. Ibid., 14ff.

89. Ibid., 132.

for Barth, is the guide for understanding that Jesus Christ is at the same time "very God and very man."[90]

Nonetheless, Barth having history in mind and the issues that led to the development of his treatises warns against Ebionitism, Docetism and other misinterpretations of who Jesus Christ is. For Barth, these early Christological misconceptions or heresies are in some way repeated in some of the liberal Protestants who equate Jesus' divinity with the highest expression or development of human nature.[91] Such warning signs guide us in our attempt to develop a Christology for the ethnic Akan so that we do not fall prey to the same misconceptions. To this end, we will seek to work much more closely with Pobee and Bediako in their application of the ancestral categories. The concern here is to see if they are able to incorporate the biblical witness to both the humanity and divinity of Christ.

Barth buttresses his point on the objective revelation of God with this statement: "God's freedom for us men is a fact in Jesus Christ, according to the witness of Holy Scripture. The first and the last thing to be said about the bearer of this name is that He is very God and very man. In this unity, he is the objective reality of divine revelation."[92] With this statement, Barth emphasizes that there is no possibility of true knowledge of God, of humankind, or of their relationship to one another apart from Jesus Christ. This is an affirmation of the Council of Chalcedon (A.D. 451) and, of course, the early church's stance on the divinity and humanity of the God-man, Jesus Christ. Pobee's line of thought also reaffirms both the divinity and humanity of Jesus Christ in some ways. However, for Pobee, the early church Councils provides us with abstract and philosophical thought with which we should not engage. He is interested in the biblical witness to Jesus because he is convinced that they are both concrete and functional in their approach. Barth speaks about this functional and concrete aspect of the revelation of God in the scripture in following words:

> Revelation itself is needed for knowing that God is hidden and man blind. Revelation and it alone really and finally separates God and man by bringing them together. For by bringing them together it informs man about God and about himself, it reveals God as the Lord of eternity, as the Creator, Reconciler and Redeemer, and characterizes man as a creature, as a sinner, as one devoted to

90. Ibid.

91. Ibid., 134ff.

92. Ibid., 25.

> death. It does that by telling him that God is free for us, that God has created and sustains him, that He forgives his sin that He saves him from death. But it tells him that this God (no other) is free for this man (no other).[93]

Thus, for Barth, we are faced with the reality that the possibility of revelation is founded on the fact that in his freedom God manifests Himself in Jesus Christ. Such a possibility means the following for Barth:

> We infer from the reality of Jesus Christ that God is free for us in the sense that revelation on His side becomes possible in such a way that He is God not only in Himself but also in and among us, in our cosmos, as one of the realities that meets us. The reality of Jesus Christ, consisting in the fact that God is this Man and this Man is God, invariably asserts that God can cross the boundary between Himself and us; or expressed in general terms, between His own existence and the existence of that which is not identical with Himself. . . .it is no obstacle to Him in the act of His revelation.[94]

At this point, Barth is dealing with the mystery of the divine condescension in the Incarnation. He reveals Himself to us in such a way that His Word or His Son becomes a man—not God the Father, and not God the Holy Spirit.[95] Barth also emphasizes that "God in His entire divinity became man."[96]

Further, for Barth, the fact that God revealed himself in human flesh within human history shows that God reveals himself "in such a way that God's Son or Word assumes a form at least known to us, such that He can become cognizable by us by analogy with other forms known to us."[97] This point is very meaningful for the attempts to explore Christology from forms known to us. Barth gives us a clue as to how to cautiously move within the boundaries of analogy. This is because he also points out that the fact of the Word becoming flesh is first, an original and dominating sign of all signs. He therefore explains that beginning with the humanity of Jesus Christ, God has ordained that certain objects of the created world should become the means of effecting a relationship with himself. Can we include

93. Ibid., 29.

94. Ibid., 31.

95. Ibid., 33.

96. Ibid., 33ff.

97. Ibid., 35.

the ancestral category here? We should, however, note that Barth also insists that God's incarnation does not in any way diminish his divinity:

> We gather that revelation is possible on God's side, that God is free for us, in such a way that His Word by becoming Man at the same time is and remains what He is, the true and eternal God, the same as He is in Himself as the Father's right hand for ever and ever. The kenosis, passion, humiliation which He takes upon Himself by becoming man, signifies no loss in divine majesty but, considered in the light its goal, actually its triumph.[98]

Thus, his condescension does not in any way reduce his original divine status. He was God, he became God-man, still in his God-ness and now still God. We cannot in any way reduce him to any other status because he died as a man. In closing, we now take a look at the last point Barth discusses on the reality of God's revelation in Jesus Christ.

Finally, Barth points out that we can conclude from the reality of Jesus Christ that God's revelation becomes possible in such a way that God's Son or Word becomes Man. "He does not become any kind of natural being. He becomes what we ourselves are."[99] This concluding point is very essential for us just as the four earlier ones. According to Barth, we do not have to know what we are on the basis of anthropology; we are what we are because of what the Word of God declares to us. We are flesh. For Barth it is also what the Word of God becomes in his revelation; he becomes flesh (John 1:14). Barth points out that it does not say generally, "man," but concretely, "flesh." Flesh, he explains, denotes humankind, humanity or man-ness, but not in such a way that by this designation a fuller content is added to a conception of a human already familiar or to a conception which can be acquired from other sources.[100]

With these brief discussions on some aspects of the theology of Karl Barth, we have attempted to elucidate the factors that brought about the rise of his new theological pursuits, his strong stance in the face of the issues that he confronted, his dependence on the Word of God as a methodological concept, and the three-fold form he uses to explicate the Word of God. In the next section, a conversation between some of Barth's theological themes with the theological methods of our selected Ghanaian

98. Ibid., 37.

99. Ibid., 39–40.

100. Ibid., 40.

theologians for this project—John Samuel Pobee and Kwame Bediako, will be undertaken.

John Pobee in Theological Conversation with Karl Barth

Theological conversations between Western and African theologians with regard to doing theology *in* Africa *by* Africans *for* Africans using primarily African cultural categories may not be welcomed by some African theologians, though others may welcome the idea with full enthusiasm. For instance, Appiah-Kubi declares in our introductory chapter: "Our question must not be what Karl Barth, Karl Rahner, or any other Karl has to say, but rather what God would have us do in our living concrete condition. Rather, it is time to answer the critical question of Jesus Christ: 'Who do you (African Christians) say that I am?'"[101]

Thus, the impression created here is that Kofi Appiah-Kubi desires a theology without the influence of Western theology, both past and current. Fundamentally, the argument is that the African is capable of constructing indigenous Christologies in answer to the question or encounter with Christ. Kofi Appiah-Kubi may be right, but how feasible is it? What do other African theologians say about this? John Mbiti, the first African to realize that the African Christian Church lacked theologians and theological concern was also the first to boldly suggest the ways Africans must engage in theological endeavors. His position, as stated earlier, is the following: "African theologies need to be within the overall traditions of the church and that theologies emerging from Africa need to be assembled and engaged with the Church universal."[102]

Thus, Mbiti wants a theology for Africa that answers the Christological questions reiterated by Appiah-Kubi, but he argues that such theologies must, while expressed in terms of African thought, philosophies, or religio-cultural categories should be rooted in the Christian tradition. John Samuel Pobee, one of the theologians whose work is to be put into conversation with the theology of Karl Barth, argued elsewhere on the need to discuss theology with the older churches and theologies. This means that the plumb line for determining emerging African theologies must necessarily take into account theologies received from the universal church as well. In other words, it must involve the overall theology of the church.

101. Kofi Appiah-Kubi, *African Theology Enroute*, viii.

102. Mbiti, *Bible and Theology in African Christianity*, 15.

It is in light of the above arguments that we engage the well-known-Western theologian, Karl Barth, in this new Christological endeavor for the ethnic Akan. In this chapter, observations on the respective methodological concepts employed by Pobee and Barth are presented, with the intent of eliciting some thoughts that will facilitate our task of constructing a Christology of Akan Christians. We thus proceed with the theological conversation between Samuel Pobee and Karl Barth.

Earlier in this project, we stated that Pobee's prime motive was to search for an appropriate Christology within African theology. Let us refresh our thought with the questions posed by Pobee, which also indicate to a large extent the motive of his search for Christology:

> Who is Jesus Christ? What manner of man is he? How does he affect my life? Why should an Akan relate to Jesus of Nazareth, who does not belong to his clan, family, tribe, and nation? These are the matters concerning us in Christology. The answers to these questions determine, to some extent at any rate, the rooting of Christianity in the new setting.[103]

In search of answers to these questions, Pobee sought to translate Christology into what he calls, "genuine African categories." Pobee's Christological questions and his statement of methodology seem to find its parallel in the origins of Barth's theology. According to Herbert Hartwell,

> Barth in his twelve years of pastoral ministry, first in Geneva (1909–1911) and then in Safenwil (1911–1921), the young Swiss pastor, born at Basel in 1886, wrestled with the problem of how he could genuinely preach the Word of God, in other words, how he could prevent his sermon from being merely his own words.[104]

Thus, we see that both Barth and Pobee are attempting to seek something "genuine." At the same time, their methodologies differ from one another. For instance, the question of who Jesus is; what manner of man he is; how does he affect one's life, may be issues which both theologians can respond to without difficulty. However, the issue of why an Akan relates to Jesus who is of a different tribe and nationality poses some real challenges for Pobee, as he turns to apply the ancestral and chieftain/linguist paradigms for the construction of Christology for the ethnic Akan. In our commentary on Pobee's work in chapter three, we pointed out that such

103. Pobee, *Toward an African Theology*, 81.

104. Hartwell, *Karl Barth: An Introduction*, 3.

applications do not really measure up to what Jesus Christ truly is and they reduce him to a subordinate level, which Pobee might not have intended. Here one encounters one of the methodological differences between Barth's and Pobee's approaches. Pobee seeks to "shape" Christ so that he becomes "acceptable" to an ethnic Akan. Barth would argue that the movement should be in the reverse, that the challenge comes from Christ to the Akan, and that it is the Akan who should respond to him as he presents himself in the Gospel message.

The question that Pobee raises in response is that the Christ who was presented to the Akan for his or her response was the Christ of those who had already been "shaped" by those who formulated the Creeds. As noted earlier, Pobee holds that the Creedal formula was an attempt of a predominantly Hellenistic society to articulate its belief in Jesus in terms of the language and concepts of its day. He comments: "who today, theologian and philosopher included, normally uses terms such as a "person" or "substance" or "hypostasis in their technical Chalcedonian sense?"[105] For Pobee, "the Creed was an attempt to translate the biblical faith into contemporary language and thought forms."[106] He points out that any Christology must be "tested against the plumb-line of biblical faith."[107] Pobee's methodology keeps what the Bible teaches on Christology. In this sense, it is important to note that Pobee's argument does not entertain the Christological controversies of the early church in relation to the metaphysical language used. Thus, he distinguishes his Christology from the metaphysical speculations in the determination of the divinity and humanity of Jesus Christ. The interesting issue is how Pobee develops his ancestral/linguist Christology with the humanity and divinity of Jesus Christ without reference to the earlier Christological controversies.

Here one can find an interesting meeting point between Barth and Pobee. Both insist on the Bible as the basis of their Christology. However they appear to have opposite responses to the Creedal formulations. As noted above, Barth, attempts to be a theologian of the Word of God. But he affirms the Chalcedonian formula despite its language and thought forms. Whereas Pobee accepts the Chalcedonian formula, in some sense, Barth accepts and works with it almost fully. For Barth, it is impossible to begin

105. Pobee, *Toward an African Theology*, 82.

106. Ibid.

107. Ibid.

Christological work as Schleiermacher[108] and Ritschl[109] did in their time with the historical Jesus. Barth's premise for doing theology is the fact that Jesus Christ is the incarnate Word of God in the strict sense of John 1.14. In other words, "Jesus Christ as the very God and very man...God the Son become man in the man Jesus of Nazareth."[110] This for Barth cannot be argued but must be accepted and interpreted on faith. Pobee agrees when he states that "the divinity and humanity of Jesus are the two non-negotiables of any authentic Christology."[111] This is because, for Pobee,in the divinity of Jesus Christ finds its true expression in *Onyame* or the Supreme Being. The Johannine statement is essential for Pobee's Christological articulation, but he rejects the metaphysical speculations used to determine the divinity of Jesus Christ. This he finds problematic for the ethnic Akan who prefers concreteness to abstraction. Therefore, as part of his methodology, Pobee depends on Akan wisdom sayings and proverbs, something that we find inadequate for the explication of who Jesus is.

Barth argues that it is in the Son of God that Jesus Christ has his exclusive existence as man. As far as Barth is concerned, this is the "central mystery of the Incarnation, revealed in the resurrection of Jesus Christ, as it means that in Jesus Christ not only God and man, divine nature and human nature, became one in an inconceivable manner but that in Him the

108. Schleiermacher, Friedrich Ernst Daniel during the beginning of the 19th century redirected the focus of religion and theology. In his book, *On Religion: Speeches to Its Cultured Despisers,* he rejected the idea of either dogma or ethics as the locus of religion. Rather, for Schleiermacher, religion is a matter of feeling, either of feeling, in general, or of the feeling of absolute dependence. It must be pointed out that Schleiermacher's formulation was in large part a reaction to the work of Immanuel Kant. Although Kant was a philosopher rather than a theologian, his three famous critiques—*The Critique of Pure Reason* (1781), *The Critique of Practical Reason* (1788), and *The Critique of Judgment* (1790)—had an enormous impact on the philosophy of religion. In the first of these, he refuted the idea that it is possible to have theoretical knowledge of objects that transcend sense experience. This of course disposed of the possibility of any real knowledge of a cognitive basis for religion as traditionally understood. Rather, Kant determined that religion is an object of practical reason. He deemed that God, norms, and the immortal life are necessary as postulates without which morality cannot function. Thus, religion became a matter of ethics.

109. Ritschl Albrecht, a theologian of the 19th century, applied these Kantian views of religion to Christian theology by arguing that religion is a matter of moral judgment. It is to such applications rendering theology to anthropology, human ethics and feelings that gave rise to Karl Barth's theology of the Word.

110. Barth, *Church Dogmatics* I/2, 10ff.

111. Pobee, *Toward an African Theology*, 83.

creator has become Himself a creature."[112] That is, God has become human. On the issue of the Creator becoming a creature, there is some resonance for Pobee who also finds the creature aspect of Jesus Christ essential to the elucidation of his divinity. But on this issue of the two natures of Jesus Christ, Barth admits that its mystery was neither solved nor meant to be solved by the Chalcedon formula (A.D. 451). However, he adopts it and uses it to explain how the divine and human are related to each other in the person of Jesus Christ."[113] From Pobee's perspective, he, instead, will use Akan anthropology.

For Barth, the human nature of Jesus Christ has no independent existence *(an-hypostasis)* but acquires and has existence exclusively in the Son of God who assumed human nature and existence in Him *(en-hypostasis).* This means that for Barth, as far as Jesus Christ's person is concerned, it is not a question of the adoption by the Son of God of an already existing human being or of idealizing or deifying a particular man.[114] Barth, on the other hand, acknowledges that this teaching does not mean a denial of the humanity of Jesus Christ who is said not to lack humanity but human existence or being of its own.[115] Though it is difficult to explain to the two natures of Jesus, for Barth, the difficulty is part of the mystery of the Incarnation.

On his part, Pobee concurs on the difficulty of the explanation of the two natures of Jesus Christ, though he complains about the tendency to discuss Christology in metaphysical abstractions. This is because Pobee finds that resorting to metaphysics is not what the Bible does. He states, "The biblical approach is different in that the metaphysical speculations about the relations within the Godhead are absent.[116] Barth supports Pobee's assertion with a strong emphasis that Christology must not be made from the thinking of humankind (philosophical abstractions). Rather, he goes further and vehemently opposes "anything which has its structure as a human being (anthropology), in his thinking (philosophy) and his experience (man's religion and culture)."[117] Here, Pobee moves away from Barth. He wants to pursue theology on the basis of humankind's religion and culture.

112. Barth, *Church Dogmatics* I/2, 10ff.

113. Ibid., 122ff.

114. Ibid., 20, 147ff.

115. Ibid., 164.

116. Pobee, *Toward an African Theology*, 82.

117. Barth, *Church Dogmatics* I/1,164.

Are these two theologians speaking of the same thing and in agreement at this point? Initially, one may argue in the affirmative, however, a critical analysis will reveal the negative. On the one hand, since metaphysical speculations and philosophical abstractions are one and the same thing, we can say that the two theologians are in agreement. On the other hand, they appear to mean different things when they speakabout speculations and abstractions. Pobee on his part argues that the Johannine statement on "The Word was God (John 1:1)"[118] does not speculate on how the Word could be God, but rather, he is interested in the concrete reality that the "Word became flesh and dwelt among us, full of grace and truth; we beheld his glory (John 1:14)."[119] So for Pobee, Christology in the bible is not done from above but on the basis of the earthly activities of Jesus Christ. He thus discusses Christology in "functional terms . . . . in terms of Jesus's activities."[120]

Based on this, Pobee looks to the Akan wisdom sayings and proverbs as the key method to describe Jesus' activities in functional terms and as such to determine his divinity. However, it is difficult to fully grasp what Pobee means by "functional terms" and to see how the proverbs, even though they are about concrete aspects of life, provide an adequate basis to develop a Christology. Barth preffered to discuss the "Word became flesh" in terms of revelation and faith than in "functional terms." Pobee points out that functionality, is more effective in any Christological discussion relative to the Akan. Thus, we see another key difference in the methodology of Pobee and Barth. Whereas Barth remains close to Protestant Orthodoxy on the issue of "the Word became Flesh," Pobee seems to be interested in his conviction that "Flesh became an ancestor."

Barth holds a strong conviction about humankind's ability to know the truth about God, the world and humankind. He looks to revelation for the answer. For him, humanity cannot do it through anthropology, culture,e or even religious experience. For him, humanity needs the enlightenment of the Holy Spirit through faith in order to know and express the knowledge of the truth of God. Faith is thus the presupposition, the basis, the point of departure or the starting point of all theological thinking. In Barth's theology as in that of Anselm of Canterbury, faith *(credere)* precedes knowledge *(intelligere)* and, on the other hand, knowledge, of necessity, follows faith

118. Ibid., 82.

119. Ibid.

120. Ibid.

(*fides quaerens intellectum*). This is the epistemological principle underlying his theology. So for Barth, the concrete message of the Word of God cannot be "anticipated with, nor can it be explained on even philosophy of religion."[121]

For Barth, Pobee's first two theological questions, 'Who is Jesus Christ?' and 'What manner of man is he?', can be answered in the light of his quotation of the Johannine statement: "the Word became flesh." Barth has this to suggest: "The Word became flesh is a particular, concrete and a rational event."[122] This particular concrete event for Barth is "the revelation of God in the God-man, Jesus Christ."[123] Nonetheless, he explicates that the real understanding of this particular event has to go beyond the birth of the man, Jesus. He points out:

> The revelation is not to be confined to the fact of the birth of Jesus, that is to the Incarnation of the Word of God, but includes His life, His teaching, His passion, His death and, above all, from the standpoint of revelation even primarily, His resurrection as well. It is the revelation of the Triune God, of the God, that is, who, according to the witness of Holy Scripture and the Church's proclamation based upon that witness, is the Father of Jesus Christ, is Jesus Christ Himself, is the Spirit of this Father and of this Son.[124]

Christology, therefore, must first and foremost be worked out on the basis of the concrete event that has revealed the entire Godhead to humanity through the Incarnation of the Word of God in Jesus Christ. This inclusive thought resonates with both Pobee and Bediako. Though, Pobee scarcely discusses the resurrection of Jesus Christ, he works well with his life and thought. It is essential at this point to take a detailed look at what Pobee says about the birth of Jesus:

> Whatever else Jesus was, he was like other men in that a woman brought him into the world. Whatever else Jesus was, in short, he was a personality in history. However, birth is, perhaps, the least in establishing the humanity of Jesus. For after all, the lower creation also gives birth. Besides, in Semitic as in African societies it was believed possible for divinities to take human form. Left to ourselves, we would skirt the birth, because not only is it inconclusive

121. Barth, *Church Dogmatics* I/1, 325; I/2, 483.

122. Ibid., 327ff.

123. Ibid., 327ff.

124. Barth, *Church Dogmatics* I/1, 134, 334.

> evidence of the humanity of Jesus but also because we do not wish to be bogged down by the problems raised by the biblical claim that Jesus' birth was miraculous (I refer to the story or theology of the Virgin Birth).[125]

Pobee's phrase "whatever else Jesus was" calls for further inquiry into what he thinks of the birth of Jesus. Precisely the fact that he moves away from the Virgin birth strikes a crucial difference between his thought, Barth, Bediako and Protestant Orthodoxy. This is because, for Barth, the divinity of Jesus Christ is explained particularly from the Virgin birth.

However, this does not mean Pobee situates the divinity of Jesus as something parallel to the divinities within the Akan spiritual universe. It is important to make this point clear because of the statement he makes that "in Semitic as in African societies it was believed possible for divinities to take human form." Pobee, however, will not equate Jesus Christ to such divinities. As explained in the chapter on Akan Cosmology (chapter two), the divinities are lesser deities or lesser gods *(abosom)* who do not in any way come close to *Onyame* or the Supreme Being.

As stated earlier, Pobee wants to develop a Christology based primarily on the humanity of Jesus Christ rather than on his divinity. Partly because of this interest in affirming the true humanity of Jesus (as man, like any Akan) and partly in view of biblical criticism, Pobee moves away from the Virgin birth. Despite his commitment to use the Bible as the plumb line, he looks upon the issue of the Virgin birth as inconclusive, and does not use it as one of his arguments for either the humanity or the divinity of Christ, and states that he does not want to be bogged down by the problems raised by the biblical claims that Jesus' birth was miraculous. But it is difficult to see how he can avoid the Virgin birth as an "inconclusive" issue in developing his Christology because some of the "genuine African categories" that he would use later would also easily fall into that category. As noted earlier, some of the African categories that Pobee uses to construct his Akan Christology include the wisdom sayings, chieftain, and linguist.

For Karl Barth, the doctrine of the Virgin birth is a pointer to the revelation of God in the Incarnation of the Word of God in Jesus Christ of Nazareth. He describes the Virgin birth, the conception of Jesus Christ by the Holy Spirit, and, the birth of the Virgin Mary as "the miracle of Christmas."[126] While Pobee would prefer to skirt the Virgin Birth, Barth on

125. Pobee, *Toward an African Theology*, 83.

126. Barth, *Church Dogmatics* I/2, 207.

his part declares: "it is (Virgin Birth) a necessary sign which accompanies and indicates the mystery of the revelation of God in Jesus Christ, of the Son of God come in the flesh, and for that reason is essential to the true understanding of the Christian revelation."[127] In this case, Barth would not think about how inconclusive or problematic the Birth of the God-man Jesus Christ is, but rather, for him it is already the single, concrete, and particularly decisive event of human history.

Also, Barth emphasizes first of all, that the *vere Deus vere homo* (very God and very man) concept cannot be understood intellectually but spiritually. Secondly, God alone is the Author of the new creation of the God-man Jesus Christ. For Barth even the Virgin Mary in some limited sense had not much part in the birth of Jesus. The Virgin Mary, according to Barth, "only accepted in obedience what God has willed for her and created in her by the power of the Holy Spirit."[128] So, Barth avoids any intellectual discussions on the Virgin birth and accepts in obedience what the Bible teaches about it. Pobee suggests that "there are more and clearer indications of the humanity of Jesus besides the problematic Virgin birth. He, therefore, searches for Jesus' humanity in terms of Akan anthropology.

Pobee discovers Jesus' true humanity by comparing the biblical anthropology to Akan anthropology. In these comparisons, Pobee relates the fact that Jesus had spirit, flesh, and body to the soul, spirit, and body of the Akan person. For him, the Akan can understand the humanity of Jesus very well because they both bear similar components. Again, as far as Pobee is concerned, Jesus and the Akan, because they were both flesh, had the tendency to sin, even though Jesus, on his part, did not yield to sin; he could have sinned because he was sent "in the likeness of sinful flesh (Romans 8:3)."

Barth concurs with Pobee that the Word of God became flesh, was real man, the Son of God assuming our human nature with all its limitations and weaknesses, including its sinfulness. However, "though his humanity was our own familiar humanity, the Son of God could not sin; for he could not be in enmity towards himself."[129] Barth continues "in assuming sinful nature he sanctified it so that sin was excluded."[130] Does it mean for Barth that God intentionally gave us sinful unsanctified human nature? The

127. Barth, *Church Dogmatics* I/1, 337.

128. Barth, *Church Dogmatics* I/2, 185ff

129. Barth, *Church Dogmatics* I/2, 40ff.

130. Barth, *Church Dogmatics* I/2, 147ff.

kenotic passage (Philippians 2) addresses Jesus' uniqueness in his obedience to the will of God and to the bitterest end of the death on the cross. Here, Pobee uses the kenotic passage to address Jesus' humanity yet he fails to give a coherent account of his death on the cross and its significance for human relations with God. Yet, what Akan Christology seeks is Jesus Christ whose cross speaks to the spiritual realities. This also accounts for the fact that his Christology is inadequate for speaking and dealing with ethnic Akan realities.

In Barth's Christology, there is the argument that in Jesus Christ, in his person and work, no reduction takes place either of his deity or of his humanity. However, in Pobee's Christology we see clearly some elements of the subordination of Jesus Christ. For instance, on the issue of the kenosis, Barth understands it to mean "the renunciation or self-deprivation of his being in the form of God alone, assuming the form of a servant without detracting from his being in the form of God."[131] Pobee has no reference to what actually happened to his deity in the kenotic passage. Rather, Pobee intends to emphasize Jesus' devotion to the will of God to explain his humanity.

Barth contends that Jesus Christ in his self-emptying did not any way cease as man to be who he is, that is, the Son of God, but took it upon himself to be the Son of God in a way quite other than that which corresponds and belongs to his form as God, that is, to be the Son of God in the form of a servant, thereby concealing his divine glory from the world, until it was revealed in his resurrection. Barth also has something to say in relation to Jesus' resurrection. That is, for Barth, by becoming a servant-man, Jesus was still God in every capacity. In this sense, for Barth there was no subordination.

Since Pobee has brought the issue of knowledge of God through creation, let us see how Barth views it. We have already indicated from Barth's Christocentric theology that anything that will give humankind the opportunity to determine who God, the universe, and humankind are, other than through the revelation of God in the Incarnate Word of God in Jesus Christ, attested in Holy Scripture, they have departed from the only sure foundation for devising theology. Such a departure leads the theologian or the philosopher away from grace to nature or natural theology.

Natural theology, as understood by Barth, "is the teaching that makes man in himself understand by nature and not by grace, possess the capacity

131. Barth, *Church Dogmatics* I/1, 337ff.

and power to inform himself about God, the world, and humankind."[132] Karl Barth believes that "natural theology is a radical error on the part of humankind."[133] He declares that there is no way humankind can know God, the universe and humanity, as they really are without God's particular and concrete revelation in Jesus Christ. Barth argues that whether through humankind's innate capacities and endowments or whether he thinks that he can gain it on the ground of a general revelation in creation or history, there is no way humankind can achieve this knowledge using these categories.

For Barth, Natural theology is practiced in direct opposition to a theology based on the Word of God. Such 'knowledge' of God, the universe, and humanity derived from natural theology is, according to Barth, entirely different from God's own revelation in Jesus Christ and, therefore, amounts to error and falsehood. For him, "every natural theology is incontrovertibly impossible."[134] Barth's reasons for rejecting natural theology are listed below.

Firstly, he points out that "it is only by the self-revelation of God in Jesus Christ and through the power of the Holy Spirit and, therefore, only by an act of God's free grace and by faith that man can know God as he himself has actually shown himself to be according to the witness of Holy Scripture."[135] Barth explains that God is the Triune God in his three modes of being as Father, Son, and Holy Spirit, in the one undivided form, the Creator, Reconciler and Redeemer. He states that God is not only the God who is for us, but also the God who in Jesus Christ is 'with us' and in him assumed our human nature. He points out that humankind could not possibly know, God, apart from that revelation. Barth postulates, that "in the face of the cross of Christ it is monstrous to describe the uniqueness of God as an object of natural theology. In the face of the cross of Christ we are bound to say that knowledge of the one and only God is gained only by the begetting of men anew by the Holy Spirit."[136]

Secondly, Barth maintains that the possibility of natural theology is excluded by the work of reconciliation as an act of divine sovereignty and of the free grace of God in Jesus Christ. It is intriguing that Pobee fails to discuss anything in relation to humankind's separation from God in the act

132. Barth, *Natural Theology*, 67ff.

133. Ibid., 69.

134. Barth, *Church Dogmatics* II/1, 85.

135. Barth, *Natural Theology*, 71.

136. Barth, *Church Dogmatics* II/1, 453.

of his sinful nature and God's reconciling work in Jesus Christ through the Cross. Though Pobee speaks of the sinless life, he does not go into how to separate humanity from the sinful nature into the new life in God, the Son. Even though Pobee speaks about sin, he only speaks of it in terms of demonstrating Jesus' divinity and humanity but not as effecting reconciliation between humankind and God. Though Pobee points to Jesus Christ as the Great and Greatest Ancestor, he does not make mention of his mediating role between the Akan and God as Bediako does. This is because such a role will also render Jesus Christ to a subordinate position.

For Barth, the work of reconciliation demonstrates the impossibility of natural theology: "When God assumed human nature in Jesus Christ, the Son of Man who is also and primarily the Son of God, he ceased to all eternity to be God only, assuming and having and maintaining to all eternity human nature as well."[137] Thus, God left his glorious estate and took the form of humanity and lived as a human being among us, in order to save, deliver and restore humanity to the rightful position. He argues further that "Since then he, the risen Lord, the Living Christ, is, God in the flesh."[138] Also, he labors the point that "God is God in this association with the human nature of Jesus Christ. To know God in this form is however impossible for any natural theology."[139]

Finally, Barth contends that natural theology is incompatible with the free and sovereign grace of God in Jesus Christ. Again, Barth states that, "if God's revelation in Jesus Christ and, therefore, his free and gracious action in his revelation is used as a source of knowledge alongside knowledge of God proper to man as such, it is no longer the free and gracious revelation of God."[140] For Barth, the revelation of God in Jesus Christ the Incarnate Word of God attested to in the Holy Scriptures is the only source through which all must be known.

Pobee, on his part agrees that "in Jesus Christ all things came to be and that no single thing ever was created without him."[141] He also admits that Jesus as Creator is the medium of revelation about God. But Pobee constructs his African Christology on the basis of the kinship of Jesus. He chose this method because he wants to develop a Christology, based on the

137. Barth, *Church Dogmatics* IV/2, 100.

138. Ibid., 101.

139. Ibid., 103ff.

140. Ibid., 103ff.

141. Pobee, *Toward an African Theology*, 87.

activities of Christ, which also works well with his humanity. For Pobee, "Jesus' identity as a man was well demonstrated by his relationship with Mary who gave him status and membership in a lineage and clan."[142]

One notes that in Pobee's Christology, lineage and clan are very important. But what have these two to do with Christ's humanity and divinity? Pobee's primary interest in his Christology is not to establish Christ's humanity and divinity but to discuss Christology in terms of the Akan understanding of the Ancestor. Therefore, he attempts to express the elements involved in claiming that Jesus is truly human in Akan thought forms. If Jesus is truly human in Akan thought forms then he must have a tribe, clan and lineage. This is the reason for posing the question: "Why should an Akan relate to Jesus who does not belong to his clan?" Therefore, his primary interest in Mary and Joseph is to establish that Jesus also belonged to a clan and had a lineage.

Pobee also tries to claim Jesus' divinity through his humanity. He discerned the following elements in the divinity of Jesus—his sinless-ness, his authority and power, not only as the agent of creation but also as judge at the end, pre-existence, and eternity. Under his treatment of Jesus' divinity, one of the prominent elements is his power and authority to judge which is his prerogative as the Supreme Being. Yet, even though he speaks about Jesus as the center of creation, his pre-existence and eternity, he does not think of him as God.

Also, Pobee asserts that in Akan society, the Supreme Being and the ancestors provide the sanctions for the good life and punish evil. He states that the ancestors hold that authority as ministers of the Supreme Being. On the basis of this, Pobee declares: " . . . our approach would be to look on Jesus as the Great and Greatest Ancestor—in Akan language, *Nana.* Pobee agrees that even if he terms Jesus as ancestor, he is superior to all other ancestors because "Jesus is closer to God and as God." Is there a difference between "as God" and "is God?" This is one of the main areas of ambiguity in Pobee's theology. While he is able to speak of Jesus "as God," he would still want to call him the Greatest Ancestor. In the Akan tradition, however, the ancestor is not the Supreme Being, but still a human being living in the other world. An ancestor is still the "living dead." It is clear that here Barth and Pobee part company, because the ancestral level is far below Jesus' rank in the Godhead, where Barth sees Christ as the second person of the Trinity.

142. Ibid., 88.

The parting of company becomes even more evident when in Pobee's Christology Jesus is also considered as the linguist of the Supreme Being. This is because, in the Akan religion, the Supreme Being is conceived of as a great paramount chief who is "so big" that he has to be approached through sub-chiefs and his official spokesman called the linguist. In the discussion of Pobee's theology, we have noted that he does not want to subordinate Christ to the Supreme Being. However, in his interest in assigning the role of mediation to Christ, and finding the linguist as one that plays this role in the Akan culture, he seeks to interpret Christ also as the linguist. However, by assigning this title to Christ, Pobee does end up moving against his own inclination,thus moving even further away from Barth's convictions about Christ and his place within Godhead.

Clearly Barth and Pobee, although they appear to be on the same mission of responding to their contexts, are in fact, engaged in very different missions. While Barth wants to call the Christian faith back to the Word of God and to make the theological task bound by it, Pobee begins with the Word of God, but is out on a mission to make the faith intelligible within the Akan culture. In so doing, he adopts cultural images and concepts that take him beyond the biblical faith which he claims has to be the plumb line for any theological task.

For our part, we feel that the images that Pobee had chosen, ancestor and the linguist, are not adequate even for the legitimate task that he set out to do, for we believe that they do not do justice to the biblical witness to Christ and what he has accomplished for the Akan. We would, however, return to a fuller analysis of this problem in the next chapter. In the meantime we turn to the task of facilitating a conversation between Barth and Bediako.

Kwame Bediako in Theological Conversation with Karl Barth

In the previous subsection we thoroughly discussed various issues that come out prominently in the theologies of John Samuel Pobee and Karl Barth which are also essential for the purpose of this research. In this subsection, our task is to facilitate a similar theological conversation between Kwame Bediako and Karl Barth on some key points that are pertinent to our task of constructing an Akan Christology.

In so doing, however, we do not intend to repeat much that has already been taken up in the conversation between Barth and Pobee. Both Pobee and Bediako are on a similar mission and even turn to common resources within the Akan for doing their Christology. But they have different starting points and methodologies. We shall, therefore, seek to identify specific areas for conversation between Barth and Bediako and join their conversation where appropriate to do so.

Bediako begins with the affirmation that Jesus Christ, in his universality, is no stranger to the African heritage and that "the incarnation was the incarnation of the savior of all people."[143] With this in mind, Bediako asserts that our true humanity in the image and likeness of God cannot be understood in the way Pobee frames his questions in terms of "clan, lineage, tribe or nationality"[144] but, in Jesus Christ, himself.

However, Bediako maintains that "the way in which Jesus Christ relates to the importance and function of the 'spirit fathers' or ancestors is crucial."[145] He argues that until now "the churches have avoided the question of Jesus Christ's relation to the spirit fathers and have presented the Gospel as though it was concerned with an entirely different compartment of life unrelated to traditional religious piety."[146] His point is that the messages preached in the churches are inadequate to fulfill the needs of the Akan people. For this reason, many Akans are uncertain about how Jesus Christ of the church's preaching saves them from the terrors and fears that they experience in their traditional world view. Thus, for him, it is paramount to relate Christian understanding and experience to the realm of the ancestors, because for Africans, this is where the problems with fears and terrors usually originate.

Bediako, however, does not completely dismiss what the churches have been able to achieve through the communication of the Gospel: "The vitality of Christian communities (in Africa) bears witness to the fact that the Gospel was really communicated, however inadequate we may now consider that communication to have been."[147] And yet, Bediako is clear that the communication of the Gospel is truly effective only where it is

143. Bediako, *Jesus and the Gospel in Africa*, 24.

144. Pobee, *Toward an African Theology*, 79.

145. Bediako, *Jesus and the Gospel in Africa*, 22.

146. Ibid., 23.

147. Ibid., 20.

preached in ways that are relevant to the experiences of the people which are shaped by their cultural location.

Does the Holy Scripture not interpret itself in spite of all human experiences? Here we already arrive at an area where disagreements between Barth and those who do theology in a cultural context begin to emerge. For Barth, "the Bible unfolds to us as we are met, guided, drawn on and made to grow by the grace of God."[148] He further suggests that history, morality, and religion are all to be found in the Bible and that we look to the Bible for guidance rather than raise issues about its relevance:

> It is not the right human thoughts about God which form the content of the Bible, but the right divine thoughts about men. The Bible tells us not how we should talk about God but what he says to us; not how we find the way to him, but how he has sought and found the way to us; not the right relation in which we must place ourselves to him, but the covenant which he has made with all who are Abraham's spiritual children and which he has sealed once and for all in Jesus Christ. It is this which is within the Bible. The word of God is within the Bible.[149]

So, then, for Barth, it may not be how we relate our traditional world view and the realm of ancestors to the Christian understanding and particularly to the Word of God, but rather, how we seek divine thoughts about ourselves. Secondly, we are not informed about how we should talk about God, but how he has sought and found the way through the incarnate Word of God in Jesus Christ to us.

Bediako holds that the covenant which God has made with all who are Abraham's spiritual children in Jesus Christ has made way for all, including the Akan. For him, the consequence of this belief is that God would speak to all within their cultures, and he attempts a way to seek how God has sought the Akan in their primal understanding. It is clear that Barth and Bediako, while making the same affirmations, are drawing different conclusions. We see this divergence also in the way that the two approach the issue of Revelation.

On the issue of revelation, Bediako places enormous significance to the revelation of God in Jesus Christ. Nevertheless, he also gives importance to the general revelation from the creation of Adam to formulate a basis for the development of his Akan Christology from the concepts and

148. Barth, *Word of God and The Word of Man*, 34.

149. Ibid., 43.

functions of the ancestors. On the basis of his understanding of revelation, he disagrees with Pobee on his Christological preoccupation with lineage and clan. For him, it is important to liberate ourselves from the closed system that clan and lineage impose on us in order to rediscover who we truly are on a universal horizon. He suggests:

> We are to understand our creation as the original revelation of God to us and covenant with us. It was in the creation of the universe and especially of man that God first revealed his Kingship to our ancestors and called them to freely obey him. Working from this insight, we, from African primal tradition, are given a biblical basis for discovering more about God within the framework of the high doctrine of God as Creator and Sustainer that is deeply rooted in our heritage. More significantly, we are enabled to discover ourselves in Adam and come out of the isolation which the closed system of clan, lineage, and family imposes, so that we can rediscover universal horizons.[150]

Thus, for him, God grants humankind revelation through creation. We are enabled to rediscover ourselves in the first Adam. Our heritage is not necessarily found within our restrictive clan and lineage but rather in the high doctrine of God as Creator and Sustainer.

Why does Bediako, having begun like Barth with the firm belief in the revelation of God in Jesus Christ, move so quickly to Adam? This is an important issue because it would have been possible for him to argue for universality also based on the universality of the revelation in Jesus Christ. It is of interest that Barth celebrates the particularity of Jesus as a Jew and builds his universality of Christ on it. Bediako, however, believes that once we begin with particularity, Jesus' particularity as a Jew will set the tone of the discussion, and the achievement of Jesus as the universal savior would be lost. By beginning with universality, and if universality of Jesus is affirmed on that basis, then the Incarnation becomes the incarnation of the Savior of all people, of all nations and of all periods.[151] Such explanation, in his view, will help all Africans not only to identify with their heritage but also with the world and with Jesus Christ, the God-man.

What has Barth to say to revelation? Will he begin the way Bediako does? We have already indicated in the above pages that Barth's theological basis is thoroughly Christocentric. Right from the beginning of the

150. Bediako, *Jesus and the Gospel in Africa*, 25.

151. Ibid., 24.

Prolegomena, Barth affirms that "the task of dogmatic theology is to discover the extent to which the church's language about God point toward the decisive revelation of God in Jesus Christ, who is both the 'essence of the Church' and the norm and measure of her theology."[152] He maintains that since Jesus Christ, himself, is the way, the truth and the life (John 14:6), "theology's overriding concern must be to witness faithfully to his significance for understanding all of the relationships between God and man and between man and his fellowman."[153]

In this conversation, Barth suggests that if we really want to follow the biblical truth strictly, then we must keep in mind that it is Jesus Christ, the Second Adam, who must be considered the final criterion of every revelation of God to humanity and for that matter for every theological endeavor. Here we see not only a difference between Bediako and Barth but also a difference that also sets Barth's theology from that of traditional Christian thought. For the former is basically Christocentric and begins his theological work with Jesus Christ. The latter begins with revelation in creation. The very task he sets out to do drives Bediako to begin with creation as the first source of revelation.

Barth suggests: "Revelation in fact does not differ from the Person of Jesus Christ, and again does not differ from the reconciliation that took place in Him. To say revelation is to say 'the Word became flesh.'"[154] Kwame Bediako has no problem with the fact that the "Word became flesh" is revelation. In fact, when he connects the universality of Jesus Christ to his particularity as a Jew, Abraham becomes a link, and all who have faith get linked up to the work Christ has done for the whole world.

Bediako links the universal significance with significance of Christ such that he argues from general revelation also to the spiritual reality of the Akan. He points out that the "experience of ambiguity that comes from regarding lesser deities and ancestral spirits as both beneficent and malevolent, can only be resolved in a genuine Incarnation of the Savior from the realm beyond."[155] Here Bediako not only affirms the incarnation but also the work it is able to accomplish within the Akan spiritual worldview. He also sees Jesus' incarnation as the incarnation from the Supreme Being,

152. Barth, *Church Dogmatics* I/1, 11–12.

153. Ibid.

154. Ibid., 134.

155. Bediako, *Jesus and the Gospel in Africa*, 25.

Onyankopong, or God. He maintains that through Jesus' death we are freed from the wrongs we did while the first covenant was still in force.

But how does this death relate to our story and particularly our natural "spirit fathers?"[156] As pointed out earlier, for Bediako, "Jesus Christ is our true Elder Brother whose death has placed him in the presence of his Father and our Father; he displaces the mediatorial function of our natural 'spirit fathers' and takes over their functions as saviors and protectors. It is of interest that both Bediako and Pobee focus exclusively on the post resurrection work of Christ. Barth's theology, rooted in the Trinity, depends a great deal on the assumptions about the place and status of Christ, before becoming the Word that spoke to humankind.

Reflecting on the saving work of Jesus Christ, Bediako maintains that "the ancestors need saving, having originated from among us."[157] He comments:

> It is known from African missionary history that one of the first actions of new converts was to pray for their ancestors who had passed on before the Gospel was proclaimed. This is an important testimony to the depth of their understanding of Jesus as sole Lord and Savior. Jesus Christ, 'the Second Adam' from heaven (1 Corinthians 15:47) becomes for us the only mediator between God and ourselves (cf. 1 Timothy 2:5). He is the 'mediator of a better covenant' (Hebrew 8:6), relating our human destiny directly to God. He is truly our high priest who meets our needs to the full.[158]

Thus, according to Bediako, a prayer request is made on behalf of the 'spirit-fathers' indicating the depth of the understanding of the new converts. But this reveals something important about Akan Christian belief that even the ancestors or 'spirit-fathers' are not saved and are in need of Christ's salvation.

In the previous chapter we noted Bediako's thoughts on the myth-making imagination of the community with regards to the ancestors. Thus, for Bediako even the work that has been ascribed to the ancestors is based on myth. For him, Christ is the reality that goes beyond this myth-making. Therefore for him Jesus Christ, as savior, "surpasses our natural ancestors also by virtue of who he is in himself."[159] Bediako points out, that Jesus

156. Ibid., 26.

157. Ibid.

158. Ibid.

159. Ibid., 27.

Christ ensures an infinitely more effective ministry to human beings that cannot be said of merely human ancestral spirits. Thus, Bediako's understanding of Jesus as ancestor also surpasses the traditional Akan concept of the ancestor. For him: "Jesus Christ is the only real and true Ancestor and source of life for all mankind, fulfilling and transcending the benefits believed to be bestowed by lineage ancestors."[160]

It is clear from the discussion above that despite the attempts Bediako makes to expand the concept of the ancestor from the confines of a tribe or clan and to see the salvation offered by God in Christ to be unique and universal, Bediako is in a world that Barth will find difficult to inhabit. For Barth, the initiative is always with God, and what humans can do is only to respond in faith. Barth is not looking for an explanation of the Gospel but its proclamation. He declares:

> The language about God to be found in the Church is meant to be proclamation, so far as it is directed towards man in the form of preaching and sacrament, with the claim and in an atmosphere of expectation that in accordance with its commission it has to tell him the Word of God to be heard in faith.[161]

Barth states further that what the preacher or the theologian has to proclaim is already given, and the task of the theologian is to confirm it and call people to obedience to the demand it makes on them:

> The Word of God is God Himself in the proclamation of the Church of Jesus Christ. In so far as God gives the Church the commission to speak about Him, and the Church discharges this commission, it is God Himself who declares His revelation in His witnesses. The proclamation of the Church is pure doctrine when the human word spoken in it in confirmation of the biblical witness to revelation offers and creates obedience to the Word of God.[162]

Thus, for Barth, it is not a question of who Jesus is in traditional or customary terms. He would even see the work of Bediako and Pobee as moving away from the Word of God to the word of man, a movement that he had set himself up to resist. This is because unlike Bediako, who wants intentionally to begin with general revelation, Barth would begin only with

160. Ibid., 31.

161. Barth, *Church Dogmatics* I/1, 51.

162. Ibid., 743.

God's self- revelation in Jesus Christ. Christology is the lens through which he saw all other doctrines, including Creation:

> It is by Him, Jesus Christ, and for Him and to Him, that the universe is created as a theatre for God's dealing with man and man's dealings with God. The being of God is His being, and similarly the being of man is originally His being. And there is nothing that is not from Him and by Him and to Him. He is the Word of God in whose truth everything is disclosed and whose truth cannot be over-reached or conditioned by any other word.[163]

An Assessment of the Conversation

It is clear from the conversations we had facilitated between Barth and the two indigenous Akan theologians, Pobee and Bediako, that they are engaged in two different tasks. It is true that Barth's theology was also responding to what he saw as a crisis in his culture and he positioned himself to engage a theology that would make the Word of God incarnate speak relevantly to the situation. However, Barth's problem is that the gospel had been overly absorbed, domesticated, and distorted by the culture. Pobee and Bediako, on the contrary, in the post-colonial African context, were facing a situation in which the Gospel appeared to be foreign and alien to the culture into which it was brought during the missionary era. The power of the Gospel message was such that it was still making a significant impact on the life of the community. And yet, it was a European gospel in an African setting.

The struggle that Pobee and Bediako were engaging is to ask the question whether the universality of the Gospel message can indeed find genuine expression in African cultural concepts and traditions. Since the tasks were different, they appear to have had different starting points and assumptions that have made the conversation difficult.

Barth was so alienated by the way the Gospel was compromised within culture and German nationalism that he moved to the extreme of rejecting any form of natural theology or use of cultural elements for the interpretation of Christ. Clearly, Pobee and Bediako are in disagreement with Barth on this and are willing to look within the African cultural resources along with the Bible as sources for the construction of indigenous theology.

163. Barth, *Church Dogmatics* II/2, 94.

At the same time, Barth, as well as Pobee and Bediako, share a number of common concerns. The three theologians give central place to the Bible; they all see the centrality of Jesus Christ in the theological task. In addition, they are keen to affirm the humanity and divinity of Christ and the saving work God had done through him for all humankind. The conversation shows that the tasks that Christian theologians face at different times and places are not the same, but that there are some central symbols and themes that are essential for doing Christian theology and which are evident in their work.

The conversation also shows that there are limits to the freedom one could take in doing theology and that, by and large; it is the Bible that can keep the theologian accountable to the tradition. And yet, it is also clear that the approach to the Bible itself can be influenced by the task that the theologian seeks to undertake.

The conversation between Barth and the two theologians, however, is not on the central theme of the work of the two theologians whose primary interest is in the concept of the ancestor as a possible entry point to an Akan Christology. It is to this that we turn in the last chapter, to examine the strengths and weaknesses and to make some of our own proposals.

4

Conclusion: Towards an Akan Christology

Introduction

Our discussions in the earlier chapters have elucidated, among other issues, the African theologies articulated mainly with the ancestral paradigm. We have studied the theologies of the selected Akan theologians—John Pobee and Kwame Bediako which have pointed out the various agreements and disagreements in the application of the ancestral categories for the construction of African Christology. A conversation between these theologians and Karl Barth was also facilitated with the view to bring out some of the issues that are relevant for developing African theology in the context of the African realities and the theological tradition inherited by the churches in Africa.

In this chapter, some of the problems that are inherent in the proposals made by Pobee and Bediako in relation to churches in Africa and to the church universal are highlighted. We would then make some proposals for a possible Akan Christological endeavor that might meet the spiritual needs of the Akan people.

Toward a Method of Christological Exploration for Akan Theological Endeavor

In order to discover a method for Christological exploration for the Akan, we will begin with an important question that should inform our theological exploration: What kind of Christology can truly respond to African hopes and aspirations? For us, this question, though basic and primary, is very meaningful for any Christological endeavor in Africa today. We have noted above that the theologies developed thus far, with African cultural resources and a particular reading of the Bible in reality has not touched the spiritual universe of the Africans. They have also not become part of the life and teachings of the churches. We therefore begin with some of the elements that should be part of the theological endeavor in the African context.

The Local and the Universal

The first principle to consider in any *Christologia Akan* must be that it should be relevant to the Akan context and, at the same time, remain firmly rooted in the overall tradition of the church so that Christians in all parts of the world can look upon one another and accept one other. Despite all the cultural and other differences the churches in Africa are part of the one Church Universal. We are convinced that the African theological quest must be within the parameters of Jesus' prayer: "That they all may be one, so that the world may believe that you sent me" (John 17) which calls for oneness, a call for unity in our diverse contexts.

Two essential elements stand out from this statement. First, a theological evaluation of all theological traditions developed in Africa, including the ones that we have examined, must include the question whether they stay within some of the basic elements of the traditions of the church. Secondly, such an understanding of the traditions of the church means that theology could not arise only out of the cultural experiences of human life but also must respond to what we believe God has done in relation to all of human life. And, if we believe that our knowledge of what God has done for humankind is rooted primarily in the Biblical witness, then, this means that Akan theology should arises not only from the resources of the culture but also from the biblical witness of Jesus Christ. For this reason, many of the liberation, inculturation, and Africanization theologians have drawn so much criticism. Even though their theological efforts highlight the significance of African cultural elements for doing theology and are responsive to the needs of the Africans in the areas of poverty, hunger and deprivation, oppression and exploitation, they often fail because they do not make the necessary connection to biblical witness to Christ.

Further, one also needs to look closely in the African context to the relationship between the theological reflections in Africa and the reality of the Church. The Church is not only a historical reality from the past, but also a present reality that expresses the life of the Christian community today. We cannot, therefore, develop a Christology that does not take seriously the reality of the Church in Africa. Whatever Christology is developed for the Akan is to be done *within* the church and *for* the church. In so doing, one should also be aware that in Christian understanding, the Church is not just a human or sociological community, but one that understands itself as called by God for a purpose.

Role of the Bible

We should also take a closer look at what it means to say that African theology must be biblical. The Bible plays different roles in the theological traditions developed in different parts of the world. As far as Africa is concerned, the Bible continues to play the central role in Christian thinking, worship and spirituality. This leads us to our second main principle that whatever Christological principle we develop must be biblical; it is the Christian faith that we wish to communicate and none other. This is also important because despite the variety of theologies developed in different parts of the world, the Bible continues to remain the common heritage of the Christian Church. Therefore, it stands to reason that a Christology for the Akan must also remain within the boundaries of the biblical faith. Here we take a cue from Samuel Pobee's earlier comment that: "whatever we develop must be tested against the plumb-line of biblical faith."[1] And it has to respond to the question of the nature of the uniqueness of Christ that makes him relevant for the Akan across the centuries.

"Biblical basis" or "biblical faith" is difficult to define because the Bible has been subjected to many interpretations. Throughout history, very diverse theological traditions have claimed to have drawn their inspiration from the Bible. Further, the bible has been subjected to critical study with the results that there is no agreement among theologians and biblical scholars on which parts or teachings of the Bible are more central to the Christian faith.

Notwithstanding the problems involved, the church had created and adopted the Bible as a canon that constitutes the teachings that set

1. Pobee, *Toward an African Theology*, 83.

the boundaries of the Christian faith. The churches in Africa, based on the teachings of the missionaries who brought the faith to them, have accepted the whole Bible, the Old and the New Testaments, as defining the faith. Today, it would be difficult for them to accept a teaching as 'Christian' unless they are helped to see that it arises from or is based on the Bible. It is important that they are shown why a teaching, even if it is interpreted with symbols and concepts of the African tradition, are consistent with what the Bible has to say on it.

For the purpose of this project, we would identify what we consider to be some of the elements that a Christian in Africa would see as setting the boundaries of the faith. First among them is the belief in the oneness of God as the creator of the whole universe and as one who cares for all people. The second would be the belief that this God had revealed himself to the world in Jesus Christ, and that it is something that is unique in that God offers God's salvation to the world through him. The belief in Jesus Christ, for the African, includes that he was incarnated through Virgin Mary, that he suffered and died for us on the cross, and that he rose again from the dead and is with God. It would also involve the belief that he is active in the world through the power of the Holy Spirit and that he has called the church into being as witnesses to him. Theologically, it also means that the Bible teaches the humanity and divinity of Jesus Christ. Any Christology that has attempted to interpret Jesus only in human terms would be seen in Africa as non-biblical.

We recognize that theologians give different weight to different aspects of the above affirmations, but by "biblical" we mean that theology needs to take the above as some of the key assumptions for doing theology. Even if we were to begin with the full humanity of Christ as the starting point for doing Christology, in Africa, the expectation would be that it should also affirm the divinity of Christ for it to be biblical. Pobee had put the emphasis on both the humanity and divinity of Christ, but he ends up with a Christology where Jesus' divine status appears to be compromised. The question is whether Pobee lives up to the "biblical plumb line he set for himself." We shall discuss this later in the chapter.

It is in this respect that Barth brings an important challenge to Akan Christology, by placing the primacy of the act of God, it communicates in scripture and is understood as witness to the Word of God as the reason and source for doing theology. In this view, Christology begins with God's decisive action. It is not a Christology of humankind about God, but a response to the initiative taken by God. Christology thus is not an abstract reflection but must constitute the appropriate response on the part of humans to God that speaks through the mediation of Scripture and preaching (as noted in his three-fold form of the Word of God) to humanity.

This is also the main burden of the Bible, where prophets do not speak on their own authority but speak in response to God's call. Within this thinking, human beings cannot by their own effort reach out to God; it is God who reaches out to humankind in a concrete and practical way for their salvation from sin and guilt, deliverance from the powers of darkness, and restoration of health and soundness. If this, as Barth would argue, is the main focus of the Biblical witness, one needs to ask whether Christology done in Africa can so easily move away from this orientation.

However, Barth's methodology is only one of the possible ways to do theology. The indigenous theologians in many cultures have challenged Barth's methodology and have insisted on beginning with the human realities in which they find themselves. The theologians of Africa have also insisted that they begin with life situations and use indigenous categories and symbols to expound the faith. We have no problem with this different starting point. However, this makes it all the more important that they stay within an overall biblical framework in their theology.

In the light of the above, our proposals do not begin where Karl Barth does but, in fact, constitute some level of disagreement with him with regard to the relevance to the spiritual wants and desires of the Akan, as the primary guiding principle for an authentic African Christology and natural revelation as ground for the Akan knowledge of *Onyame* to constitute a genuine knowledge of the God of the bible. This also points out that the Akan's traditional knowledge of the gospel of Jesus Christ is, indeed, knowledge of the God of the Bible and so of the God known in Jesus Christ.

Gospel and Culture

Our third main principle is that all indigenization, adaptation, inculturation, and Africanization of Christology should address actual spiritual realities of the people. Nothing rings home in the ears of the Akan more than a spiritual force that can operate and overcome the forces of darkness. The Ancestor paradigm, while serving other purposes, does not serve this important purpose. According to tradition, the ancestors do not have such power over the forces of evil. This means that one has to exercise restraint in the application of the so-called genuine African categories for the construction of Christology in African context.

This raises an important question in relation to the Gospel and culture. Much of the indigenous theologies look primarily at how the Gospel can be transformed in the context of the culture. However, long debates on Gospel and Culture speak of a double movement. While the presentation of the Gospel which comes in the Western mode into Africa needs to be transformed, the encounter of the Gospel should also result in the critical transformation of the cultures that Christ encounters. There is no need for romantic notions about culture because all religions and cultures are ambiguous. This is the point that eludes many indigenous theologians in their work. The re-adaptation of Jesus Christ into our cultures does not necessarily mean reducing Jesus Christ to simply fit into a particular cultural mode.

For instance, the gods or the lesser deities are more powerful in the Akan spiritual universe than the ancestors. Akans look for a reality that can overpower the nefarious power and activities of these lesser deities or the spiritual beings. If Jesus Christ is subordinated to the level of Ancestor, how can he, in any way, destroy the works of these lesser deities or the spiritual beings? The Akan, therefore, expects a Christology in which Jesus Christ will be seen to wield that supernatural power to deal with evil power, magic, sorcery, or witchcraft that plagues the society. According to Mbiti, "when something goes wrong in the welfare of the individual or his family, he immediately wonders who has caused it to happen."[2] It is common belief that retrogression, disaster, or some forms of accidents are caused by people who dabble in and use evil magic, sorcery, or witchcraft. If the Akan would understand Christology, it will be a type that has the power to overcome and deal with such evil forces.

By interpreting Jesus as the ancestor, one reduces him to the level of parent and grandparent, which would leave the Akan with little or no interest in him. When Christ is forced into existing cultural types and his significance is defined only within the cultural milieu, it is difficult to articulate the fullness of what the Gospel message has to say about him and his significance. As long as Akan Christology presents Christ with the power to heal from disease (because the Akan has medicine men who cure), and deliver people from the power of darkness and evil forces (because there are a lot of priests and priestesses who exorcise) he would be welcomed.

2. Mbiti, *Introduction to African Religion*, 166.

Thus the presentation of Jesus Christ in cultural symbols should do full justice to the expectations Akans have of a deliverer or savior.

We understand that the concept of the ancestor, among other cultural symbols among the Akan, lends itself towards developing a Christology. This is the reasons why not only Pobee and Bediako but, also, some other theologians in Africa have attempted to develop a Christology around this concept. However, we want to argue that there are limitations to a Christology that seeks to make Jesus Christ conform to the image of the ancestor. We would argue this from two angles. In the first instance, what we know about Christ from the biblical witness does not permit us to attribute ancestor-ship to him. It would be difficult for an Akan to accept him as an ancestor. Secondly, we would also argue, that the biblical witness that we have of Jesus and, what we believe God to have accomplished through him, will not fit into the category of the ancestor.

Christ and the Trinity

Our last reflection on the principles for the development of the Akan Christological formula is on the Trinitarian faith of the church. The Akan Christology that sees Jesus Christ as the ancestor may consciously move towards emphasizing the humanity of Christ. Yet, in so doing, we would move away from the traditions of the church that has held on to some understanding of the divinity of Christ, as an important element of Christology. The concept of the Trinity was developed in an attempt to avoid any ontological subordination of Jesus Christ to the Supreme Being. The importance of attributing divinity to Christ in the tradition has also to do with the work of Christ in the salvation of the world. Presenting Christ as the savior is also in the interest of Pobee and Bediako. We believe that according the ancestor position to him does not serve this purpose.

In the African tradition, the ancestor is subordinated to the Supreme Being, and therefore, any ancestral categorization does not fully provide adequate ground to speak of the divinity of Christ in a meaningful way. Once Christ is framed in the ancestral image, he cannot, at the same time, have equal status with the Supreme Being or *Onyankopong*, the Creator and sustainer of the universe. The Biblical interpretations of Christ have also struggled with the issue, as seen in the kenotic passage in Philippians, which says that Jesus Christ being God thought it not robbery to be equal to God but humbled himself and took the form of humankind. And yet, the passage goes on to speak about Christ's elevation again to the high level so that he is given the name above every name so that every knee, in heaven and earth would bow before him. The image of the ancestor shuts down the possibility of an African cultural exploration of the meaning of the Divinity of Christ.

Some Factors Essential for Doing Akan Theology

Our point of departure for the method of Christological exploration, therefore, will not be the category of the ancestor, Akan proverbs and sayings, as most of the elements of Akan culture do not lend themselves to be developed for an adequate representation of Christ to the Akan. Rather, we turn to the Akan concept of God or the Supreme Being among the Akan who is believed to be the same God that the Bible also talks about. It is a common belief of all Africans that "God created the universe, sustains it, provides for it, rules and controls it."[3] According to John Mbiti, some of the traditions even hold that "God created the universe out of nothing."[4] Again, in most African societies he is believed to be "the Molder, Begetter, Bearer, Maker, Potter, Fashioner, Architect, Carpenter, Originator, Constructor and so on."[5]

Right from the introduction of Christianity, the Akan Christian easily understood who Jesus Christ was in God. This is because the works and attributes of Jesus Christ taught by the missionaries were very similar to what the indigenous people knew about the Supreme Being. Almost everything the early Akan Christians learned about Jesus Christ was just what they had known and experienced of the Supreme Being. Moral attributes such as "goodness, love, kindness, holiness and righteousness, faithfulness, and mercifulness"[6] were ascribed to the Supreme Being. In addition, all of the three eternal and intrinsic attributes of "omnipotence, omniscience, and omnipresence with the ideas of sovereignty, limitlessness and self-existence and the first cause of all things"[7] are all attributed to the one and only Supreme Being.

3. Ibid., 51–52.

4. Ibid., 52.

5. Ibid., 49.

6. Ibid., 54–55.

7. Mbiti, *African Religions and Philosophy*, 30–31; Mbiti, *Introduction to African Religion*, 56–57.

Ever since the missions began among the Akan people, they were taught that Jesus Christ bore all these attributes, which meant that Jesus Christ was of the Supreme Being. This simple understanding is what made evangelization of the Akan very easy. Even many traditional priests left their shrines to join the church. Since the Akan related creation to the Supreme Being, even to the traditionalists, John's statement that Jesus, as the Logos, was the creator "through whom all things were made, and without whom nothing was made" (John 1:3) would not have been difficult to comprehend.

Another factor worth mentioning is that since the coming of Christianity into the Akan territory over two hundred years ago, it has grown from strength to strength until it has taken center stage in the religious life of Africa. Pointing to this reality, Andrews Walls of the Center for the Study of Christianity in the Non-Western World at the University of Edinburgh, remarks: "the center of gravity of Christianity has shifted from the Northern Hemisphere to the Southern Hemisphere."[8] This remark is an indication of the degree to which Christianity has in the Southern Hemisphere, in general, and in Africa, in particular. The kind of theological or spiritual factors that are facilitating and expediting the advancement of Christianity in Africa must necessarily be part of developing any Christological endeavor. There is no doubt that Jesus Christ already has a central place in African churches.

Because of this, one might question the urgency of the Christological question discussed by Appiah-Kubi that we have discussed in the previous chapters. For the sake of clarity, we would like to re-quote the entire statement:

> How can I sing the Lord's song in a strange land, (in a strange language, in a strange thought, in a strange ideology)?' (cf. Psalm 137:4) For more than a decade now the cry of the psalmist has been the cry of many African Christians. We demand to serve the Lord in our own terms and without being turned into Euro-American or Semitic bastards before we do so. That the Gospel has come to remain in Africa cannot be denied, but now our theological reflections must be addressed to the real contextual African situations. Our question must not be what Karl Barth, Karl Rahner, or any other Karl has to say, but rather what God would have us do in our living concrete condition. For too long African Christian theologians and scholars have been preoccupied with what missionary A

8. Walls, "Expansion of Christianity."

> or theologian B or Scholar C has told us about God and the Lord Jesus Christ. ...the struggle of African theologians, scholars, and other Christians in ventures such as this...is to find a theology that speaks to our people where we are, to enable us to answer the critical question of our Lord Jesus Christ: Who do you (African Christians) say that I am? [9]

We do not think that the Christological question is about "Who is he?" Rather, one needs to work on a wider theological task of placing Jesus Christ in relation to the Supreme Being. We think that our question should rather stand as follows: How do we understand the person and work of Christ in relation to the Supreme Being, acknowledged and worshipped in Africa, long before the coming of the missionaries? We note that in the Akan oral tradition, God, the Supreme Being, is known as spirit, invisible, and everlasting. According to Mbiti, some call the Supreme Being, "the Spirit, or the Fathomless Spirit."[10]

It is also important to be clear about the purpose of the Christological task. In the African context, the purpose of Christology is not merely an intellectual struggle to arrive at a theoretical understanding about Jesus Christ in the cultural idiom of the people. Rather, the purpose needs to build commitment and faith in Jesus Christ. The theologian, himself, needs to be aware that the task is for and on behalf of the church and to help the people in their daily struggles. Therefore, the theological effort must not only seek to build spiritual commitment but also must arise from such commitment—something that both Pobee and Bediako also seek in different ways.

In the history of the church, some of the great theologians of the past and present such as St. Augustine, St. Thomas Aquinas, Karl Barth, Karl Rahner, H. de Lubac, Paul Tillich and others, became great theologians because they accepted the demands of thought and action imposed on them by their own concrete situation. Thus, here, it may not necessarily be that we follow the questions and the thought pattern of the above mentioned theologians. Rather, what we seek to imply here is that African theology should also emerge out of deep struggle with the spiritual challenges faced by the African people.

Therefore, relevant African theology should not only be "African" but should also respond to the spiritual struggles of the African people.

9. Appiah-Kubi and Torres, *African Theology Enroute*, viii.

10. Mbiti, *Introduction to African Religion*, 59.

Because of this, Christ will be viewed in Akan culture in 'practical terms.' The practicality of Jesus Christ must be demonstrated by the power he has over the spirit of the sea, water, rock, mountains, mermaids, witches, wizards, cosmic powers and the other spiritual hosts of wickedness. No god (divinities) or lesser deities, either of high or low status, has the capacity to handle the myriad of evil spiritual forces inhabiting the spiritual universe of the ethnic Akan. Unless Jesus Christ is seen as being able to accomplish the work of overcoming these evil forces, he cannot be fully comprehended in the Akan spiritual thought and more so cannot inhabit the spiritual universe of the Akan.

For this reason some of the elements of the teachings about Christ in some of the traditional theologies would speak directly to the Akan people. They would easily understand the notion of the *Logos* condescending to become flesh for the sake of the people. They would accept the notion that he took flesh and blood so that through his death, he would destroy the one who has power over death, that is, the Devil, and release those who, through fear of death, were subject to bondage. Deliverance from spiritual bondage is the most sought after thing in the Akan world and to find Jesus Christ's capacity to deal with it will work well for the Akan believer. Thus, the Word *(Logos)* taking flesh is meaningful to the Akan.

Akans believe that some of these spirits are dangerous to the prosperity and progress of the individual. The Akan is always seeking a force that can truly destroy these wicked and mysterious forces, which may be inborn in a person, inherited, or acquired in various ways. These beliefs and fears can be used to manipulate some people without their awareness. Those who engage in witchcraft, for example, whether deliberately or out of their own ignorance exploit these fears. It is important that those who engage in doing African theology have the essential tools necessary to understand the psychological, sociological, and religious realities that are at play in shaping the spiritual quests of the people.

Another factor that is essential for doing Akan theology is the community involvement of the African theologian. The theologian, in Akan thinking, does theology on behalf of the community and for its benefit. This demands that the theologians be involved in their community and their social participation must be as active as possible. Such participation will put the theologians in a position to gain a deeper grasp of the cultural issues posed by their community and the living conditions of their contemporaries. This will also help the theologians to pay due attention to the real questions raised by the people and to the appearance of new values in a given society.

Finally, the Akan expect that those who do theology or Christology are to be deeply involved in the ecclesial life of the church. One of the facets of African Religious thought is the belief in religious officials or leaders. These are mostly trained people who conduct religious matters such as ceremonies, sacrifices, official prayers and divination. They are deeply involved in all the activities in which they officiate. Writing about African religious officials and leaders, John Mbiti comments as follows:

> They know more about religious affairs than other people, and are respected by their community. They hold offices as priest, rainmakers, ritual elders, diviners, medicine men, and even kings and rulers. These officials may or may not be paid for their duties, but in most cases people give them presents and gifts to show their gratitude.[11]

Thus, we see that the Akan Christian convert will expect the theologian to hold office in the community of faith. The theologian is not expected to be an outsider. As far as he or she is the one who is the expert in the issues of the development of the faith community, he or she must necessarily be part and parcel of that community. Again, Mbiti reveals the importance of religious officials, which supports our assertion of the value of the theologian for the Akan believer:

> Without them, religious activities would neither survive nor function properly, and much of the religious wisdom of the people would be forgotten. They are specialists and experts in religious matters; they are the human keepers of the religious heritage. They are an essential part of the African Religion since without them it would grind to a halt and people would not benefit from it in practical terms.[12]

The value of the theologian is, therefore, measured according to his or her involvement and participation in church. Thus, we see the value and commitment of both Pobee and Bediako who demonstrated such commitments in the Ghanaian Anglican and Presbyterian Churches respectively. In addition, African theologians are expected to preserve and sustain the

11. Mbiti, *Introduction to African Religion*, 12.

12. Ibid., 12

church's heritage. On this note, we now go further into the exploration of some proposals for Christology in the Akan theological endeavor.

Some Proposals for Christology in Akan Theological Endeavor

Having outlined some of the factors essential for developing Christology in the Akan context we now move on to make some proposals for African theology in general and specifically for Akan Christology. Here, we work on three issues that facilitate the emergence of Akan Christology. These include the reduction of the foreignness of the church, the need to enrich the concept of community that is central to African life and a proposal for an understanding of the meaning and significance of Christ that speaks to the longings of the Akan people. We expect that these three factors will cohere into forming a meaningful Christology for the Akan group of people.

Foreignness of the Church

The importance of reducing the foreign aspect of the church is without question one of the foremost mechanisms through which the church in African can truly be indigenized. In order to make the church truly African, much has to be done in the areas of indigenization of the ethos, preaching, worship and the general liturgical life of the Church. We must draw from the cultural and traditional dimensions of those elements that enhance the worship life of the church in Africa. Use of indigenous language will be an important assert in this effort. Thus, Kwame Bediako's argument in support of "vernacularization,"[13] is very helpful.

This is based on the belief that all genuine theology has an inalienable relationship to worship. A genuine Akan theology and Christology can arise only in the context of a church and worship which is rooted in the Akan culture. Theology that arises outside this context may be intellectually stimulating, but it would not speak to the hearts and minds of the Akan people. In other words, Akan Christology must arise from and be rooted in the Akan church and worship life. This means that the Akan language must be used in church proclamation, worship, and all practices. Songs of worship in the English Language must all be translated into Akan languages just as the Bible is translated in some languages.

13. Bediako, *Jesus in African Culture*, 119.

The missionaries may have distorted Christianity, but not the Gospel. Indeed, Christianity may have been at the service of colonial and cultural imperialists, but not the Gospel. Christianity may have been and was, indeed, foreign, but not the Gospel. According to Bediako, it is the failure to distinguish Christianity from the Gospel that has caused African theologians to be unduly "haunted by the foreignness of Christianity, and having started from that foreignness, were never able to arrive at indigeneity."[14] For Bediako, the whole point rests on a fallacious premise. Yet, apart from asserting the falsity of the premise, Bediako's approach does not adequately addresses the issue the way he claims to pursue. But the point is that even in today's Akan church, the foreignness of Christianity is still evident. Most Akan Christians continue to experience Christianity as foreign. Thus, indigenization of the ethos of the church and its worship life is our foremost task.

Enriching the Understanding of Community

Secondly, one of the greatest contributions that African cultures can bring into the Christian Faith is the profound understanding of community and its concept of ancestral veneration. At the same time, the Christian theology also has much to say about community. The church is not only a sociological grouping but is also the body of Christ. In Christian understanding, the church as a whole community is the inheritor of the mission and ministry of the church.

St. Paul speaks of the church as body in which all the members belong to one another and that the gifts anyone within the community has is for the benefit of all. Further, the church as the community is understood as the foretaste of the eschatological hope for the whole human community. Thus, Christian theology has much to contribute to the already rich understanding of community within the Akan culture. Because of this close relationship between the church and Christ, it is inappropriate to do a Christology in the African context that is not rooted in a strong teaching on community. At the same time, the temptation in Africa is for the tribe or a community around a specific cultural group to become a community defined against other tribes and communities. One of the contributions that the Christian faith can make is to help the church in Africa to widen its understanding of community.

14. Ibid., 117.

The Akan practice of admiration of ancestors can also make an enormous contribution, especially to the Protestant understanding of the church as a community. Protestant theology has not adequately developed the concept of the communion of saints that transcends the barrier of death. Even though the tradition is aware that the church is a community that includes the ancestors, it has not quite found a way to express this faith or to develop the theological significance of that faith.

Probably, within the whole concept of ancestors we may be able to delineate the relationship between the church militant and the church triumphant. It is our view that the use of the image of the ancestor is inadequate to develop a strong Christology. But it can be very useful to further develop our understanding of the church that transcends all barriers of class, tribe, nation and even the boundaries of death.

Before we move to make some proposal on the interpretation of Christ in the Akan culture, one should be aware that African theology must also be done within the context of the teachings of the independent and non-denominational Protestant, Pentecostal, and Charismatic churches. Over the last fifty years, the teachings and ethos of these churches have taken the center stage of Christianity in Ghana.

These teachings point in the direction of deliverance, restoration, healing, prosperity, justification, sanctification, salvation, and Christian character. They all find their expression in the one person, Jesus Christ. The attempt of these churches to maintain a preaching that focuses on Jesus Christ cannot be overemphasized. The concept of faith in Jesus Christ is that which gives hope to the Akan Christian. Our Christological proposals, therefore, need to be made with the awareness of this reality.

Jesus as One Who Incarnates Mediation

We have argued that understanding of Jesus in terms of ancestral veneration does not meet the biblical witness to Jesus Christ as one in whom God revealed himself. More specifically, we find that the interpretations that Pobee and Bediako have given do not do full justice to their own commitment to uphold the humanity and divinity of Christ. This inadequacy arises, as stated earlier, from two sources. To begin with, the Akan would not find the marks of the ancestor in Jesus. As stated earlier, not all Akan who die are elevated to be ancestors. They must have had a full life to an appreciable age; they must have had children; and should not have had a violent death as Jesus had. Therefore, while the Akan can understand Jesus' violent death in terms of atonement and may even look up to the cross as a sign of their salvation, and Jesus, as their savior, it would be difficult to easily associate him with an ancestor in the manner that both Pobee and Bediako have appropriated. Neither Pobee nor Bediako do the necessary reinterpretation of the life of Jesus or of the concept of the ancestor to deal with this deficit.

Again, the ancestor concept does not do justice to Jesus' divinity, because the ancestor, in Akan thinking, is lower than the gods and divinities, which are themselves, lower than the Supreme Being. Thus, the ancestor is far removed from the Supreme Being and do not carry the weight of divinity ascribed to him. Neither of them, but especially Pobee, appears to re-interpret the concept to be able to meet these issues. This is surprising because both of them, in theory, are committed to the humanity and divinity of Christ as essential elements of Christology.

Nonetheless, the ancestor category could have been applied to Jesus Christ from the point of view of the Supreme Being—*Onyame*. This is because in traditional thought, it is god—*Onyam*e who is referred to as "Grand Ancestor." this is pointed out by Kofi Asare Opoku as stated in chapter two: "*Tetekwaframoa*—he who is there now as from ancient times; *Nana*—Grand Ancestor."[15] This means Pobee and Bediako could employ the grand ancestor category to bring out who Jesus Christ is in terms of his divinity depicting his pre-incarnation and pre-existence. Appropriating Jesus Christ in this manner could also overcome some of the limitations found in the works of the two Akan theologians.

A study of the Akan cosmology in the earlier chapters identified the Akan Supreme Being as *Onyankopong, Oboadee* or Creator and Sustainer of the universe. In Akan thinking, the whole spiritual universe is based on the Supreme Being. As mentioned above, venerated as they are, ancestors do not have the kind of reality or access to the Supreme Being to be of Christological interest. They also do not have the power to resolve the problems of Akan life because they do not have the role of mediating between the Akan and the Supreme Being.

The absence of any mediating power between the Akan and the Supreme Being gives rise to an enormous amount of superstition among the Akan. Here I do not mean by superstition the reality of the Akan spiritual world but the belief that witchcraft, mediums, spiritual forces behind objects etc. can play this role of mediation. This belief is exploited by those

15. Opoku, *West African Traditional Religion*, 15.

who falsely claim to have the power and access to the Supreme Being or to the lesser divinities through these media. This reality, however, shows that what the Akan longs for is someone who can mediate the Supreme Being to them.

The challenge and opportunity to Akan Christology therefore is to interpret the significance of Jesus Christ as a kind of mediator that is distinctively different from the mediations that have been proposed within the culture with traditional categories. The concept of the Grand Ancestor does not overcome some of the limitations that we have discussed about the ancestor category to interpret Christ. I have, however, chosen to go beyond it to interpret Christ primarily in terms of mediation so that the Akan can be assured of the full and immediate presence of the Supreme Being among them. Therefore, one of the challenges of African Christianity will be to develop a concept of Jesus Christ as mediator that goes beyond the classical understanding of Jesus Christ as mediator to one in whom the fullness of the Supreme Being is made accessible to the people.

The concept of mediation and an understanding of Christ as mediator are not new to Christology. But what is needed in the Akan context is a concept of mediation that goes well beyond the traditional concepts of mediation. In the Western tradition, meditation is primarily drawn from the legal metaphor which relates primarily to sin and guilt. The African understanding of mediator also has a mediatorial function only in terms of prayers and intercessions. In doing Akan Christology, perhaps we should turn to Paul's vision of Christ in II Corinthians 5, which speaks about the fact that "God was in Christ." This understanding of the fullness of God being made available in concrete terms would be the function of Christology within the Akan tradition.

What we need is to interpret Christ as One in whom the Supreme Being has come to dwell within the community and this full presence of God among them is mediated in Christ. "In him the fullness of God has come to dwell with you, so that no powers of earth or sky can hurt you" would be the message that would give confidence to the Akan. By thinking of the Supreme Being being present in Christ for the people, and by looking at Christ as mediating the fullness of the Supreme Being, we meet some of the issues that have prompted the need for a Trinitarian doctrine. It is also easy to move from this to speak of the presence of the Supreme Being in Christ as the power of the Spirit that we experience in our lives.

These need much further elaboration, but this move would help the Akan to overcome the fears of the spirit world; it would help them to overcome the sense of remoteness they feel from the Supreme Being; it would also undermine the powers of the nefarious activities that claim to mediate between them and the Supreme Being.

This can then move us beyond the classical controversies over the humanity and divinity of Christ and speak in terms of actualization of the presence of the Supreme Being within the community. In other words, Akan Christology should not be built on mediation in the sense of a go-between, but as a reality through which the Supreme Being dwells with the people so that, as mentioned above, their fears and anxieties are put to rest—this is what they crave for in a Savior. Jesus Christ, in this thinking, would be seen as One in whom the presence of God with the people would be celebrated and around whom a community of faith could be built.

Much more work needs to be done to further develop this concept and to give it a fuller Christological profile. This, however, lies beyond the scope of what we had set out to do and needs to remain a project for the future.

APPENDIX A

The "No!" and "Yes!"—To Jesus Christ as Ancestor

Introduction

THE ISSUE OF INTERPRETING Jesus as ancestor for the development of an Akan Christology has been affirmed and contested for a long period. There are those who say emphatically 'no' to Jesus being ancestor and those who say emphatically 'yes.' Therefore, we make an addendum to the dissertation that introduces a section where we bring out some of the issues from an interview conducted by Diane Stinton.

Diane B. Stinton, a Canadian with a PhD from the Center for the Study of Christianity in the Non-Western World at the University of Edinburgh, is professor of theology at Daystar University, Nairobi, Kenya. In her book, *Jesus of Africa: Voices of Contemporary African Christology,* she explores Christologies from French and English- speaking African scholars and clergy while also reporting on how African lay people view Jesus. It is the combination of some of the views about whether or not Jesus Christ is our ancestor from the laity, clergy and theologians of African descent that we turn to her book. In her concluding statement she pointed that:

> Finally, the fact that African Christians portray local 'faces' of Jesus, articulating what they find appealing and relevant in him, forms a significant contribution to world Christianity. The fundament reality is that no single cultural context can claim a monopoly on understanding Jesus Christ. Rather, the multiplicity of Christological images arising in African enhances the discovery of

> the fullness of Christ, which transcends all cultural constructs of the gospel.[1]

The arguments, complexities and ambiguities relating to the subject-matter of Jesus Christ as Ancestor have been extensively presented by many of the leading African theological and philosophical studies most prominently by John Pobee's *Toward African Theology* (1979), Kwame Bediako's *Jesus in Africa: The Christian Gospel in African History and Experience.* Also prominently featuring Jesus as Ancestor are the theological works of the Tanzanian Catholic theologian, Charles Nyamiti's *Christ as our ancestor,* and Benezet Bujo's *Christmas: God Becomes Man in Black Africa.*

Though the works of some of these theologians are beyond the scope of this research, we have put some excerpts here with the intent that readers understand Kwame Bediako and John Pobee are not alone. Also, we have included some of the interviews conducted by Diane Stinton and recorded in her book about those who object to the idea of Jesus Christ as Ancestor for various reasons as well as those who welcome it. Thus, in this section, we will outline what some African theologians, non-theologians, pastors and laity are saying about the ancestor-ship of Jesus that give them enough reason to either objectively or subjectively declare emphatically "No!" or "Yes!" to Jesus Christ as Ancestor.

One of the voices, who happens to be a doyen of religious tradition, is the Ghanaian Catholic theologian and retired priest, Archbishop Emeritus Peter Kwasi Sarpong. He postulates: "the ancestor is very restrictive because it is an ethnocentric concept."[2] According to Archbishop Emeritus Sarpong, "You don't have the ancestors of the Asantes; you have the ancestors for the clans. My father is my ancestor; he's not your ancestor. And so before you adopt Jesus as an ancestor, you must be able first of all to convince the whole world that Christians are one family."[3] In his own book, *Asante Christology,* Kwasi Sarpong develops his thought around the characteristics of the Asante Kings who established the Asante Kingdom and the new Kingdom that Jesus Christ established. But he does not use the concept of ancestors to develop a Christology because for him it would be an overly ethnocentric Christology.

Diane Stinton points out that even though Archbishop Sarpong admits that using the ancestral category to define Christology could be done,

1. Stinton, *Jesus of Africa*, 253.
2. Kwesi Sarpong, quoted in Stinton, *Jesus of Africa*, 132.
3. Ibid.

he cautions using the African family as a model for the church. Here is his full statement:

> It can be very good and it can be very dangerous, in the sense that the African family is characterized by love, sharing, sensitivity to one another, sharing problems, joint ownership of property, and so on. These are all excellent things. But, at the same time, the African family excludes other families. It's very ethnocentric. And what is happening in the African world, in Rwanda, in Burundi, is all an enlargement of the idea of the African family. The person who is outside my family is not as important as those in my family. I can band together with my own family members against another person from another family. When somebody from my family has done something, no matter how obnoxious, I support him or her, you see? So whereas the concept of the family can be used beautifully as for the church, in some respects it can be very dangerous.[4]

However, Ghanaian Catholic Bishop Palmer-Buckle attested to the following:

> Because I grew up in a Christian environment, the role of the ancestors was overshadowed already at a very early age by the saints on the Catholic faith and by Jesus Christ. So I've never had a very big, call it reverence of ancestors as such. But I grew up in Accra. Maybe that's another negative aspect of it that I grew up in the urban area, so something like pouring libation, calling on the ancestors, something like a stool, ancestral stools, never played much of a role in my life.[5]

Another objection is raised on the grounds that Jesus Christ as a person does not qualify on the grounds of traditional merits. Diane Stinton's research points this out clearly: "In addition to physical lineage, objections were raised on the grounds that Jesus did not fulfill the traditional requirements of an ancestor in terms of age, marriage, and offspring."[6] She points out what a Kenyan Protestant lay person Ole Ronkei, of the Maasai ethnic group maintains:

> Christ can't be an ancestor! No! How can he be? He was a young kid—culturally speaking. An ancestor has this connotation of age, where I come from. You need to reach a certain stage, you

4. Ibid.
5. Ibid., 130.
6. Ibid.

> pass away, and we classify you as one of our ancestors. If a young person dies, he will just go into historical oblivion! An ancestor is somebody who is here, he's one of us, born, raised his own family until he passed away, and so we're looking at him as an ancestor as a line that we've come through. Then Christ even becomes more problematic. He didn't have a wife! He didn't have children! Where are the offspring? Ancestor! It is very problematic where I come from.[7]

Obviously this sentiment expressed by an East African ethnic person runs through the entire Africa. The Akan has the same traditional requirements for the determination of who an ancestor is. This is not to admit that the ultimate objective of Africans is to one day become an ancestor. In the traditional thought of the Akan, a man should live a full life and die before he can attain ancestor status. Full life here means having a wife or wives and biological child or children before death. Within this understanding, Jesus does not qualify as Ancestor.

Another point that Diane Stinton's interview reveals is the requirement of a 'good death': "One last requirement traditionally held for African ancestors is a 'good death.'[8] Jesus died on the cross; he was hung. Not only a death of this nature but also, in some cases, accidental deaths are not considered 'good death.' Diane Stinton points out a question posed by a Ghanaian woman named Asabea: "Would Jesus' death be considered so (good death) in African understanding . . . unless it was underscored as a sacrificial death."[9]

Those who condemned Jesus Christ death on the cross found him guilty of high treason. He was considered a revolutionary in the eyes of the traditional government of his time. He was single, gathered men around him; he claimed to announce a new Kingdom and had thoughts, insights and understanding for life that challenged the traditional views of his time. His ideas and philosophy challenged the status quo, and all of his acts went directly opposite the rulers of his day. Even if these were legitimate actions on the part of one who wanted to bring about a newer and fuller understanding of life, they are not associated with one who would be hailed as an ancestor.

7. Ibid., 132–33.

8. Ibid., 133.

9. Ibid.

As long as Jesus is seen as an ordinary man like one of us, he would not qualify as ancestor on the basis of African traditionally acclaimed laws and requirements of ancestor-hood. On the issue of 'sacrificial death,' as pointed out in Asabea's comments above, being 'sacrificial' would not, in itself, be seen as a qualification for an ancestor; it would be something that will be held in high regard, but would not be seen as consideration for Ancestor-ship.

Another point that will raise theological problems according to Diane Stinton, is that the characteristics of ancestors are very different to those associated with Jesus. She points out some of them from the comments provided by those whom she interviewed:

> Kenyan Protestant Bishop Kivunzi and Ghanaian Protestant clergyman Oduro both stressed that ancestors are creatures while Jesus is the creator of the ancestors; hence, he cannot even be called ancestor par excellence. Ghanaian PACWA member Florence Y. B. Yeboah added that although Jesus represents believers in heaven, he does so as creator and not as an ancestor from who she comes. Therefore 'even though he's condescended to come and dwell within us, he's still our Lord, our creator, our maker.[10]

Thus those whom she interviewed point to the fact that Jesus is known as the creator of the ancestors. If he is the creator of the ancestors, then he could not be considered an ancestor himself. Again, if Christ is the creator of the ancestors then he cannot "displace the mediatorial functions of our natural 'spirit fathers'"[11] as intimated by Kwame Bediako. Some may argue that because Jesus was truly human, it is possible for him to become an ancestor. However, we cannot depend on his humanity alone to give him the ancestral status. The issue of Jesus as ancestor par excellence is the position of Benezet Bujo's theology and the interviewee reacts against that assertion.

Another most common objection which we have indicated already above is the point that ancestors are "dead and buried while Jesus is alive."[12] Kenyan Archbishop David Gitari, according to Diane Stintion says: "to the African, the living and the dead are very important. They are part of the family. But Jesus died and rose again, and he's living. Therefore he is more

10. Ibid.

11. Bediako, *Jesus in African Culture*, 26.

12. Stinton, *Jesus of Africa*, 133.

than an ancestor."[13] Thus the fact of Jesus' resurrection separates him from what we know and accept as ancestor:

> I would picture him as rather much bigger than an ancestor. I see ancestors as, in the traditional concept, living in ghost land—vaguely alive, but hardly having bodies and not being able to interact with people. Jesus as ancestor would only mean to me that he's died and gone, but my difficulty with the use of that word ancestor for Jesus Christ has to do with my understanding of who Jesus is. You see, he died, but he rose again! And therefore I can't relate with ancestors, but can relate with Christ.[14]

Yet another Kenyan Catholic lay man Wanjohi pointed out to Diane Stinton that Jesus as ancestor does not make much impact on him personally because for him Jesus had knowledge which surpasses any knowledge that an ancestor would have.[15] Similarly, Ole Ronkei, in reference to the Old Testament approach to prayer, which points to God as "the God of Abraham, the God of Isaac, the God of Jacob" to signify the ongoing covenant relationship with him, says:

> We pray exactly the same way to the God of our forefathers. Then we name them, according to the generations, not an individual person. I think you say, "The God of Isaac," and you're talking about this Isaac and his own entire generation. But, we talk about it in terms of those age groups. So, we say, "The God of that age group, and the God of the next age group," to show that we have not deviated, that we are still believing in exactly the same God that our ancestors believed in. Do you want to put Christ in that category when you talk about ancestors? See, if I put Christ there and he's God, he can't fall in that category! He has to be above![16]

According to Diane Stinton, the Protestant lay woman, Irene Odotei, voiced a similar concern that Jesus Christ is irreplaceable. Therefore there is the danger of making him part of the hordes of other ancestors. Though to some extent, she pointed out the possibility of distinguishing him as ancestor, par excellence, or proto-ancestor, she nonetheless cautions thusly:

> There's no group with only one ancestor. There are so many of them. And even the gods, there are so many gods, and there are

13. Ibid.
14. Ibid., 133–34.
15. Ibid., 134.
16. Ibid.

> so many ancestors. And if you come to Accra and they're praying through libation, they mention so many names of the 'spirit fathers' and the gods, declaring: 'From this place to that place, from the east to the west,' then they call all of them and say, 'I don't even know your number, so come, all of you, come, both great and small.' Now, getting Jesus mixed up of the plethora of ancestors, and calling all to come for a drink takes away the uniqueness of Jesus Christ.

Diane Stinton, thus point out that "These theological problems contributed to the conviction that Jesus is above the ancestors and must remain so to be on par with God."[17] In conclusion, she points out that for some respondents, presenting him as ancestor even distinguishing him as ancestor par excellence, or proto-ancestor, risks compromising his divinity."[18] Stinton's position is valid, however, because the ancestral status assigned to Jesus does not in any way make him fully human nor does it actually help in identifying him as a divine. His humanity and divinity cannot be ascertained by his ancestral status at this point.

On the contrary, there are theologians and non-theologians, pastors and laity who speak of Jesus as ancestor in various ways for their own theological constructions which lend support to both Pobee's and Bediako's assertions. One such theologian is Benezet Bujo who uses the term, proto-ancestor, to describe Jesus Christ. From the point of view, the life Africans receive from God is mediated through the ancestors, Bujo points out the following:

> For the secret of life is to be found above all in the hallowed attitudes and practices of the ancestors. In their wisdom is to be found the key to a better and fuller life, and it is therefore crucial that the rites, actions, words and laws which the ancestors have bequeathed to their descendants be scrupulously observed: they are the indispensable instruments of salvation. The way a person treats this inheritance is decisive, for life or for death. The ancestral traditions are gifts of God. They have a truly sacramental character. The life-giving traditions of the past must determine the present and the future since in them alone is salvation found. [19]

17. Ibid., 134.
18. Ibid.
19. Bujo, *African Theology in its Social Context,* 27.

It is true that Africans relate and depend on their living-dead, but do they do so for their salvation? There is ample evidence that the wisdom of the ancestors is sought for the development and progress of both the individuals and the nation. But what is their salvific effect? Bujo, the theologian, who proposes the image of Jesus Christ as the ancestor, par excellence, or the proto-ancestor, comments:

> If we look back on the historical Jesus of Nazareth, we can see in him, not only one who lived the African ancestor-ideal in the highest degree, but one who brought that ideal to an altogether new fulfillment. Jesus worked miracles, healing the sick, opening the eyes of the blind, raising the dead to life. In short, he brought life, and life-force, in its fullness.[20]

A Ghanaian Protestant clergyman, Samuel Aboa, who granted an interview to Diane Stinton, makes this statement:

> Well I think of Christ as an ancestor, because we believe that our ancestors are also mediators. Those who have died before us continue at least in spirit, and they can mediate between us and the gods or other ancestral spirits, or other powers. And it becomes more meaningful to me when it's said that Christ has died for us and he mediates for us. In this way, I equate him with our understanding of the ancestors.[21]

In the end notes of her book, Diane Stinton rightly addresses the issue of the use of the term, 'equate,' in these words: "Although Aboa used the term equate in the passage cited, the context of conversation makes clear that he does not equate Jesus with the African ancestors literally but only analogously."[22]

Aboa has already used the term, 'mediator,' (a term reserved exclusively for Jesus Christ in terms of his salvific functions) two times in the same conversation and, finally, declared Christ as ancestor. Aboa has then, intently equated Jesus Christ with the ancestors. Contextually, it is without doubt that, for Aboa, Jesus and the ancestors perform the same function as mediators. On the same page, Aboa is quoted as saying "the notion of Jesus as ancestor helps him to understand the vicarious death and the

20. Ibid., 79
21. Stinton, *Jesus of Africa*, 127.
22. Ibid., 281.

resurrection of Jesus . . . our traditional worldview gives us the idea of how to comprehend these biblical affirmations."[23]

In another interview Diane Stinton represents the argument made by the Kenyan Catholic, Sister Marie Gacambi in the following words:

> After all, in the scripture we say he's the firstborn of all creation . . . someone that has an interest in us. Our ancestors have an interest in the wellbeing of the family. They are the mediators between us and God. So really, Jesus is the ancestor, from that perspective, because he's the one that has this whole human link with the transcendent.[24]

There is an interesting point here between the statements of Aboa and Sister Marie Gacambi that is valid for critical analysis. Whereas Aboa thinks of the ancestors as mediators between the gods or spirits and the living human beings, Gacambi maintains that the ancestors' mediatorial function is between human beings and God. So who is giving us the right information here? It is important to ascertain the truth here for obvious reasons. We have a situation where the gods or the spirits are said to be the initiators of both malevolent and benevolent acts on those they like and those they dislike respectively. Hence the ancestors are said to mediate on the behalf of the human beings whom they have left behind. But, according to the myth of the Akan, and the African, in general, sometimes the ancestors are not able to make any changes because they themselves need a higher God to mediate their issues for them.

Abraham Akrong, a Presbyterian clergyman and lecturer at the Department of African Studies at the University of Ghana, Legon, Accra, who also granted an interview to Diane Stinton, makes the following assertion:

> It's a meaningful category to me, in a way, because the ancestors stand for what we call fullness of life. You know, it's the ideal life. If you want to ask the African, 'what is your ideal?' It's to grow up, go through the rites of passage, and die and become an ancestor! That's the ideal. So the ideal nature of the ancestors for me would be a way in which we could also articulate the ideal nature that Jesus Christ came to teach us about what we really ought to be.[25]

23. Ibid., 127.
24. Ibid.
25. Ibid., 129

The main import of Akrong's statement does not seem consistent with the African Cosmology we have researched and described in chapter two. For Africans do not just live to grow, die and become ancestors. This is not the ideal life. Rather, there is the idea that the life cycle has virtue and validity in African thought: birth, growth, rites of passage, death, ancestor, reincarnation. Is Akrong attempting to speak about the cycle of life or the ideal life for the African? The ideal life for the African is the anticipation of growth, prosperity, and having a family. This obviously does not include becoming an ancestor as Akrong portrays.

Akrong is quoted as saying: "Among the Akan, the ancestral thought is very deep and strong. The ancestral symbol is the underlying paradigm of all social interactions."[26] This is true of the Akan. In his University of Ghana office he granted me (as his former teaching assistant at the Central University College) an interview in 2009. In this interview he confirmed what he had told Stinton:

> It is so deep! The African culture controls us. Don't be deceived by anything. Don't be deceived by their cars, the external Westernization. I mean deep, deep down, we're moving into the world from an African premise, deep, deep, deep down. . . . the ancestral image could help us to reveal the mystery of Christ, because I believe that Christ is a mystery and you cannot exhaust him. It's a mere attempt to understand. We produce our ways by which we can build traditional bridges, where we don't tax them too much. They're contributing to, in a deep way these traditional symbols are powerful in terms of capturing that mystery.[27]

One needs to distinguish between using Ancestor as a cultural symbol to understand Christ and using it to build a Christology.

Emmanuel Martey, a Ghanaian Protestant clergyman and theologian spoke of the ancestral image as theologically appealing because, for him "if you read the scripture, and the African concept of ancestry, it fits." Further, he points out that: "This is an image which can explain who Jesus is better, because the African understand the concept of ancestry. Every analogy breaks down at a point. We are not saying that Jesus is an African ancestor, per se. What we are saying is that we're taking the concept, that image, the metaphor, to explain to the African who Jesus Christ is."[28]

26. Ibid., 136.

27. Ibid.

28. Ibid., 138.

According to the interview, Martey stressed this in answer to the Christological question in Mark 8:

> The disciples of Jesus Christ use their previous religious knowledge and experience to answer the reality of Jesus. So what African theologians are arguing is that in answering the Christological question, one cannot ignore one's previous religious understanding and experience. That's why some of us go back into African traditional religion and African culture, to see what images, what symbols, are there, which will help us to understand who Jesus Christ is for the African.[29]

Thus Martey concluded that the ancestral concept is especially significant for explaining Christ to Africans. Another theologian, Waliggo, cautions that the use of the ancestor paradigm as inadequate, nonetheless, validates the image. He, however, has this to say to the general concept of using indigenous thought: "I always object to any theology which tries to be either merely liberation, because you cannot have enculturation without liberating, and you cannot have liberation theology without enculturation. I would want to see all the different models interacting and being interplayed, rather than taking any title at the exclusion of another."[30]

Charles Nyamiti, a Tanzanian Roman Catholic theologian who works fully on the concept of Jesus as our ancestor, uses the ancestral category as a point of departure for theological endeavor. Somehow, like Kwame Bediako, Nyamiti also depicts Jesus Christ as 'brother-ancestor,' based on the type of ancestor-ship which exists between a dead individual and his fellow brothers and sisters in a nuclear family.

With these in view, we leave the rest of the discussions to the readers to make their own theological assertions.

29. Ibid.

30. Ibid.

Bibliography

Akinade, Akintunde E. "Who Do You Say That I Am?—An Assessment of Some Christological Constructs in Africa." *Asia Journal of Theology* 9.1 (1995) 181–200.

Akrong, Abraham. "Christology from an African Perspective." In *Exploring Afro Christology*, edited by John Samuel Pobee. New York: Peter Lang, 1992.

———. "The Empowering Christ: A Postcolonial African Christology." Unpublished work.

———. "Introduction to African Traditional Religion." Paper presented to the department of religion at McCormick Theological Seminary, Chicago, April 25, 2005.

Amoah, Elizabeth. *Moral and Social Significance of Proverbs*. Maryknoll, NY: Orbis, 1986.

Antobam, Kofi. *Ghana's Heritage of Culture*. Leipzig: Koehler, 1963.

Antonio Edward P., editor. *Inculturation and Postcolonial Discourse in African Theology*. New York: Peter Lang, 2006.

Appiah-Kubi, Kofi. "Christology." In *A Reader in African Christian Theology*, edited by John Parratt, 69–81. London: SPCK, 1987.

Appiah-Kubi, Kofi, and Sergio Torres, editors. *African Theology En Route*. Maryknoll, NY: Orbis, 1979.

Atiemo, Abamfo O. *The Rise of the Charismatic Movement in the Mainline Churches in Ghana*. Accra, Ghana: Asempa, 1993.

Baeta, Christian G. *Prophetism in Ghana*. London: SCM, 1962.

———. *A Study of Contemporary Ghana: Some Aspects of Social Structure*. London: Allen & Union, 1967.

———. *Christianity in Tropical Africa*. London: International African Institute, 1968.

Barth Karl. *Church Dogmatics* I/1. Edited by G. W. Bromiley and T. F. Torrance. London: T. & T. Clark, 1957/2000.

———. *Church Dogmatics* I/2. Edited by G. W. Bromiley and T. F. Torrance. London: T. & T. Clark, 1957/2000.

———. *Church Dogmatics* II/1. Edited by G. W. Bromiley and T. F. Torrance. London: T. & T. Clark, 1957/2000.

———.*Church Dogmatics* II/2. Edited by G. W. Bromiley and T. F. Torrance. London: T. & T. Clark, 1957/2000.

———. *Church Dogmatics* II/3. Edited by G. W. Bromiley and T. F. Torrance. London: T. & T. Clark, 1957/2000.

———. *Church Dogmatics* III/1. Edited by G. W. Bromiley and T. F. Torrance. London: T. & T. Clark, 1957/2000.

———. *Church Dogmatics* III/2. Edited by G. W. Bromiley and T. F. Torrance. London: T. & T. Clark, 1957/2000.

———. *Church Dogmatics* IV/1. Edited by G. W. Bromiley and T. F. Torrance. London: T. & T. Clark, 1957/2000.
———. *Church Dogmatics* IV/2. Edited by G. W. Bromiley and T. F. Torrance. London: T. & T. Clark, 1957/2000.
———. *Dogmatics in Outline.* New York: Harper & Row, 1959.
———. *God in Action: Theological Address.* Translated by E. G. Homrighausen and Karl J. Ernst. New York: Round Table, 1936.
———. *Evangelical Theology: An Introduction.* Grand Rapids: Eerdmans, 1963/2000.
———. *The Humanity of God.* Richmond, VA: John Knox, 1960.
———. "No!" In *Natural Theology: Comprising "Nature and Grace" by Emil Brunner and the reply "No!" by Karl Barth.* Translated by Peter Fraenkel. London: Centenary, 1946.
———. *The Word of God and the Word of Man.* Translated by Douglas Horton. New York: Pilgrims, 1928.
Baum, Robert. *Africana: Encyclopedia of African and African American Experience.* Edited by Kwame Anthony Appiah and Henry Louis Gates Jr. New York: Basic Civitas, 1999.
Bediako, Kwame. "Africa and Christianity on the Threshold of the Third Millennium: The Religious Dimension." *African Affairs* 99.395 (2000) 303–23.
———. "Biblical Christologies in the Context of African Traditional Religions." In *Sharing Jesus in the Two Thirds World*, edited by Vinay Samuel and Chris Sugden, 115–75. Bangalore: Partnership in Mission-Asia, 1983.
———. *Christianity in Africa: The Renewal of a Non-Western Religion.* Maryknoll, NY: Orbis, 1995.
———. *Jesus and the Gospel in Africa: History and Experience.* Maryknoll, NY: Orbis, 2004.
———. *Jesus in Africa: The Christian Gospel in African History and Experience.* Yaoundé, Camorron: Editions Clé, 2000.
———. *Jesus in African Culture: A Ghanaian Perspective.* Accra: Asempa, 1990.
———, editor. *Missionary Inheritance in Christianity-A World faith.* Keely: R. Lion, 1986.
———. *Theology and Identity—The impact of culture upon Christian Thought in the Second Century and in Modern Africa.* Cumbria, U.K: Regnum, 1999.
———. "Understanding African Theology in the Twentieth Century." *Bulletin for Contextual Theology* 3.2 (1996) 1–11.
Bloesch, Donald G. *Essentials of Evangelical Theology.* Vol. 1. San Francisco: Harper & Row, 1978.
Brokensha, David W. *Social Change at Larteh, Ghana.* Oxford: Clarendon, 1966.
Bujo, Bénézet. *African Theology in its Social Context.* Translated by John O'Donohue. Maryknoll, NY: Orbis, 1992.
———, and Juvenal Ilunga Muya. *African Theology in the 21st Century: The Contribution of the Pioneers.* Nairobi, Kenya: Paulines Africa, 2002.
Busia, Kofi Abrefa. *Africa in Search of Democracy.* London: Routledge & Kegan Paul, 1967.
———. *The Position of the Chief in the Modern Political System of Ashanti.* London: Oxford University Press, 1951.
Carson, D. A. *Showing the Spirit: A Theological Exposition of 1 Corinthians 12–14.* Grand Rapids: Baker, 1987.
Christenson, J. B. *The Role of Proverbs in Fante Culture in Peoples and Cultures of Africa.* Edited by E. P. Skinner. Garden City, NY: Doubleday, 1973.

Cone, James H. *Liberation: A Black Theology of Liberation*. Philadelphia: J. B. Lippincott, 1970.

Danquah, J. B. *The Akan Doctrine of God*. 2nd ed. London: White Friars, 1968.

Debrunner, Hans W. *A Church between Colonial Powers*. London: Lutterworth, 1965.

———. *A History of Christianity in Ghana*. Accra, Ghana: Waterville, 1967.

Dickson, Kwesi A. *Theology in Africa*.Maryknoll, New York: Orbis, 1984.

Ela, Jean-Marc. "Ancestors and Christian Faith: An African Problem." In *Liturgy and Cultural Religious Traditions*, edited by Herman Schmidt and David Power, 34–50. New York: Seabury, 1977.

———. "Christianity and Liberation in Africa." In *Paths of African Theology*, edited by Rosino Gibellini, 136–53. Maryknoll, NY: Orbis, 1994.

———. "The Memory of the African People and the Cross of Christ." In *The Scandal of a Crucified World: Perspectives on the Cross and Suffering*, translated and edited by Yacob Tesfai, 17–35. Maryknoll, NY: Orbis, 1994.

———. *My Faith as an African*. Translated by John Pairman Brown and Susan Perry. Maryknoll, NY: Orbis, 1988.

Erickson, Millard J. *Christian Theology*. 2nd ed. Grand Rapids: Baker, 1998.

Evans-Pritchard, Edward. *Witchcraft, Oracles, and Magic among the Azande*. Oxford: Oxford University Press, 1937.

Fackre, Gabriel. *Christology in Context: The Christian Story*. Grand Rapids: Eerdmans, 2006.

Field, Margaret. *Religion and Medicine of the Ga People*. 2nd ed. Oxford: Oxford University Press, 1961.

Forde, Daryll. *African Worlds: Studies in the Cosmological Ideas and Social Values of African Peoples*. London: Oxford University Press, 1968.

Gairdner, W. H. T. *An Account and Interpretation of the World Missionary Conference*. London: Oliphant, Anderson & Ferrier, 1910.

Gelphi, Donald L. *Experiencing God: A Theology of Human Emergence*. New York: Paulist, 1971.

Gollwitzer Helmut. *Karl Barth: Church Dogmatics—A selection with Introduction*. Louisville: John Knox, 1961.

Gruchy John W. *Theology and Ministry in Context and Crisis: A South African Perspective*. Grand Rapids: Eerdmans, 1987.

Guthrie, Donald. *New Testament Theology*. Leicester: Inter Varsity, 1981.

Guthrie, Shirley C., Jr. *Christian Doctrine*. Louisville: Westminster John Knox, 1994.

Harris, William Thomas, and Harry Sawyerr. *The Springs of Mende Belief and Conduct: A Discussion of the Influence of the Belief in the Supernatural among the Mende*. Freetown, Sierra Leone: African University Press, 1968.

Hart, Trevor. *Regarding Karl Barth: Toward a Reading of His Theology*. Eugene, OR: Wipf & Stock, 2005.

Hartwell, Herbert. *The Theology of Karl Barth: An Introduction*. London: Gerald Duckworth, 1968.

Hastings, A. *African Christianity*. London: Geoffrey Chapman, 1976.

Healey, Joseph G. *A Fifth Gospel: The Experience of Black Christian Values*. Maryknoll, NY: Orbis, 1981.

Healey, Joseph, and Donald Sybertz. *Towards an African Narrative Theology*. Maryknoll, NY: Orbis, 1996.

Henry, Carl F. H. *The Identity of Jesus of Nazareth*. Nashville: Broadman, 1992.

Hilman, Eugene. *Toward An African Christianity: Inculturation Applied.* Mahwah, NJ: Paulist, 1993.
Hodge, Charles. *Systematic Theology.* 3 vols. Grand Rapids: Eerdmans, 1993.
Hodge, Melvin L. *The Indigenous Church.* Springfield, MO: Gospel, 1977.
Hunsinger George. *How to Read Karl Barth: The Shape of His Theology.* Oxford: Oxford University Press, 1991.
Idowu, E. Bolaji *African Traditional Religion: A Definition.* Maryknoll, NY: Orbis, 1973.
———. *Olódùmarè: God in Yoruba Belief.* New York: Praeger, 1963.
———. *Towards an Indigenous Church.* London: OUP, 1965.
Jahn, Janheinz. *Muntu: An Outline of Neo-African Culture.* London: Faber & Faber, 1961.
Jones, Paul D. *The Humanity of Christ: Christology in Karl Barth's Church Dogmatics.* London: T. & T. Clark, 2008.
Kabasele, Françoise. *Christ as Chief In Faces of Jesus in Africa.* Edited by Robert J. Schreiter, Maryknoll, NY: Orbis, 1991.
Katongole Emmanuel, editor. *African Theology Today.* Scranton, PA: University of Scranton Press, 2002.
Kelly, J. N. D. *Early Christian Doctrines.* New York: Harper & Row, 1978.
King, Noel Q. *African Cosmos: An Introduction to Religion in African.* Belmont, CA: Wadsworth, 1986.
Kirwen, Michael C. *The Missionary and the Diviner: Contending Theologies of Christian and African Religions.* Maryknoll, NY: Orbis, 1987.
Kuma, Afua. *Jesus of the Deep Forest: Prayers and Praises of Afua Kuma.* Translated by Jon Kirby. Accra: Asempa, 1981.
———. *Kwaebirentuw Ase Yesu: Afua Kuma Ayeyi ne Mpaebo.* Accra: Asempa, 1980.
Larbi, Kingsley E. *Pentecostalism: The Eddies of Ghanaian Christianity.* Accra, Ghana: Blessed, 2001.
Little K. *The Mende of Sierra Leone.* London: Routeledge & Kegan Paul, 1951.
Manus Ukachukwu, Chris. "African Christologies: The Centre-piece of African Christian Theology." *Zeitschrift Für Missionswissenschaft Und Religionswissenschaft* 82 (1998) 3–23.
———. *Christ, the African King: New Testament Christology.* Frankfurt: Peter Lang, 1993.
Marsh, Thomas. *The Triune God.* Mystic, CT: Twenty-Third, 1994.
Martey, Emmanuel. *African Theology: Inculturation and Liberation.* Maryknoll, NY: Orbis, 1993.
Mbogu, Ibeawuchi Nicholas. *Christology and Religious Pluralism: A Review of John Hick's Theocentric Model of Christology and the Emergence of African Inculturation Christologies.* Berlin: LIT, 2006.
Mbiti, John S. *African Religions and Philosophy.* Nairobi: Heinemann Educational, 1969.
———. *African Religions and Philosophy.* 2nd ed. Portsmough, NH: Heinemann, 1990.
———. *Bible and Theology in African Christianity.* Oxford: Oxford University Press, 1986.
———. *Concepts of God in Africa.* London: SPCK, 1970.
———. "The Encounter between Christianity and African Religion." *Temenos* 12 (1976) 125–35.
———. *Introduction to African Religion.* 2nd ed. Nairobi, Kenya: East African Educational, 1992.
———. "Our Savior as an African Experience." In *Christ and the Spirit in the New Testament, Essays in Honor of C. F. D. Moule,* edited by B. Lindars and S. Smalley, 397–414. Cambridge: Cambridge University Press, 1973.

———. *The Prayers of African Religion.* Maryknoll, NY: Orbis, 1976.
———. "Some African Concepts of Christology." In *Christ and the Younger Churches*, edited by Georg F. Vicedom. London: SPCK, 1972.
McCormack, Bruce L. *Karl Barth's Critically Realistic Dialectical Theology: Its Genesis and Development 1909–1936.* New York: Clarendon, 1995.
McDowell, John C., and Mike Higton. *Conversing with Karl Barth.* Hampshire, England: Ashgate, 2004.
McGrath, Alister E. *Christian Theology.* Oxford: Blackwell, 1994.
Mofokeng, Takatso Alfred. *The Crucified among the Crossbearers: Towards a Black Christology.* Kampen: Uitgeversmaatschppij J. H. Kok, 1983.
Moore Basil, editor. *The Challenge of Black Theology in South Africa.* Atlanta: John Knox, 1973.
Mueller, David L. *Karl Barth.* Makers of the Modern Theological Mind. Waco, TX: Word, 1972.
Mugambi, J. N. K. *African Christian Theology: An Introduction.*Nairobi: East African Educational, 1989.
Mugambi, J. N. K, and Laurenti Magesa, editors. *Jesus in African Christianity: Experimentation and Diversity in African Christology.* African Christianity Series, Nairobi: Initiatives, 1989.
Muzorewa, Gwinyai. *The Origins and Development of African Theology.* Maryknoll, NY: Orbis, 1985.
Noel, King Q. *African Cosmos: An Introduction to Religion in Africa.* Belmont, CA: Wadsworth, 1986.
Nolan, Albert. *God in South Africa: The Challenge of the Gospel.* Gweru, Zimbabwe: Mambo, 1988.
Nyamiti Charles. "African Christologies Today." In *Jesus in African Christianity: Experimentation and Diversity in African Christology*, edited by J. N. K Mugambi and Laurenti Magesa. African Christianity Series, Nairobi: Initiatives, 1989.
———. *Christ as Our Ancestor: Christology from an African Perspective.* Gweru, Zimbabwe: Mambo, 1984.
Oduyoye, Mercy. "The Church of the Future in Africa: Its Mission and Theology." In *The Church and Reconstruction of Africa*, edited by J. N. K. Mugambi, 66–83. Nairobi, Kenya: AACC, 1997.
———. *Hearing and Knowing: Theological Reflections on Christianity in Africa.* Maryknoll, NY: Orbis, 1986.
Opoku, Kofi Asare. "The Challenge of Witchcraft." *Ibadan Journal of Religious Studies* 4.1 (1970).
———. "The Idea of an African Philosopher: The Concept of 'Spirit' in African Metaphysics." *An African Journal of Philosophy* 2.1 (1973) 7–88.
———. "Traditional Religious Beliefs and Spiritual Churches in Ghana: A Preliminary Statement." *Research Review* 4:2 (1968).
———. *West African Traditional Religion.* Accra, Ghana: FEP International, 1978.
Otabil, Kwesi. *West African Traditional Religion.* Accra: Ghana, 1994.
Ott, Martin. *African Theology in Images.* Zomba, Malawi: Kachere Series, 2007.
Palma, Robert J. *Karl Barth's Theology of Culture: The Freedom of Culture for the Praise of God.* Allison Park, PA: Pickwick, 1983.
Parker, T. H. L. *Karl Barth.* Grand Rapids: Eerdmans, 1970.
Parratt, John, editor. *A Reader in African Christian Theology.* London: SPCK, 1987.

———. *Reinventing Christianity: African Theology Today*. Grand Rapids: Eerdmans, 1995.

Parrinder, Geoffrey. *African Mythology.* London: Hamlyn, 1975.

———. *African Traditional Religion.* Hutchinson, UK: Hutchinson's University Press, 1954.

———. *West African Religion.* London: Epworth, 1969.

Paul, Gifford. *Ghana's New Christianity—Pentecostalism in a Globalizing African Economy.* Bloomington: Indiana University Press, 2004.

Pobee, John Samuel, editor. *Exploring Afro-Christology*. Frankfurt am Main: P. Lang, 1992.

———. "Jesus Christ—The Life of the World: An African Perspective." Ministerial Formation 21 (January 1983) 5–8.

———. *Skenosis: Christian Faith in an Africa Context.* Gweru, Zimbabwe: Mambo, 1992.

———. *Toward an African Theology*. Nashville: Abingdon, 1979.

———. *West Africa: Christ Would Be an African Too.* Geneva: WCC Publications, 1996.

Pobee John Samuel, and Amirtham Samuel, editors. *Theology by the People: Reflections on Doing Theology in Community*. Geneva: World Council of Churches, 1986.

Pobee John Samuel, and Carl F. Hallencreutz, editors. *Variations in Christian Theology in Africa.* Nairobi: Uzima, 1986.

Quarcoopome, T. N. O. *West African Traditional Religion.* Ibadan, Nigeria: African University Press, 1987.

Rattray, R. S. *Ashanti.* Oxford: Oxford University Press, 1969.

———. *Religion and Art in Ashanti.* Oxford: Oxford University Press, 1927.

Ray, Benjamin C. *African Religions: Symbol, Ritual and Community*. Upper Saddle River, NJ: Prentice Hall 2000.

Sarpong, Peter Kwasi. *Anthropology and Inculturation in Action.* Tamale: Unpublished Paper, 1993.

———. "Asante Christology." *Studia Missionalia* 45 (1996) 1–19.

———. *Ghana in Retrospect: Some Aspects of Ghanaian Culture.* Tema: Ghana Publishing Corporation, 1974.

Sauter, Gerhard. *Protestant Theology at the Crossroads: How to Face the Crucial Tasks for Theology in the Twenty-First Century.* Grand Rapids: Eerdmans, 2007.

Schoffeleers, Matthew. "Christ in African Folk Theology: The Nganga Paradigm." In *Religion in Africa: Experience and Expression*, edited by Thomas D. Blakely, Walter E. A. van Beek, and Dennis L. Thomson. 73–88. London: James Currey, 1994.

Schönborn, Christoph, OP. *God's Human Face: The Christ-Icon.* Translated by Lothar Krauth. San Francisco: Ignatius, 1994.

Schreiter, Robert J. *Constructing Local Theologies*. London: SCM, 1985.

———, editor. *Faces of Jesus in Africa*. Faith and Cultures Series. Maryknoll, NY: Orbis, 1991.

Shorter, Aylward. *African Christian Theology*. Maryknoll, NY: Orbis, 1977.

———. *African Culture and the Christian Church.* London: Geoffrey Chapman, 1973.

———. *Ancestor Veneration Revisited. AFER* 25.4 (1983) 197–203.

———. *Folk Christianity and Functional Christology. AFER* 24.31 (982) 133–37.

———. *Jesus and the Witchdoctor: An Approach to Healing and Wholeness*. Maryknoll, NY: Orbis, 1985.

———. *Toward a Theology of Inculturation*. Maryknoll, NY: Orbis, 1989.

Smart, James D. *The Divided Mind of Modern Theology: Karl Barth and Rudolf Bultmann, 1908–1933*. Philadelphia: West Minster, 1967.

Smith, Huston. *The Religions of Man.* New York: Harper & Row, 1965.

Stinton, Diane B. *Jesus of Africa: Voices of Contemporary African Christology.* Maryknoll, NY: Orbis, 2004.
Taylor, John V. *The Primal Vision: Christian Presence amid African Religion.* London: SCM, 1963.
Taylor John B., editor. *Primal World Views: Christian Dialogue with Traditional Thought Forms.* Ibadan, Nigeria: Daystar, 1976.
Torrance, T. F. *Christian Doctrine of God: One Being Tree Persons.* Edinburgh, UK: T. & T. Clark, 1996.
———. "The Problem of Natural Theology in the Thought of Karl Barth." *Religious Studies* 6 (1970) 121–35.
———. *Theology in Reconciliation.* London: Geoffrey Chapman, 1975.
———. *Theology in Reconstruction.* London, UK: SCM, 1965.
———, editor. *Theological Dialogue between Orthodox and Reformed Churches.* Edinburgh: Scottish Academic, 1993.
———. *Trinitarian Perspectives: Towards Doctrinal Agreement.* Edinburgh: T. & T. Clark, 1994.
Turner, W. H. "The Primal Religions of the World and their Study." In *Australian Essays in World Religions,* edited by Victor C. Hayes, 27–37. Bedford Park: Australian Association for World Religions, 1977.
Udoh, Enyi Ben. *Guest Christology: AN Interpretative View of the Christological Problem in Africa.* New York: Peter Lang, 1988.
Upong, Justin S. "Christology and Inculturation: A New Testament Perspective." In *Paths of African Theology,* edited by Rosino Gibellini, 40–71. Maryknoll, NY: Orbis, 1994.
Waliggo, John M. "African Christology in a Situation of Suffering." In *Jesus in African Christianity.* Edited by J. N. K. Mugambi and Laurenti Magesa, 93–111. Nairobi, Kenya: Initiatives, 1989.
Walls, Andrew. "Africa and Christian Identity." *Mission Focus* 6.7,1 (978) 11–13.
———. "African in Christian History: Retrospect and Prospect." *Journal of African Christian Thought* 1.1 (1985) 2–15.
———. "Expansion of Christianity: An Interview with Andrew Walls." *The Christian Century* (August 2000) 792–99. Online: http://www.religion-online.org/showarticle.asp?title=2052.
———. "Towards Understanding Africa's Place in Christian History." In *Religion in a Pluralistic Society,* edited by J. S. Pobee, 180–89. Leiden: E. J. Brill, 1976.
Webster, John, editor. *The Cambridge Companion to Karl Barth.* Cambridge: Cambridge University Press, 2000.
———. *Karl Barth: Outstanding Christian Thinkers.* New York: Continuum, 2000.
Welbourn, F. B. "Some Problems of African Christianity: Guilt and Shame." In *Christianity in Tropical Africa,* edited by C. G. Baeta, 182–99. London: Oxford University Press, 1968.
World Student Christian Federation. *A New Look at Christianity in Africa.* Geneva: World Student Christian Federation, 1972.
Wendland, Ernst. "Who Do People Say I Am?: Contextualizing Christology in Africa." *AJET* 10.2 (1991) 13–32.
Williamson, Sidney George. *Akan Religion and the Christian Faith: Comparative Study of the Impact of Two Religions.* Accra: Ghana University Press, 1965.
Wingren, Gustaf. *Theology in Conflict: Nyrgren, Barth, Bultmann.* Translated by Eric H. Wahlstrom. Philadelphia: Muhlenberg, 1958

Young, Josiah U., III. *African Theology: A Critical Analysis and Annotated Bibliography*. Westport, CT: Greenwood, 1993.

Yusufu, Obaje Ameh. "Theocentric Christology." In *Exploring Afro Christology*, edited by John Samuel Pobee. New York: Peter Lang 1992.

Zahan, Dominique. *The Religion, Spirituality, and Thought of Traditional Africa*. Translated by Kate Ezra Martin and Lawrence M. Martin. Chicago: University of Chicago Press, 1970.

Index

C

D

E

F

G

H

I

J

K

L

M

P

Q

R

S

T